ALSO BY NEELI CHERKOVSKI

POETRY

Don't Make a Move
The Waters Reborn
Public Notice
Love Proof
Juggler Within
Clear Wind
Animal
Elegy for Bob Kaufman
Leaning Against Time
Naming the Nameless
From the Canyon Outward
From the Middle Woods
Manila Poems
The Crow and I
Elegy for My Beat Generation
Hang on to The Yangtze River

BIOGRAPHY & MEMOIR

Ferlinghetti: A Biography
Whitman's Wild Children
Hank: The Life of Charles Bukowski
Coolidge and Cherkovski in Conversation

BUKOWSKI: A LIFE

BUKOWSKI
A LIFE: THE CENTENNIAL EDITION

NEELI CHERKOVSKI

BOSTON
BLACK SPARROW PRESS
2020

Published in 2020 by Black Sparrow Press

DAVID R. GODINE, *Publisher*
Boston, Massachusetts
www.godine.com

First published in hardcover in 1991 in a different version under the title
Hank: The Life of Charles Bukowski by Random House, New York.

LIBRARY OF CONGRESS CATALOGING-IN-PUBLICATION DATA
Names: Cherkovski, Neeli, author.
Title: Bukowski : a life / Neeli Cherkovski. |
Other titles: Hank
Identifiers: LCCN 2020010476
ISBN 978-1-57423-241-7 (paperback) |
ISBN 978-1-57423-242-4 (ebook)
Subjects: LCSH: Bukowski, Charles. |
Authors, American–20th century–Biography. |
Beats (Persons)–Biography.
Classification: LCC PS3552.U4 Z6 2020 | DDC 811/.54 [B]–dc23
LC record available at https://lccn.loc.gov/2020010476

Cover Illustration: Joe McKendry (after a photograph by Sam Cherry)
Cover Design: Alex Camlin
Frontispiece Photograph: Sam Cherry

FIRST PRINTING, 2020
Printed in Canada

For my partner
JESSE CABRERA

THIS THING UPON ME
IS NOT DEATH

Reflections on the Bicentennial of Charles Bukowski

E ARLY IN my adolescence in the 1950s, Los Angeles was a kind of
Xanadu, a foreboding grid of long boulevards, aging palm trees,
and Hollywood glitz. My family used to drive into town on a route that
passed the long-gone Brew 102 brewery, Union Station, and City Hall,
one of the lone skyscrapers in the downtown back then. I was already
a poet myself by 1959 when I began reading the yet-undiscovered
bard of that mythical metropolis, Charles Bukowski.

Hidden from mainstream literary life, Bukowski could only be
found if you sought out the little magazines published in tiny print
runs around the country, often in small towns, and with little to no
financial resources. They had names like *Quicksilver*, *Epos*, and *Midwest*. These journals seemed to have existed forever and were a cottage
industry of their own. Some were mimeographed, others done with
low-cost photo offset. They published poetry of all kinds, but Bukowski stood out.

From the mid-1950s he emerged, offering images of the sprawling
Los Angeles basin. His poems were characterized as hard-edged and
desperate. Many of the editors sensed that they had hit upon an entirely
new voice. Positive reviews were posted, and profiles published. Early
critics dubbed him "a poet of skid row," which he was not, a hard-drinking bard, also not true; nor was he the usual proletarian writer shack-
led to left-wing ideologies. Bukowski's original impulse to write came

ix

largely from the usual suspects: John Dos Passos, John Fante, William Faulkner, Ernest Hemingway, Carson McCullers, and William Saroyan. Robinson Jeffers left a lasting impression on him, as he was drawn to that poet's sense of isolation from the literary scene.

What did I feel when Bukowski's poetry came into my possession? He spoke directly to me. It felt like listening to one of my father's old pals, that straight-shooting manner: an ace is an ace, a spade a spade. The work was tough, but there was an underlying sense that the man who wrote these poems had compassion for the world at large. I could feel the rented rooms he described and the dead-end neighborhoods he walked. Truth was spoken, unvarnished and realistic. I had been reading the poems of Carl Sandburg, which had the same earthy quality, and Walt Whitman, who had prepared the way with his wide-open poetics.

Bukowski's books in the early 1960s, published off dining room tables and in cramped workspaces, had appealing titles, such as *Flower, Fist and Bestial Wail*, *Longshot Pomes for Broke Players*, and *Run with the Hunted.* These were done in simple, saddle-stapled editions of 300 copies or less. I still remember my high school English teacher reacting in horror to the title *Longshot Pomes for Broke Players*. She was offended by the word "pomes," quick to assume it was a typo, the glaring mistake of all mistakes. It was no use explaining that the word choice was a statement about poetry itself.

One of Hank's poems from those early years affected me deeply; I memorized it and recited often. "Old Man, Dead in a Room" is a product of the poet's thirty-ninth year, when his reputation was slowly growing. He had lost both his father and mother. Death weighed on him. He knew poetry was a hedge against mortality, and he made use of that: "this thing upon me is not death / but it's as real / and as landlords full of maggots / pound for rent / I eat walnuts in the sheath / of my privacy / and listen for more important / drummers…"

In this centennial year of Bukowski's birth, his books are read all over the world in many languages, especially his novels. He offers a view of America's underbelly. His alter-ego Henry Chinaski is a heroic figure to young readers at home and abroad. Bookstores in Mexico City and Buenos Aires carry stack of his books, literary events celebrating him take place across Europe. New collections of his writing seem to arrive each year. His prose echoes with a lost Los Angeles in these compilations. This voluminous outpouring of poetry is a testing-ground for young writers.

1920 is a long way from 2020. The chasm between those years is crammed with war and revolution, with immigration and vast social changes. Add the Great Depression and the bourgeoning of suburban America, and the changes are a cosmic headache. This book is a kind of time capsule as it looks back on one man's life. Biography is history. It can tell you the story is over, when it may be just beginning. I offer no great revelations. My bias is toward the positive aspects of my subject's life, and I even figure personally throughout the book, which makes it feel at times like something of a memoir of my friendship with Bukowski. The deed is done; I look forward.

As I reread my biography/memoir—not an easy task as I tend to go on and not look back—I find myself being reintroduced to my old friend. I also find myself wishing I had spent more time with people who knew Hank as a young man, people who are now long since gone. I regret not having spent more time with Bukowski's high school buddy. I only knew him as Baldy, when he showed up at Hank's little bungalow in the mid-1960s. Indeed, he was bald. In Hank's autobiographical novel *Ham on Rye* he figures as one of the gang who runs with the book's antihero, Chinaski. We went out to dinner that night at the nearby Shakey's pizza parlor. Baldy talked non-stop of old times, but I couldn't glean much from it. He said nothing of Hank's mother, though he did tell me his father was a tough customer. When the conversation turned to parents, Bukowski told Baldy, "Neeli is lucky. He has good parents. They support his every move." That was true, and Hank brought it up often. I did try to speak with other high school classmates, but they all denied knowing Bukowski. One interviewee said, "He was kind of a shadow figure not easily approachable, although he did hang around with some of the guys. I think he was very intelligent, sure of himself." It's not much, but it's sure better than, "Oh, he was a nice guy." I wish I had gone over his childhood with a little more daring.

Bukowski was in his early sixties when he sat down and wrote the story of his youth in *Ham on Rye*. He was acutely conscious of being an elder. As he wrote the novel he knew he was delving into the truly gone world of Los Angeles's past. Still, he explained that something mysterious remained: memories of betrayals by the rich and powerful, the theft of the land stolen from the common people. This is well-explained in his early poem "Crucifix in a Deathhand," which is both elegy and dirge: "...this land punched-in, cuffed-out, divided..." It is a tone poem to the grim, deep, and sustaining noir of Los Angeles. He begins it "out in a willow" and then blooms in the basin, even mentioning the long-gone Spaniards. The rap his city got as a mess is what intrigued Hank: the sprawl, the clogged roads, the cramped shopping malls with their glitzy neon. He points to this with pride. It is the sounds, as he once said, "of hamburgers sizzling in the pan."

When I was first preparing to write this book, I spent many hours taping Hank. We had practice: we'd made hours and hours cassette recordings of our conversations through the 1960s and early 1970s. Those were interesting times. We could be serious, humorous, nasty and sometimes—I would like to think—brilliant. The diminutive recorder seemed to tremble back then. Now I think of those recordings as groundwork for what came later. I asked myself as I began the research to write this book, "Do I really want this manner of relationship with an old friend, and mentor to boot?" Hank and I had only reconnected, after all, in the mid-1980s after many years of not seeing one another. I thought, "Perhaps I should not go down this path." But he and his wife Linda kept encouraging me, and curiosity actually drove me on. Writing a biography of Bukowski's life would, I realized, answer questions I'd held on to for decades. And the best way to build on our past conversations was to, again, rely on new tape-recorded conversations.

A lot of what Bukowski offered to the public was pure showmanship. From Hemingway he not only learned about how to nail human emotion on the page, but also how to cultivate a public. The working-class background was more what I'd call middle-class poverty. The hard-drinking bard is mostly fictional. When I think of the essence of Charles Bukowski, I think of the day he met my partner Jesse Cabrera when we visited him at his house. There was no tough-guy surprise that I was gay. Hank took me aside and said, "I'm so glad you are with somebody, man." Then he asked if we would stay the night. He and

Linda had a room prepared, and there were fresh-cut flowers in a vase on the nightstand. None of this surprised me—Hank accepted people.

Bukowski was a disciplined writer with an understanding of what it takes. He had the same dreams as many young writers of his generation: write the "Great American Novel." In many of our early conversations Hank spoke of the "literary gods" as if they were superhumans, gifted with special literary powers. He loved the proto-surreal prose of Saroyan's *The Daring Young Man on the Flying Trapeze* and Fante's short fiction collection, *Dago Red*. Bukowski proclaimed: "John Fante is my God." I strove to keep a record of his influences. I make it clear that Hank wanted to write a poetry equivalent to the gutsy prose of James T. Farrell's *Studs Lonigan* trilogy and John Dos Passos's *U.S.A.* trilogy.

Bukowski often used boxing terminology to express his feelings about the writing process: "You have to lace the gloves and enter the ring" and "You need to go 12 rounds and score a knockout." Along these lines he said, "In the end, you have to be so good they can't deny you." He told younger writers not to fear rejection. "I used to get hundreds of rejection slips. All I could think was, 'What fools these editors are.'" One of my old cassettes contains a brief conversation between my mother and Bukowski. I had lured him over for a visit. My mother, easily as competitive as Hank, said, "Poets are born that way." Hank countered, "No, Clare. Life makes you a poet. And on such a delving day I wrote about a man who shot people out of the sky. He had an iron hand. It was Baron Manfred von Richthofen."

Where do I stand with Bukowski on the centennial of his birth? It's been 25 years since he passed, and my thoughts have had plenty of time to mature. I can still picture Hank in the 1960s, sitting at his writing desk at the old typewriter. He called it his "typer." Many afternoons I'd walk up to the front door of his bungalow and pause when I heard the typer clattering away. If I listened for a moment, then turned and left, perhaps I did it in the service of literature. If I knocked, however, he would answer the door and tease, "Man, you ruined it." I always admired his devotion to the work at hand, and I still do. I know Hank would have written even without an audience.

But where do I stand?

I still feel that his early poems stand out for their clarity and concision. Bukowski had a truth to tell and he told it in the language of the streets. Those early poems are his very best. Later, the poems seem to have lost something. Yet, they always entertained and left an important impression: Bukowski poems reminded people that in their so-called ordinary lives extra-ordinary things can happen. Hank has always mirrored back to his readers those traits that keep us human.

I was just eighteen years old when I held a copy of Bukowski's *It Catches My Heart in Its Hands*—his first letterpress-printed book—and read the language of the streets speaking clearly through my book-lined bedroom. All these years later—after all the tapes and the years and years of conversations and phone calls and letters—Charles Bukowski's words still reach out, and I am listening even now.

— NEELI CHERKOVSKI
San Francisco, 2020

TALKING WITH BUKOWSKI

An Introduction

IN THE 1960s there was a time when Charles Bukowski and I used to go to L.A.'s Olympic Auditorium for boxing, wrestling, the whole gambit. It got so that we knew the names of even the most obscure contenders. The wrestler's theatrics, often quite insane, had us howling with laughter. Staged though it was, we were excited observing the fake poundings the fighters took. They were good at what they did. We'd guzzle beer, devour hot dogs, damned if the mustard got on our shirts, damned if the ketchup stained our sleeves. Bukowski praised or cursed the wrestlers, encouraging a slam to the mat, a thrust against the ropes. At the boxing matches, which were in deadly earnest, we talked to the other fans, especially those who looked as if they might be fighters themselves. Often, when I'd go for more beer, leaving Hank at his seat, I'd be asked if he fought, too. I'd tell them he'd gone under the name "Kid Henry." Nobody considered that I might be kidding. All they had to do was take one look at that face. As one guy put it, "He looks like a killer. I'd hate to be caught in the ring with him." When I told that to Hank, he said, "Don't they know about me. I've got the face of an angel."

Hank rarely went to bars in those days, but there were a few run-down cocktail lounges on the fringe of downtown Los Angeles where I could entice him to go. Most were little more than Skid Row hangouts smelling of beer and urine. A few reflected a vanished glory. These were my favorites. To Hank, none of it mattered. He felt uncomfortable, as if he were slumming, but after the fights, it only seemed natural to stop off for a drink or two. On several occasions he spoke with convincing familiarity of Joe Louis, Max Schmelling and other famous boxers of his youth. Inevitably, some barfly would pipe-up with a memory or two of Rocky Marciano or Archie Moore. Hank had his own vest-pocket wisdom to impart: "You need tenacity to win. Of course you have to have talent to go with it," he'd pronounce in a bar on Main Street, not far from the big Greyhound Bus Terminal. "By the way, that's what a writer needs too," he'd whisper.

The Olympic was pretty decrepit even back then. I realize now that we never talked poetry when we attended the fights. Our minds were focused on the fighters. Shop-talk vanished in the magic. It may have come up on the drive over—but once there, we entered another world. In general, Hank maintained an anti-intellectual stance; it rose to the surface at the fights. He liked the illusion of exhibition wrestling and he enjoyed the fact that the wrestlers appealed to people who would never go to an opera, or attend a symphony. Hank held out the hope that some of them might read his poetry and stories. "I write for the girlie magazines," he told me as we walked to the parking lot after a championship match. "I think they'd find my poetry easy to read and understand." One will not come across the type of sermonizing Henry Miller makes use of in *Tropic of Cancer* or *Tropic of Capricorn*. Hank saw the disintegration of post-World War II American life almost before it began. In his written work, he's a hero, a fall guy, a comic character, a womanizing lush, a wise old dog. His readers do more than glimpse his many-sidedness. For some, it's a deep experience. They feel as if his writing opens places inside of themselves they might never have seen otherwise. Often a reader comes away feeling heroic, because the poet has shown them that their ordinary lives are imbued with drama.

In later years his readers found Bukowski sailing along the freeways, still writing poetry, but hardly living on the bottom rungs of society. "It's a good life," he said. "A home, a wife, a swimming pool, a deck, a garden, and a tax accountant."

Hank's writings were sometimes Falstaffian—reflecting the larger-than-life hail and farewell brawler who can drink with the best of them—with a touch of Balzac thrown in. Hank needed beer and cigarettes to maintain his productivity. After he had made money and settled into his own house near the age of sixty, fine wine replaced the beer. One evening while standing in front of the swimming pool he had installed just outside of the sliding glass door of his living room, he said to me, "You know, famous or not famous, rich or poor, all I wanted was to write, and I did it." The first sentence of his autobiographical novel *Post Office* reads, "It began as a mistake." Keeping the postal job all through the 60s he viewed as an error. But it was a job he needed at the time, and it kept him in beer and typewriter ribbon, pens, envelopes, stamps and money for the horses at Santa Anita, Del Mar, and Hollywood Park. Once in the 60s we were swinging onto Santa Monica Boulevard, heading toward the setting sun on our way to Barney's Beanery, when he said to me, "You know, kid. Here we are, two grown men, and we're still writing these things called poems. It doesn't make much sense, when you think about it."

Since the early 1960s I have been in a conversation with Charles Bukowski. When we first met the talk came mostly from him, advice from an older man to a younger one. He would often apologize, hoping that he wasn't being overbearing or preachy. Still he felt he knew things that might be of value to a writer just starting out. He advised me to forget what I'd learned in school. "They're lying to you." As time went on, the twenty-five year difference in age seemed to melt away. Hank and I spent countless evenings in his East Hollywood apartment discussing life and literature. He treated me as he would a contemporary, occasionally pulling rank as the "major poet" of the duo.

Our one-on-one conversations echo through the years and continue to reverberate. Some are recorded on tapes grown brittle with age. When I listen to them, I picture us surrounded by empty beer cans, talking about Ernest Hemingway, our fellow poets, and various social and political issues. Those who knew Hank in this way often testify to his magnetic personality, the gentle power of his speaking voice, and his devotion to the art of the rejoinder. He loved to toss out a concept and wait for a response, one he could then pounce on, eliciting further response. "Come on, kid. Give it to me." We'd spend entire evenings going back and forth with gentle jibes, spontaneous epigram, and the occasional left hook to the cerebral cortex.

On a given evening, he might focus on his job at the post office, his difficult childhood (over and over again describing his father and mother as unfeeling people), or on the world of the small poetry journals in which he was published. I was fascinated by the glimpse Hank offered of the Roosevelt era and the Great Depression, as well as by descriptions of how much he had suffered trying to define himself as a writer in the 1940s. I found it hard to reconcile the beefy, healthy-looking man sitting across the room from me with the image he painted of a thin, wild-haired, twenty-five year old restlessly moving from city to city, leaving a trail of short stories behind. Hank recounted these episodes with humor, just as he does in print. No matter how bad things got, his ironic, wry view of the world, and his ability to laugh at its most extreme situations, kept him going. He had a goal in mind: to become a self-sufficient writer.

Bukowski had a way of dominating, while still allowing others to have the floor. He absorbed everything, taking mental notes of each word they used. Days later he could play it all back if needed, blow by blow. He spoke in such a way that you felt he had naturally learned to see each word before speaking it. Only when he was drunk did he sometimes wander. I realized that one of the reasons the stories came to him so easily was that he spent a lot of time listening to others. He liked to talk, but he felt just as comfortable listening. Hank had a natural filmic sensibility and a remarkable memory—he recorded what he witnessed in life and stored it away.

I have had another kind of conversation with Bukowski, as a reader, carrying on a private dialogue between myself and what he put onto the page. Usually we read someone who is, more often than not, a total stranger, and at times we leave the page feeling as if we had struck up a lasting friendship. Many readers come away from Henry Miller's sprawling opus convinced that he is their buddy, either a companion of the streets or a free-minded father figure. They forget that they only know him as a voice coming from a book. How many young people maintain a personal relationship with Jack Kerouac for the same reason? There is evidence that an entire generation of college-age rebels saw him on these personal terms—reader to writer. When I first read Bukowski I had only to peruse four or five poems to feel as if his voice, laid down on the page, was that of a soul mate.

This reader's conversation continues. Despite Hank's passing, he continues, through his writings, to tell me of his daily trials, pointing to the foibles and shortcomings of others as well. The big motifs of his poetry and prose come through clearly. One encounters the literary outsider, the tough-minded lover who will not let a woman get too close, the keen observer who may, at any moment, ferret out some simple truth, the L.A. tough guy who exudes a sense of personal danger. Henry Chinaski, that character who bounces through most of Bukowski's fiction, is an intimate of the reader. He is, to borrow from computer terminology, user-friendly. People appreciate him because he talks straight and demands honesty from others. Shame and self-abasement are never far off and he does not hide from either his comic or foolish side. The public image of Bukowski as madman and recluse was orchestrated by the writer himself, and sometimes lived. His uncompromising cynicism serves as an anchor. Concerns are voiced that readers might feel, but either cannot articulate or are afraid to. Chinaski/Bukowski comes across as the man who dares to challenge propriety, who remains unafraid of striking out at social and literary icons. For me, that's been the most interesting part of this reader's conversation.

As Bukowski's biographer I have spent hours taping his life, asking specific questions and letting him answer them one by one, a conversation. More than one hundred pages of these questions and answers exist. As I wrote this biography, we often talked on the telephone. Most of the time he was answering questions about one part of his life or another. Hank gave me permission to recreate our earlier dialogues. He had admired my sketch of him in *Whitman's Wild Children*, a collection of critical memoirs on ten American poets, and I was encouraged to go back and reinvent some of our conversations. The biographer's convention is often difficult in that a tremendous responsibility lies on his shoulders to balance a factual rendering of a person's life with that "other life" that takes hold in the course of writing. One evening Hank said, "You always had a problem listening, but somehow you absorbed enough of our talk. Go with it, baby," after which we proceeded to get drunk on expensive red wine, rather than on the beer of the writer's working-class days.

When I published *Hank*, the life of a then still living author, I felt constrained by certain conventions. Just how personal should I be? Is there a line of propriety one must avoid crossing, even if my subject is the self-described "dirty old man" of American letters? When I first began the project, Hank asked that I keep a distance from certain incidents. When he read the finished book, however, he commented, "I wish you had put in those wilder stories." This revised edition retains a history of Bukowski's coming of age as a writer, as well as providing a more expansive account of our life and times together. It is what I wanted it to be initially, an interweaving of biography and memoir.

Recently, a poet in my writing workshop said that she found a spiritual element in Bukowski. We discussed certain poems that have the quality of all lasting writing, an ability to render the world in a new way. Shortly after talking to my student, I came across an interview in which Hank spoke of Los Angeles as a spiritual city. I realized that this non-religious man, by virtue of his being a poet, possessed many of the characteristics of a spiritual guide. The pugnacious side of Bukowski would cringe at the thought, I am sure, but it is there. In his death, I hear him clearly. His voice comes to me resonant, full of unforced authority, a message of endurance, self-reliance, and honesty of expression. At the same time, he is also saying, "Poetry is a dirty dishrag. Keep laughing at yourself on the way out the door."

Not long after his death, I visited his grave on a hillside overlooking the harbor at San Pedro with our mutual friend, Scott Harrison. It was a warm day, with a few clouds in the sky, idyllic. Hank had once said, "Someday you'll be standing over my grave and I'll pull you down." That didn't happen, but I did put my hand to the grass under which he lay.

— NEELI CHERKOVSKI
San Francisco, 1997

ONE

I N ONE of the quieter neighborhoods, almost at dead center of Los Angeles on a warm day in the spring of 1926, a little boy with a pouty face and small, intense eyes walked toward a group of kids playing three houses down from his own. There were gardenias, pink stucco dreams, palm-lined streets, steamy grasshopper evenings, and days when the Santa Ana winds came down from the high Mojave Desert far inland, bringing echoes of the Spanish conquistadors who founded El Pueblo de Nuestra Señora la Reina de Los Angeles, September 4, 1781, on the site of the Indian settlement of Yang-Na. Beginning on this date, the local myths grew. People flocked to Los Angeles because of its sunlight and the semitropical floridness of the land, ribboned with dry gullies, graced with mountains, and often covered in strange mists. In 1869, when the railroads spanned the continent, this settlement town began to resemble a city.

The growing city searched for water. The city fathers were relentless in this activity. Growth became a religion which everyone worshipped. Los Angeles looked north, like a thirsty dragon, to the Owens River Valley, several hundred miles away. On a clear day in 1913, William Mulholland, chief engineer of the city, stood before an assembled crowd of dignitaries and just plain folk, one hundred thousand in number, and opened the spigots that had brought the water south. He proclaimed, "There it is, take it." With the new water, the city truly became a thriving metropolis, complete with sedate neighborhoods of proper, hardworking folk. A corrupt city administration welded the land, the water, and the city's future together to manipulate the populace to their own ends. While the politicians worked, a movie colony that made people laugh, told them how to feel, and stuffed them with notions of romantic love grew into a phenomena that made the L.A. suburb of Hollywood famous worldwide.

The six-year-old boy watched as a Model T Ford puttered in the opposite direction and tried to keep his eyes from catching the sun, which seemed pinned onto the pale blue sky. He peered at the sun for a moment, taking the memory of that skylamp under his eyelids and amusing himself with its transformation from an intense flame into a thin sliver of light. He walked on with his eyes wide open, wondering what those kids would say once he came close enough. They played up and down the street, tossing balls and thinking up inventive ways of passing away the long summer days. He wanted to join their games, and hoped for an invitation. The boy partially blamed his father for creating a schism between him and these kids. Henry Bukowski, Sr., chased them away whenever they stepped on his lawn. *"You kids get out here!"* he would yell. *"You have no business here!"* He loved telling his wife that those damned hooligans were destroying his beautiful rosebushes and trampling the lawn that he mowed so carefully.

Hank, as he was called by his classmates, busied himself with counting the leaves on a tree. Secretly, he envied the fact that these kids could dress as they liked. His parents demanded that his clothing remain immaculate. If there had been a contest for the best-dressed child on Virginia Road, he would have won. Katherine Bukowski wanted her son to stand out as an example of good breeding. The boy, however, saw things differently. He dreamed of running around in old dungarees.

He focused on the tree while looking out of the corner of one eye to observe the four boys, and thought about what his father had said, that he was forbidden to play with the kids. "They're not good children," Henry Bukowski advised. "I don't want to see you talking with them."

Adding to his frustration, he was constantly rebuffed by the boys. "Hey, Heinie! What are you doing, Heinie?" one of them said. "We don't want to play with you. Go back to Germany with all those other krauts." The boys jumped up and down, hurling the epithet "Heinie" at Henry Charles Bukowski, Jr. They knew how to pitch the insults, one after another with skill and bravado. Rather than run from them, Hank walked closer, hoping for an invitation to join in their games. None of them said anything. He backed off, half circling them, then turned away. The oldest, a kid with blond hair that fell over his forehead, shouted, "Hey, Heinie! Heinie! Are you gonna cry to your mama?"

Hank left the children, wishing he had not been born in Germany. He took a long, sweeping look at the lawns and houses on both sides of the street. I don't belong here, he told himself. When he walked into the house he said nothing to his mother, who busily dusted the furniture. Her indifference had taught him to rely on himself. Alone in his bedroom he reasoned that the German language caused his problems. All that strange talk that he had heard on the last visit to Grandmother Bukowski's house in Pasadena made him angry and impatient. Emilie Bukowski made it a habit to speak in her native tongue to her daughter-in-law Katherine and to her own children.

Hank knew that the boys on Virginia Road called him Heinie because he still had traces of an accent. He managed to rid himself of the German vocabulary by the time he was four and a half years of age; a few words remained, each of which he consciously blocked from his thoughts. The accent, though, took longer to leave, no matter how hard he worked at getting rid of it. Even so, "Heinie" followed him on up through the fourth grade.

While walking home, he thought of his birthplace, Andernach, a town on the Rhine River with cobblestone streets. It had a partial city wall dating back to medieval times, and many buildings over four hundred years old. A few vague impressions were about all he could remember. One person who stood out in his mind was his uncle, Heinrich Fett, whom he called "Uncle Heinie," a jovial, short, good-natured man.

Hank tried to imagine himself elsewhere, and with different parents. Closing his eyes, and lying in his bed, he drifted into a reverie in which he controlled his life. He saw himself running down a street that looked a little like Virginia Road. On either side were other boys his age, laughing and pushing one another playfully, heading toward an open field. Happily, he let this daydream run its course.

The Bukowskis lived an orderly life. The more his parents imposed their rules, the more Hank relied on the wisdom of childhood to find his happiness. His mother remained distant from him throughout his early years. He envied other children when he saw them playing happily with their parents.

Hank developed personal defenses on his own terms, learning to observe people closely, paying special attention to their body movements and facial expressions. If his parents were not available to help interpret the world, or if their teachings seemed suspect, he found that there were enough resources from within to help him define new people and strange situations.

"At four or five you start putting it together and looking around," Hank has said. "I had some pretty terrible parents, and your parents are pretty much your world. That's all there is." Hank felt caged in. His father, frustrated over his failure to find a high-paying job during the twenties, frequently beat Hank. "He wanted to be rich. But he had no talent, he had no special flair. If I made what he thought were errors, I would get a beating. He took it out on me because the world did not quite accept him as he wanted it to." Hank kept his anger, frustration, and rebellion under the surface. Not until he was an adolescent did his rebellion become apparent. Henry's treatment of his only child went far beyond the philosophy of "spare the rod, spoil the child." He offered no kindness, no instructions in how to throw a ball, no bedtime stories, no friendly pats on the back.

The day after the incident with the neighborhood kids, Hank sat in the kitchen, sensing that something was wrong. The windows didn't look right; his father's face appeared distorted. Even the way the tablecloth folded over the side of the table seemed wrong; somehow ominous. He didn't like the sound of his father's snappy, deep voice, nor his mother's shuffling around the breakfast table. She spoke with an accent, and he often heard her say things in German. His father spoke German when he wanted to, even though he was a native-born Californian, and a proud American.

"We're taking a ride today," his father said. "I've got to get the hell out of town. A man has to think." His pronouncement sounded like a challenge. Katherine merely nodded and said, "Yes, Henry. It would be very nice to take a drive."

"I work hard to feed all of us," Henry Senior said. "Now I expect us to be out of here as soon as possible. The sunlight won't last forever. A proper family has to have an outing every week." Hank knew what was coming next.

"I do a good job in my work," Henry continued. "People think being a milk delivery man is easy work. It's not. You have to run around collecting bills. You work long hours. I pull my weight, though, not like the others. Customers don't want to pay their damned bills, so I have to go after them."

"You work very hard, Henry," his wife added.

Before leaving the table, Henry surveyed the kitchen with a smug, self-satisfied air. Money would soon be within his grasp. Even if he had to work for a boss, that was okay, as long as he carried out his job in the prescribed manner. Retirement lay only thirty-five or forty years away.

Henry's morning homilies regarding the American work ethic were as regular as the sunrise. He interwove his outlook on hard work with a litany of complaints concerning his job, together with reports of route changes, his fellow employees' shortcomings, and his bosses' peculiarities. He labored as though an injustice had been dealt to him. As he continued talking about his job on this particular morning, Hank thought about the tablecloth again and considered how wrong it looked. Suddenly his father demanded, "Henry, finish your food! You didn't finish! Oh look, Mama, Look! Henry didn't finish the food you laid out for him." Katherine said, "Yes, Henry. You eat it all before we go on our outing." Hank ate sullenly, not looking forward to a drive in the heat. He made a mental note of his mother's spotless kitchen. Everything seemed so clean: no dust had settled on any of the furnishings or objects in the room, not a dish remained unwashed. Rather than go with them, he wanted to be out on the streets with kids his own age, playing games.

Henry rubbed his hands together, knitted his brows and breathed in deeply. The Sunday drives were not the whims of a nature lover, or a man who enjoyed the outdoors. They simply offered a defeated man a means of dealing with his frustration. When not working or going for a drive, he sat in his chair before the large picture window, listening to USC games on the radio, surveying his lawn and his neighbors.

These were not particularly fun outings for Hank, though they did break up some of the day-to-day monotony of staying at home or around the neighborhood. Hank felt embarrassed as they finally left the kitchen and prepared to leave the house. Could these two people really be his parents? Their voices didn't sound right. Their mouths didn't move properly. Their hands were false and awkward. Their arms were like afterthoughts to the rest of their bodies. He repeated such observations often. Far from aggravating him, they offered Hank comfort, making him feel ever more self-reliant, more able to face himself comfortably. Many things remained a mystery, but he was beginning to know himself through his rejection of others.

There were no freeways back then, nor sprawling, seemingly endless suburbs, and it didn't take long to drive from the center of the city to the orange groves surrounding Los Angeles. Dairies, bean fields, and plenty of open land lay close by. The myth of an idyllic pastoral life still clung to the palm trees and numerous mission-style buildings dominating the city's commercial districts. A little over 1,400,000 people lived in Los Angeles back in the mid-twenties. The majority of them had come from elsewhere, dreaming of charmed lives in a land of perpetual sunshine.

Even in the car, Henry's obsession with his job dominated. No matter what happened in the world, nothing could be more important than the milk route. Henry's monologues were populated by his co-workers: "Conrad didn't do his job—and McHugh is messing up." All the way out of town and on to the country road leading to the orderly rows of trees, the job was explored from every possible angle. Occasionally, one of Henry's family members came under attack: "That Ben is a good-for-nothing bum. He'll never amount to anything." Katherine, well practiced in her husband's moods, rarely failed to agree.

On and on they drove, passing gas stations with one or two red pumps in front of a roadside cafe, and the shacks of migrant workers. On these trips, Hank's mother brought along a picnic basket filled with sandwiches, fruit, potato chips, and soft drinks. There was also an old-fashioned portable icebox in which she had put fruit over dry ice. Henry occasionally showed his son and wife games that he learned to play with his ever-present pack of Camel cigarettes.

They arrived at a small park surrounded by orange groves vaguely east of Los Angeles. Katherine laid out her lunch on a table while Henry sat facing the groves, complaining that it was a damned shame the oranges were not there for the taking—as if the no trespassing signs were a personal affront. When Katherine said that lunch was ready Henry sat down with a scowl on his face. Within moments he was scolding Hank for running off far from the table.

Not all outings were to the orange groves. The family sometimes drove to Venice Beach and neighboring Ocean Park, with its big amusement pier. People paraded up and down the boardwalk, picnicked on the beach, and bought rides on the amusement pier. Children who went there with their parents were allowed to play freely— except for Hank. Henry and Katherine kept him close by their side as they promenaded on the boardwalk. Hank's memories of the beach are pleasant enough: "You would smell hamburger and onions, and you had to eat. Everybody ate hamburgers down at Venice Beach, or you had to get back in your car and get out of there. It was worse than a drug. The sand was clean. The air was clean. You breathed and you felt good. There were shells in the sand. Kids would come up with big pails full of nothing but shells. Now you have bottle caps and styrofoam."

A small dose of fatherly kindness came about before dawn once, when Henry awakened five-year-old Hank so he could watch him prepare for his milk route. The company he worked for still used horse-drawn milk wagons. Hank walked outside clothed in his pajamas and slippers. It must have been around five A.M. They walked to the milk wagon. The horse was in harness, waiting to begin the daily routine. Henry held out a sugarcube to the horse, who unceremoniously devoured it. Seeing Hank's amusement, he said, "Here, you try it next. Just hold your palm out there and the horse will take the sugarcube just like he did from me." Henry put the sugar in his son's hands and Hank held it out to the animal. He drew back for a moment, fearful that the beast might bite off his entire hand when he saw the pinkish flesh underneath the horse's parting lips. His father coaxed him closer. Hank moved on in as the horse exposed his teeth and tongue, finally taking the sugarcube. "Do it again," Henry told his son—and once more the cube disappeared into the horse's mouth.

Anna Bukowski, the wife of Hank's Uncle John, remembered her nephew as a sullen and lonely child. "I felt sorry for little Henry. It seemed as if he really needed friends—some kids his own age. I know that his parents didn't let him play with other children. He didn't speak out like most kids. Henry just didn't seem a jolly boy. When they came to visit us I could see how closely they watched over him." Anna's daughter, Katherine, pictures her cousin as a chubby kid who dressed in formal clothing. "My Aunt Katy was so fussy with him. He couldn't play like other children. I believe they were very strict. When he visited us he was dressed in an elaborate outfit. He didn't look comfortable."

For Hank's birthday parties children were welcomed into the house, given paper hats to wear and directed toward different party games like pin the tail on the donkey. But it quickly became Henry's show. He hovered over the young guests like a Prussian officer. There would be ice cream and cake, little paper napkins printed with happy birthday. Henry made sure the kids didn't spill any cake on the floor or drip ice cream on his rug. If they did, he shouted in a way guaranteed to frighten them. Katherine would stand off to one side, passively letting her husband do as he wished. Even during the games, he commanded: "You must play politely!" If they became noisy, he shouted them down, ordering them back into their chairs. After the first two or three parties, Hank began to dread them. His parents rarely surprised him with a toy. The gifts they bought were undershorts, stockings, and other articles of clothing. He was afraid to ask for toys, inwardly angry because they gave as gifts what parents are expected to provide. He knew what other kids had received for gifts, everything from miniature railroads to baseball gloves. One fine gift his father surprised him with was an Indian suit—but the other kids on Virginia Road played in cowboy outfits.

The patriarch of the Bukowski clan, Grandfather Leonard, had emigrated from Germany in the 1880s, after serving in the Kaiser's army. He made his way to Cleveland, where he met, and fell in love with eighteen-year-old Emilie Krause, an immigrant from Danzig. After their marriage, they moved to Pasadena, a suburb of Los Angeles. Many of America's wealthiest families settled there, including the Wrigleys, who made a fortune in chewing gum.

Leonard stood six feet, three inches tall, weighed more than two hundred pounds and sported a prominent mustache. Hank remembers the smell of whiskey on his breath the one time they met. When he visited his grandfather, his parents waited in the car. "My parents wouldn't come in the house. I asked them later, 'Why don't you go to see him? He's beautiful. He's a nice man.' My father yelled, 'He drinks!' " Leonard gave his seven-year-old grandson the Iron Cross he had earned in the Kaiser's army, and a gold watch.

Leonard had been attracted to Pasadena by the unlimited opportunities presented in a rapidly growing city. He worked as a carpenter, and lived in a modest house at 205 South Pasadena Avenue. He stayed in the trade until 1904, when he became a general contractor. By 1906 his firm prospered. His wife, Emilie, bore four sons and two daughters. The eldest, John, was born in 1888. He was followed in age by Charles; Henry Charles was next in age. Then there were Emma, Eleanor, and Ben.

Hank's cousin Katherine remembers a visit by Henry Bukowski and his family when she and her sister were still quite young. "We were very poor. My father didn't make much money. I think Aunt Katy looked down on my parents for that reason. I remember when she came over once and was wearing a very stylish silk scarf. It must have been obvious to her that I admired it. Probably to humor me, she let me touch it and then wear it for a while."

Henry disliked his brothers for reasons long forgotten. Ben was a quiet man, with a mischievous side to him; John lived in a small house on a sizable piece of property, and rarely had any money. Katherine and her sister Eleanor, Hank's cousins, were strangers to him. He described them years later: two very quiet, pretty girls who were scraping peanut butter from a jar.

Katherine Bukowski Woods describes her grandmother Emilie as being a conservative Baptist. "I think she eventually gave a lot of her money to the church. She left my grandfather, but not before she had taken control of most of the money he had made as a contractor—at least that is what I have heard." She said that Leonard and Emilie reconciled shortly before the old man's death from stomach cancer in the late twenties. Cousin Katherine says that her Aunt Katy, Hank's mother, took care of Leonard during his illness and that the old man stayed at his son's house in Los Angeles. "It may be so that my mother took care of him," Hank says, "but my grandfather didn't stay with us. Probably my mother went over to his place in Pasadena. I mean, I would know if he was in my house. I only saw him once."

By 1920, Emilie Bukowski lived in her own home, separately from her husband, also in Pasadena—one of several houses he owned. It was a much smaller house than she was used to. The one she raised her children in had been a rambling, two-story structure. But her home wasn't without its own charm, half hidden as it was behind an overhanging mass of pepper trees. Life in the small house centered in the kitchen, where German and American cuisine was prepared in vast quantities. There were dishes of wiener schnitzel and sauerbraten, roast beef, ham with pineapple slices—and there was always plenty of coffee being served. What Hank remembers most of all are the mounds of mashed potatoes and gravy that Emilie dished out. As she served the food she often told the family, "I will bury all of you." That is one of the few phrases he remembers her saying. There was never any hugging or kissing, never any demonstrations of grandmotherly love. A certain tension hung in the air during visits to Emilie's. That Leonard's name was never mentioned must only have made his absence that much more present.

Hank had a clear memory of Emilie's canaries: "She had many cages. They were all of different sizes and styles. One time when we were over there it was getting dark and she covered the cages with white hoods."

Emilie owned a piano, which she had taken from her husband's house. On one visit Hank sat there and began playing with it, fascinated by the varying sounds he could make come out of it. He kept on hitting the keys while his parents and Emilie talked, along with other relatives. Suddenly his father demanded that he stop playing. "Let the boy play the piano," Emilie said.

Henry Bukowski met wife-to-be, Katherine Fett, in Andernach, Germany, when he was stationed there as a young GI in 1920. Katherine's brother Heinrich managed a canteen for the American troops, and it was there that he met Henry Bukowski. The two men liked each other, and sometimes the American brought meat and other condiments to the Fett household—which, like other families in Andernach, was suffering from a lack of food brought on by the war. One day he glimpsed Heinrich's sister Katherine and wanted to meet her. Being a shy woman, she resisted, but finally Henry came for dinner at the Fett's. The tall American fell in love with the diminutive German girl, and it wasn't long before they married.

Their son, Henry Charles Bukowski, Jr., was born in Andernach on August 16, 1920.

Henry and Katherine, together with their child, stayed on in Andernach for a while after the war ended, but Henry soon felt restless for home. By the time they had come from Germany to Los Angeles, the city had entered a period of unparalleled growth. Although it was doubling its boundaries in a relatively short time, the town retained some of the flavor of its past—a wild cow town of the 1860s and 1870s, and earlier still, its Spanish past, which had become a mostly mythical history of an era of romantic Californios who ruled over vast tracts of land, raising prime cattle and horses.

Katherine rarely said much concerning growing up in Germany, or about her family. Without warning, she would sometimes tell Hank random stories. One concerned her grandfather: "He was an accomplished musician," who "drank a lot of beer." According to her, he went from bar to bar playing the violin, holding his hat out for tips. As soon as he had earned enough money he stepped to the bar and began drinking. As the evening progressed, he would be thrown out of one bar for being disorderly, and move on to the next, and the next. Hank liked this story very much and felt sure that his great-grandfather must have been equal to Leonard Bukowski, another drinker. He began to think that the older generations of his family must have really been special.

Katherine barely knew English when she arrived in the States. As Hank said in later years, "My father was conqueror of her nation. A hero. In a sense, he ruled over her. Rarely, if ever, did she contradict his various edicts." Henry Bukowski didn't just beat his son as the boy grew older, but he also inflicted physical punishment on his wife as well. "When things were really tough during the Depression," Hank says, "My old man would often beat my mother. I tried to stop him a few times, but then, after beating away at her, he would start on me."

At Virginia Road Grammar School, Hank became friendly with a lonely, cross-eyed boy his own age named David Winchell. They started talking to one another during lunch period when they happened to sit down on the same bench preparing to eat their sandwiches. They discussed what kind of sandwiches their respective mothers had prepared. David offered Hank some potato chips, who took a few and then asked for more. Before the break ended, the two kids decided to walk home together.

They were followed by a pack of first-graders who surrounded David and began calling him names. One boy knocked him to the ground. When David got up, rubbing the tears from his eyes, the biggest attacker said that *they* didn't want sissies in their school. The boy then punched David in the stomach. Next, they encircled Hank, screaming catcalls. He couldn't make out what they were saying, and then, for some reason, they pulled back and walked away.

When Hank arrived at his classmate's home, David said goodbye and disappeared into his house. From inside, the sound of Mrs. Winchell scolding her son for his messy knickers and shirt echoed through the walls and into the street. Then she told him to do his music lessons. Hank waited around a while finally hearing a violin. On his way home he thought to himself that he didn't like this new friend or the way he played the violin.

Throughout his school years, Hank found himself singled out over and over by kids like David. He concluded that the oddballs and subnormals were inexplicably attracted to him. In a strange way he *had* really taken after his father, considering his cynical view of life. Henry Senior's negative view of the world had filtered down, into his son. Hank hardly found a schoolmate with whom he felt comfortable. As far as he was concerned, he could do without an ongoing friendship. "There wasn't any escape. Home was bad. Then you'd be in school and that wasn't an escape, and then you'd be walking home and you'd be followed by the mob, guys threatening to beat the shit out of you. There was no release." Adults sensed Hank's rebellion: his eyes and facial expressions told them that he was the cool observer, that he meant to let them know that they could not pull anything over on *him*. Always in the back of his mind stood the figure of Henry C. Bukowski, Sr.

There was one basic difference in the way he and his father reacted to people. While Henry barked and yelled, Hank simply expressed by body movement, and perhaps a subtle phrase or a lowering or slowing of his voice, a general disdain. Where his father performed emotional slash-and-burn on both his wife and child, Hank withdrew into himself, radiating his rebellion, slowly building a wall of silence between himself and the object of his scorn.

In grammar school Hank was the kid with the sneer, the type of pupil whom a teacher never forgets. In the classroom itself, it became a ritual for the teacher to either send him into the hall as punishment for his classroom behavior, or to shout out, *"Wipe that sneer off of your face!"* Strangely, none of the male teachers seemed annoyed by Hank: the female teachers were the ones who were most bothered by him. "I found it strange," he says, "but the women teachers must have sensed my rebellion." He had come to believe that the majority of the teachers were acting: they didn't necessarily believe in, or practice, the lessons that they taught. He was judgmental from the moment they began to talk, and began to measure the degree of their commitment to whatever it was that they said.

One thing he had noticed when his father became angry in public, whether for some imagined slight in a movie-theater line or, more often, in a restaurant where he argued about the poor service and the bad food, was that people rarely shouted back. They didn't seem to be frightened by the big man. They'd listen, but nothing much would ever change. Watching this, day in, day out, Hank slowly learned to give his father the silent treatment, and to do it to teachers as well.

One time in his early grammar school years the family went to the neighborhood pharmacy. A clerk came up to Hank and his mother and asked Mrs. Bukowski if she knew who that horrible man was on the other side of the store: "Every time he comes in here, there's an argument."

"That's my husband," she told him. It was as if Henry Senior deliberately wanted to see how far he could go with people. Yet, Hank knew instinctively that, despite his impressive size, his father was a coward and would back down if anyone seriously offered a challenge.

Hank's parents were disinterested in his academic progress. They never asked how he felt about his studies, nor probed him about which subjects interested him more than others. He drifted along on his own, mainly concerned with getting through each day without having to fight someone. But finally, the inevitable happened: Hank got into a fight. A school bully threw the first punch. When the teacher came to stop the brawl, all the other boys, including a few who were Hank's tormentors throughout his grammar school years, said that Hank had started the fight. He was sent to the school office where he went through a grueling interview with the principal, who brought it to an end by asking Hank to shake his hand. He hesitated. The principal coaxed him with an outstretched hand, whereupon the man squeezed Hank's hand, demanding *"Am I a tough guy?"* The humiliation ended with Hank groaning "Yes," and the principal handed him a note to take home to his parents.

That note from the principal, telling of Hank's bad citizenship, began a new era. When he handed the note to his mother he headed for his room, which he always did on coming home. He lay down in bed and tried to sleep. His mother began crying loudly: *"You have disgraced us! You have brought shame on us!"* The conditioning of her petit bourgeois upbringing surfaced. When she grew up in Andernach, the teachers and school administrators received as much respect as do doctors and scientists in the United States. If a student got into trouble with the school system it meant that the student, not the teacher, had done something wrong.

Katherine asked Hank what would happen if the neighbors found out. It was as if something cataclysmic had fallen on the Bukowski household. *"How could you have done this to your mother?"* she continued. Then she invoked ultimate fear when she said, "Oh, wait until your father comes home from work." When she slammed his door shut and went back into the living room, Hank lay there reasoning that he hadn't really done anything bad and yet he was made to feel as if he had. Soon afterward, he heard his father's mean-spirited voice, which filled Hank more with revulsion than fear.

Katherine explained to her husband what had taken place, and handed him the note. Henry Senior called his son from the room and said, "All right, Henry, into the bathroom!" The boy wondered why his father didn't ask his side of the story, but he didn't bother to bring the question up. He entered the bathroom as commanded. Henry grabbed his razor strop from its hook on the wall, held it in a firm grip, and ordered his son to take his pants down. There were many blows, hard and numbing. Tears rose in Hank's eyes. Luckily, he couldn't hear the words crawling angrily from his father's mouth. All he heard, all he felt, was the strop hitting his flesh. Then he focused his mind on the rosebushes his father had grown and tended in the backyard, his pride and joy, the things he loved—and his automobile sitting securely in the garage. Hank began to cry, not wanting to, but he couldn't help it. His father finally stopped and left the room.

Hank knew enough of his father's temperament not to be too surprised by the beating. As for his mother, he somehow expected her to come to his assistance. He went up to her and told her that it wasn't right for his father to beat him, and that she knew it. She told him that father is always right, then walked away. Hank never forgave his mother for not coming to his defense on this or numerous other occasions. In later years, he would think back on her acquiescence to his father's disciplining, and feel both anger and profound disappointment. He couldn't have known that his mother was most likely the victim of her own upbringing. To have opposed her husband would have violated the fundamental rules she had grown up with: the father is the *unquestioned* master of his household, and children have absolute respect for parents' authority. It was, once again, part of the code of the German middle class. Katherine would have betrayed her own conditioning in Andernach to have taken exception to the beating, or to all the subsequent ones.

Not long after Hank began grammar school the family moved several blocks from their home on Virginia Road to a two-bedroom house at 2122 Longwood Avenue. There was a large picture window in the living room, which faced the front lawn. From his chair, which also faced outside, his father listened to sports events on the radio. At Longwood Avenue, Henry informed his son that he had now reached an age at which he must help care for the house: "Your job will be to mow the lawn." Hank must have been in the fourth or fifth grade when his father told him this. "I had been playing football with some of the neighborhood guys. For some reason they had let me join in their games." It was a Saturday morning, and Henry Bukowski had plenty of time to survey his son's work.

"You're big enough to mow the lawn, to trim the edges, and then to water the roses," Henry said. "It's time you earned your keep around here!" Hank tried to reason with him, explaining that he wanted to at least finish playing football. His father asked him if he was talking back. Hank said that he wasn't.

His mother watched from behind a curtain of the picture window. This was their normal work day. From morning until night his parents put all their passions into scrubbing, dusting, rinsing, sweeping, waxing. Hank could never quite figure out why they had to move the rug every week and wax the floor underneath it. Years later he explained it as a kind of Germanic excess.

For a kid who had not been allowed to play with other children for so many years, every chance he had to join a game meant a lot. His father told him to stop wasting his time on such worthless activities—which Hank couldn't understand, since his father listened to the ball game religiously.

Katherine continued to stand by the picture window as Henry explained to Hank the intricacies of mowing the lawn and trimming the edges. He showed him how to dump the grass from the catcher, and exactly where to begin trimming. He warned his son to wipe the unhappy look from his face, saying that, if he didn't, "I'll give you something to really be unhappy about." Hank didn't understand until a short time later what a prophet his father could be—of self-fulfilling prophecies.

He had his mind on all the other gardening implements that his father shoved into his face. Henry paraded an edge trimmer, a hose and gardening shears before him. His instructions were precise and pointed: *You go north. You go south. You double mow. You make sure your edges are trimmed neatly and in a straight line.* "Remember. Under no circumstances are you to leave one blade of grass higher than another," he warned. And that was his last instruction, put in ominous terms. Hank began to appreciate the gravity of the situation. Since he had never gardened before, he knew that it would be fairly easy to make a mistake. He said nothing of this to his father; that would have been considered insolence. What he did consider was the fact that he didn't feel as if the house belonged to the family. It was Henry Charles Bukowski, Sr.'s house, and no one else's.

Henry warned his son that he would come out to do a thorough check of all the yard work when it was finished. As Hank reports in *Ham on Rye*, the novel of his childhood and young adult years, his father warned, *"I don't want to see one hair sticking up in either the front or back lawn! Not one hair!"*

Hank set about doing the job. He knew that his father could have made it easier by letting him do it later in the day, after the game. He kept on thinking of his friends playing football, of the day waning away, of the sun going down, and him, still working on the yard.

When he began on the back lawn Katherine and Henry came onto the porch that led off the kitchen to check on his progress. He said nothing to them and continued mowing. His mother wore her special blank expression; Henry looked impatient. Hank continued mowing, thinking of how unjust his father was, wishing for a different kind of father, or none at all. He thought of Frank Sullivan, one of the neighborhood boys, with whom he had been playing football earlier in the day. He liked Frank, and envied the freedom his parents gave him.

Hank began mowing near to where his parents stood. He overheard his mother saying, "Henry, he doesn't sweat like you do when you mow the lawn. He looks so calm."

"Calm? He's not calm. He looks dead," his father answered. He then told his son to push harder, faster. Hank obliged, causing grass to fly out over the grass catcher. His father screamed, *"You son of a bitch!"*

Henry leapt from the porch and ran to the garage where his car sat. He rummaged for a moment and came bounding back with a two-by-four almost a foot in length. Hank saw it coming, but made no attempt to dodge it. He wanted to let the old man have his satisfaction. "He got me on my right leg. It was very painful, especially considering I was just this kid. My leg seemed to freeze, but I knew that I had to keep walking, so I did. I just grabbed on to the mower tighter than before. Finally, I came up to where the two-by-four had landed. I reached down, picked it up and threw it aside. The pain got worse." Henry called his son to a halt and made him go back and do the lawn over where he hadn't caught the grass in the catcher. Hank obliged, doing his best to hide the pain.

After finishing the lawn, Hank had to use the hose to clean off the driveway and then to water both the front and back yards. His father came from the house to do his inspection. This would be a ritual repeated many more times over the ensuing years, with the same results. The big man went onto the lawn, got down on his hands and knees, and put his head down next to the just cut lawn to see if any grass had been missed. Hank stood off to one side, waiting. His father sprang to his feet and ran toward the house, saying, "Ah-ha!" He called for his wife, "Mama! Oh Mama!" Katherine joined him on the front lawn. He told her that he had *found a hair*, meaning a blade of grass—in fact, he discovered *two* of them. He asked his wife to bend down and have a look. She did and told her husband that she could see them, too. Katherine then went back into the house, not looking at her son. Henry pointed to the front door and told Hank to go inside. "Into the bathroom," Henry said. Once they were there Hank was told to take his pants down. "Then the beating began. He used that same strop he had used on me that time he beat me for the problem at school. In truth, he had beat me for other infractions as well, so I had become used to it. Still, a beating is a beating, and it hurts. My father laid into me without mercy. I had failed in doing a perfect job on his goddamn lawn and could not be forgiven."

On the streets Hank found some relief from the iron rule of his father. His parents had gradually loosened the reins, and allowed him to play with the neighborhood kids. For years he had felt awkward with other children, primarily because he was not allowed to talk with them except in school. Up until this time—his last year in grammar school—he hardly knew how to throw a baseball or football correctly.

Longwood Avenue was a shaded street, with hardly any traffic; the houses had green lawns and sizable yards. It looked pretty much like any other street in the country at that time, the kind that a director wouldn't sneeze at if he were making a movie about growing up—a perfect environment for kids. One of Hank's first Longwood Avenue friends was a redheaded boy called "Red." He told Hank about his false arm and let him touch it. Hank felt the false arm, which was as hard as a rock. He asked Red if he had any friends either. None of the boys in the neighborhood played with either of them. Hank had found a soul mate—and to make things even better, Red had his own football, which he immediately brought out to the street so he and Hank could play. They took turns pretending to play various positions, throwing the ball, kicking it. The two boys had various adventures together, both on Longwood Avenue and elsewhere in the neighborhood.

Hank's fifth-grade teacher explained to her class that President Herbert Hoover was slated to appear at the Coliseum in Exposition Park, a few miles south of downtown Los Angeles and next to the USC campus. "This is a once in a lifetime opportunity," she told them. "You and your parents should attend this event as a civic duty." She asked them each to write essays about the momentous occasion. Hank didn't go, but he wrote about Hoover anyway. He put many details into his essay like how the president stood ramrod-straight, how he waved to the crowds and how his voice boomed over the sound system. He described the excited populace of L.A. assembled there, cheering their president.

When the essays were handed in, the teacher read each dutifully and told the students, "There is one bit of writing here about the visit of our president to the Coliseum written by Henry Bukowski. It is so beautiful and I want to read it to you." The kids turned and looked his way. They found it difficult to believe that the class oddball, the outsider, the loner, had been singled out for his writing ability. Once the class settled down, the teacher began reading his story.

As the other students left the class, Hank's teacher asked him to stay behind. She questioned whether he had actually been present when President Hoover gave his address. Cornered, he admitted that he had not been there. Rather than being angry, the teacher said that this fact made his essay all the more remarkable, and that she was very impressed. Hank, as young as he was, realized then that "people wanted beautiful lies, not the truth. That's what they needed. People were fools." This impression became central to his way of thinking from that time onward.

That was the first time Hank believed he was a writer. Yet rather than being encouraged to write more, he simply drew back, although it impressed him to see that all the kids in the class, even the prettiest girls and the top athletes, stared at him with admiration when the teacher finished reading his essay. Even he almost believed that he had been *at* the Coliseum.

Hank does not quite remember the circumstances, but about this time he developed a friendship with Frank Sullivan, who had been among his tormentors on Virginia Road. He was a blond-haired boy who remained Hank's friend up through the sixth grade. Because he was friendly with Frank, who had many friends, Hank was slowly accepted by the other kids and joined in their games. As he and Frank grew older they began wandering away from the immediate area of Longwood Avenue. They spent their time making their way down to the beach, riding their bicycles, sometimes walking, or sneaking onto the movie studio lots. One excursion documented was to an airshow down at Dominguez Hills, several miles from their homes.

Hank became interested in airplanes, having learned about them from Frank and from his father, who had been a World War I flying ace in Europe. The two boys walked down to Venice Boulevard to hitch a ride. They got a ride from a man of about thirty-five. When they got into the car he tried to interest the two boys in going for a swim, telling them that he knew a place where they could be alone. He interspersed this with talk of a man who was arrested for a homosexual act under the pier at Venice Beach, expressing outrage that the police would pry into what should be a citizen's right to privacy. The boys insisted on going to the air show. The man submitted, driving them there. When they parked, Hank and his pal took off running, losing themselves in the crowd.

Frank's family belonged to the Catholic Church. He attended catechism classes at Saint Agatha's Church on West Adams Boulevard. The church was within walking distance from Longwood Avenue, and Hank began going there with his friend. Henry and Katherine approved of, and encouraged, Hank's attendance. "Maybe this will straighten him out," Henry advised his wife.

Catechism class interested Hank. He enjoyed passing the time discussing religion with Frank. Little did he know that a man destined to be perhaps the greatest influence on his own work, John Fante, had undergone a Catholic upbringing in Boulder, Colorado, and, in fact, would write a book about it, *Dago Red*. This book was destined to be one of Hank's favorite pieces in his junior-college days. When he read the descriptions of the nuns, the priests, the confession box, and the religious classes, he thought of those days with Frank Sullivan attending the parish church.

When a priest told Hank and his friend that animals could not go to heaven because they didn't have souls and therefore could not be baptized, the two boys didn't take this disturbing news well. Instead, they found a dog near the church, brought him inside and sprinkled him with holy water.

Gradually, the novelty of Catholicism and its mysteries wore off, and Hank became bored. He decided that the regimentation and dogma didn't suit him, nor did he like a God who seemed so much like his father. After two weeks of Hank's skipping classes, the church sent two girls of Hank's age, blonde, blue-eyed, and dressed in flowery blouses, to see him. He told the girls that he didn't want to return to the catechism class—and that was the end of his flirtation with organized religion.

Hank began junior high school in the same year that Franklin Roosevelt became president. He listened to his father gripe about the lack of discipline at every level of society, and how this was ruining the country. He continued preaching the gospel of hard work, and the more he talked, the less Hank listened. But he did hear his father, and a lot of other people, discuss the great flood of '34, the result of the heaviest downpour in the recorded history of the region. The local newspapers reported that thirty-six people died in the 8.27-inch deluge. That storm, amidst the suffering brought on by hard times, dramatically showed the people of Los Angeles just how bad life can be.

Fifty-six years later, the poet Charles Bukowski sat down and wrote "We Ain't Got No Money Honey, but We Got Rain," a document of what times were like when the promise of the American heartland turned to dust and jobless millions waited in despair for good times to come again. The poem begins:

> *call it the greenhouse effect or whatever*
> *but it just doesn't rain like it*
> *used to.*
>
> *I particularly remember the rain of the*
> *depression era.*
> *there wasn't any money but there was*
> *plenty of rain.*
> *. . .*
> *the jobless men,*
> *failures in failing time*
> *were imprisoned in their houses with their*

wives and children
and their
pets.
. . .

the jobless men went mad
confined with their once beautiful wives.
there were terrible arguments
as notices of foreclosure
fell into the mailbox.
rain and hail, cans of beans,
bread without butter . . .
. . .

my father, never a good man
at best, beat my mother
when it rained
as I threw myself
between them,
the legs, the knees, the
screams
until they
separated.

"I'll kill you," *I screamed*
at him, "You hit her again
and I'll kill you."

"Get that son-of-a-bitching
kid out of here!"

TWO

Bukowski attended Mount Vernon Junior High School, a short walk from home. He told himself that adults, and children, too, were not very nice. Nothing deterred him from this belief. Irony, silence, and sarcasm were three weapons he put to good use. His demeanor was taciturn and guarded, at home and at school. Tainted words poured from the mouths of his teachers as they spoke what Hank knew to be rote and meaningless lessons. The lack of passion in their voices annoyed him. The only way to illuminate the darkness of the classroom was to retreat from it without leaving his seat.

Hank's father's milk delivery job came abruptly to an end because of hard times. Katherine Bukowski found employment as a cleaning woman for well-to-do families unscathed by the Depression. Hank and his fellow classmates inherited the desperation of their parents, brought on by the deepening of hard times. Not a few of his contemporaries shared the same disdain for authority that he did.

In the seventh grade he met William Eli Mullinaux, a short, small-boned boy nicknamed "Baldy." He remembers that Hank would raise his hand and tell a teacher that what he or she had just said was wrong. "Hank didn't let those teachers get away with anything," he has said. The boy had heard so much misdirected anger from his father that he had learned to appreciate honesty; he watched for it, especially from his teachers who were supposed to represent the truth.

Together with Frank Sullivan, Hank and Baldy began to explore the world of women, in the burlesque houses downtown. The three friends made their way there on the trolleys. To their amazement, none of them were ever asked their ages. They paid the admission and went inside.

Hank continued to feel like an outsider, but he did hang around with Frank and Baldy. Long walks to the beach, trips to the burlesque houses, and an inordinate amount of solitude were important aspects in his life. The pronouncements he sometimes made concerning school and society were taken seriously by his classmates. He had many years of practice as a keen observer, which gave him insights that he shared—not meaning to impress anyone, but just because he had to express them.

When he was caught for a prank at school, along with Baldy and another classmate, the principal wrote a note to Henry Bukowski, who again took his son into the bathroom, already the scene of many beatings. Although the laying on of the strop continued, which hurt like hell, Hank's response was profoundly different: his fear had gone away. A certain victory over his father had been won. For quite some time he had known that the beatings were senseless, more of a ritual in which his father satisfied his own needs than actual punishment. Hank sensed that his father understood something was different in his son's attitude. Suddenly he stopped beating him and walked to the bathroom door. "Why don't you give me some more, if it makes you feel any better," Hank asked.

Commenting on this incident in his autobiographical novel *Ham on Rye*, Hank writes:

> I looked at him. I saw folds of flesh under his chin and around his neck. I saw sad wrinkles and crevices. His face was tired putty. He was in his undershirt, and his belly sagged, wrinkling his undershirt. The eyes were no longer fierce. His eyes looked away and couldn't meet mine. Something had happened...My

father turned and walked out the door. He knew it. It was my last beating. From him.

During the summer of 1934, after graduating from junior high, Hank and his father argued over which high school he would attend. Henry insisted on Los Angeles High School on Olympic Boulevard, considered to be the best school around, and the one where the wealthy families from the affluent neighborhood of Hancock Park sent their children. He figured that the luster of the rich kids might rub off on his son. In *Ham on Rye,* Hank tends to portray himself as a lower-class kid thrown in with those from rich families. The reality, according to his classmates, was that plenty of children from poorer families attended Los Angeles High School. The school was a cross-section of the city's economic makeup, and by no means an enclave of the rich.

"You'll do well to follow the example of the rich kids," Henry said. "They're from the best families and they know how to buckle down and work."

Hank answered that it made better sense to attend Polytechnic High, because it was closer to home. He lost the argument and reluctantly registered at L.A. High School. Worse, his face began to break out with acne. But since a skin condition of this kind was normal for kids his age, no one paid much attention to it.

On the first day of school he rode his bicycle along with Baldy. Many of the older students had their own cars, and most were well dressed. For an adolescent like Hank, who identified with the poor, and who loved to sit back and listen to President Roosevelt's fireside chats, his peers seemed as if they came from a different world. Hank focused much attention on the sons and daughters of the rich, so out of place, it seemed to him, in a country ravaged by poverty.

Through the summer before Hank's sophomore year, his skin condition worsened, and as a result he felt increasingly alienated from other adolescents. Scorn for the student body grew ever more wildly within him when the affliction took a dramatic turn for the worse:

it had erupted on his upper torso and his back, as well as his face. The thought of disrobing in the locker room and then having to stand nude in the showers, subjecting himself to possible ridicule, was too much for him. Tremendously embarrassed at this prospect, he opted for ROTC. He was not gung-ho about that, but at least he didn't have to expose himself. The other boys loved their uniforms, and wore them proudly.

The acne became so bad in that first year of high school that the pustules on his shoulders became raw while he participated in ROTC drills. When drilling with his rifle, he occasionally had to bang his gun against his shoulders, quickly and hard. Blood invariably soaked through the uniform. At home his mother lined that area of his shirts with cloth.

Hank often stood before the bathroom mirror, imagining how he must look to others. "I felt as if no woman would ever want to be with me. I saw myself as some kind of freak. Remember, they were big. They dominated my face." At the end of the first term of high school, he withdrew from school. He didn't like the idea of being singled out, especially for something that was entirely beyond his control.

Henry gave him a brown salve, probably sulfur and Resorcinol pastes, and insisted that he keep the paste on his face long after the time indicated in the instructions. "It will make you better," he shouted, "I know what I'm doing." On one particular night he insisted that Hank leave it on all evening. The burning sensation that came along with it became so intense that he ran to the bathtub, filled it with cold water and washed the salve away. When his father discovered what he had done he told his wife, "That son of a bitch doesn't want to be well. Why did I have to have a son like this?"

To make matters worse, Katherine lost her job cleaning houses while Henry played a game of pretend by getting in his car each morning and driving away from the house as if he were going to work. He told his neighbors that he was an engineer, something he had always dreamed of being. Henry's lying at this time, and throughout his life, only enhanced Hank's insistence on being honest with his own emotions. "My father's lies," he has said, "caused me to value the truth in my poetry, to value the truth when writing about the human condition."

Hank trekked to Los Angeles County Hospital, clear on the other side of town. The recently completed main building, considered a showcase piece of architecture at the time, was already crowded with patients. Here Hank received one of his first tastes of bureaucracy after a tedious ride on the Los Angeles Railway's yellow car. He was sent to the fourth floor. He was told to wait in a sprawling room filled with other charity cases. The time for his appointment passed. He waited the entire day, but was never called. Late in the afternoon he handed in his appointment card and returned the following morning, again for an early appointment. When his turn came, the doctor looked at him and called in some other doctors for consultation. One of them said it was the worst case of acne vulgaris he had ever seen. Hank was amazed at their insensitivity. They talked about him as if he wasn't even present, in the most frank and insulting terms. One doctor told of a girl who had just cried, saying that she would never get a man because she would be scarred for life. If she could only see this young man, he said, she would see that she had nothing to complain about. Smarting under this kind of abuse, Hank steeled himself against the physical pain subjected upon him. The doctors went to work with ultraviolet treatments. One of the indicated treatments back in the thirties was with a narrow-bladed surgical knife, used to promote drainage. In Hank's case, an electric needle was used to drill each pustule individually. One nurse asked him what he did to occupy himself while out of school. He described going home and staying in bed because he was so ashamed of the acne. "That's awful," she said. When he suggested that girls were now out of his life she told him not to think that way. The nurse was the kindest person he had met in years. She restored his faith in the possibility of some goodness in the world. To the doctors, he was just a specimen with a bad case of acne (who couldn't pay), but the nurse made him feel like a thinking, feeling person.

The treatments dragged on for several months, unfortunately not resulting in an improvement. Hank continued to occupy himself with his looks. He thought of Baldy and the other young men he knew.

No matter what shortcomings they had, at least they weren't covered all over with these ugly boils. Henry and Katherine rarely referred to the acne after Hank completed his first treatment.

While the acne was still at its worst, and he was in his first months of treatment, he refused to see any of his friends. His classmates Jimmy Haddox and Baldy came to visit one morning while his parents were away from the house. He could hear them outside calling for him, then talking to one another. Hank hid in a closet in the hall, leaving the door slightly ajar. Just as he thought, they had entered the house through the back door, which he had left open. As they searched through the house, Hank swung the closet door open and told them to leave. When they hesitated, he said if they didn't leave he would kill them.

A breakthrough took place in Hank's treatment at the county hospital. After what seemed like countless sessions of ultraviolet treatments, and drilling into the pustules, the doctors applied a salve to his face and then covered it in bandages. His entire head lay beneath the bandages. He liked what he saw when he glanced into the mirror on a cigarette machine in the hospital waiting room.

Even though the bandages had a positive effect, Hank needed more drilling and ultraviolet treatments. After a few weeks the treatments were terminated. Hank learned that he was no longer eligible for free medical care. This came about as a result of Henry Bukowski's new job as a guard for the Los Angeles County Museum. When Henry found out that Hank's free treatments had been ended, he was furious. "Those goddamn doctors are bloodsuckers," he said. "They'll take all your money and drive home to their mansions." He sent Hank to a doctor who believed in a nutritional approach for curing acne, a viewpoint that gained in acceptance throughout the thirties. As a result, Hank began a regimen of carrot juice and other items, and avoided fried foods.

Henry had taken a test for his job, which he passed, and he lied regarding his college education, which he lacked. Hank heard his father bragging as to how he pulled the wool over the eyes of his new employers.

"It isn't right," Katherine said.

"It's okay to tell a lie when you're doing it for a job," her husband answered.

In the fall of 1935, when his acne was at its worst, Hank wrote his first short story, basing his main character on Baron Manfred Von Richthofen, the World War I flying ace. "His hand was shot off, and he kept fighting guys out of the sky. This is all psychologically impossible, I understand. But, remember, my face was breaking out in boils while everybody else was making love to their fellow students and all that. I was the ugly boy of the neighborhood, so I wrote this long story. It was a little yellow notebook. It cost me six cents. I wrote with a pencil, how this guy with the iron hand shot down this guy and that guy."

To have created this half-real, half-imaginary man excited him. From that moment on he knew that he had an escape valve, a way to fight the fear that he sensed around him, and the lack of understanding. Another thing he had learned was the value of being alone. Having endured solitude enough in his childhood, he found new value in it as an adolescent. Being forced to go into himself, to find things to do and to think over within the confines of his house during the months of convalescence, he learned to face himself more keenly than before, to seek his own counsel more easily.

Hank had missed one semester in school. Baldy was one semester ahead of Hank, and eagerly greeted his friend when he emerged again from his isolation. Hank's father proclaimed that he wanted him to become an engineer. He said that engineers helped to build the country and earned a lot of money, that it was a job one could be proud to have, whereas an artist or writer usually ended up in poverty. He also complained about the cost of the doctor he had sent Hank to and the extra time he had to put in at work to earn enough money for the special diet.

In 1937, during the last semester of the school year, Hank began drinking. Because he looked older than his age, he occasionally went

[31]

into bars in downtown L.A., and he found whiskey to his liking. He met three guys who were three or four years older than himself. One was a tall, well-built fellow with light-blond hair that fell over his forehead and was perpetually uncombed. He made his living by robbing service stations. Another was a pleasant young man called "Stinky." Hank always stuck up for him and protested against the nickname. They hung out with a married man who held down a steady job and rented a large apartment. As the oldest of the group and the one with a steady job, he supplied whiskey and kept his house open to his friends. Hank was able to articulate many of the thoughts that these three other young men had, and they admired him for it. All of society came under his scrutiny as he attacked it with relentless energy, never raising his voice to be like a soapbox orator. With an absolutely cool demeanor, he said things like, "I don't care about anything or anybody. Nothing matters."

On numerous occasions, the four of them held drinking contests. Hank usually won. The money he earned supplied him with liquor of his own. Stinky became so smashed after one of the drinking bouts that he half-crawled into the bathroom. When Hank went to check on him, he found his friend sacked out in the bathtub.

In order to meet his drinking buddies, Hank always waited until his parents turned out the lights and went to bed, which was at 8 P.M. every night, like clockwork. Once he knew they were asleep, he opened the back window, climbed out, negotiated his way over a hedge, and then caught the streetcar. Getting back home was a little more difficult. He never left sober from these get togethers with his friends. Tottering down the street to the streetcar stop, he would somehow keep on his feet, climb on board when the car came, and collapse onto a seat.

Neither of his parents seemed to know how he spent his evenings. Because he usually climbed back into the house through the same window, there was little chance of his activities being discovered. The closer Hank came to the date of his graduation, the more boldly he acted; he stopped trying to mask his morning hangovers.

"Look at him. How will he ever get a job?" Hank's father said one morning. "And what will the neighbors think? What will become of you?

"I want no more of this drinking. Do you understand me?" the old man said.

Hank didn't answer.

"If you don't stop drinking now, you'll keep doing it all of your life, and then we'll see what will become of you!" Henry shouted, hoping for a response.

Again, Hank remained silent.

A few days later he came up to the door of his parents' house and knocked, rather than going in through the back window as he usually did. Katherine opened a little window in the door and yelled, *"Henry! Oh Henry! He's drunk again!"*

Hank heard his father's booming, awful voice: *"He's drunk again?"*

Henry's footsteps resounded through the house as he ran from the bedroom up to the front door. He looked out of the small window and told Hank that he would not open the door. "You are a disgrace to your mother and your country."

Hank complained that it was cold, and warned his father he would break the door down unless he opened it immediately.

"No!" Henry said. "No, my son. You do not deserve my house ..." True to his word, Hank stepped back several paces, and then ran at breakneck speed toward the door, his shoulders lowered, his weight leaning forward. He failed to completely break the door down, although a sharp cracking sound assured him that he had damaged the lock.

Henry gave in at that point. Hank walked inside. Katherine looked at him coldly. His father's face, etched in hatred, made him sick. He wanted to tell him so. Instead, his stomach contracted and he vomited on the rug.

"You know what we do when a dog shits on the rug?" Henry asked.

"No," Hank answered.

Henry rushed forward and grabbed Hank's neck from behind.

"You are a dog," he screamed, and tried pushing Hank down to the pool of vomit.

Hank struggled to get free, not an easy matter given Henry's height. He said in a firm, commanding voice, "Stop! I'm asking you one last time, to stop."

This provoked more pressure from his father, who managed to press Hank down so that his nose almost touched the soiled rug.

Then, as if through some miraculous power, Hank swung his arm up and punched his father with a solid uppercut to his chin. The big man fell backward onto the sofa.

Katherine, who had already been screaming hysterically, dug her fingernails into her son's face, screaming, *"You hit your father! You hit your father! My God! How could you do such a thing?"*

Hank stood there feeling almost serene. "I was out of the picture, really," he recalls. "I mean, the old man had fallen, and in my mind it was all over. So I just stood there while she continued to dig into me."

Blood splattered onto the floor, mixing with the vomit and creating little pools of blood here and there. After several minutes passed, Hank, who was himself a mass of blood, asked his mother if she had finished.

"Yes," she replied.

The drinking, however, had just begun.

It was in junior high school that Hank discovered the local library. The old brownstone between Washington and Adams Boulevards, near 21st Street and La Brea Avenue, provided a safe haven from the oppressive atmosphere at home and in school. The books seemed invincible, standing side by side, row after row. The chairs and tables in the library had a pungent, beautiful smell as the sun filtered in through the windows. The shadows and tonalities of light and darkness there seemed mysterious. It took some digging to discover the books he really liked. Often he came across a title that intrigued him, such as *Bow Down to Wood and Stone*. When he sat down to read the book itself he was disappointed, finding that the text did not have the strength of the title. Instead it offered only sentimentality and melodrama. But there were enough good discoveries. "The library was another world, another people. It roared and leaped. The blood whirled anew in my beaten spirit."

Neither of his parents were able to enter that world, which didn't unsettle Hank in the least. He checked out the books, several at a time, and took them home to read. Far from being happy that his son showed an interest in literature, Henry called for lights out at eight. "I would have to read these mighty men with the bedlamp under the covers. It got hot as hell under there, but it was the only heaven I had ever felt."

Hank became a relentless and restless reader. He fell under the spell of wild and wicked words, of sentences that rang clearer than most of what he heard in school. Images of the familiar were shown in a new light, and unknown subjects were suddenly laid out before him.

The young Bukowski maintained an innate respect for the passions and prejudices of the writers he read, particularly for those who did not resign themselves to normalcy. He wanted to read the opinions that differed from the standard. The disgust he had held for so long against the rules, regulations, and norms of the adult world was shared by many of the writers he read, such as Sinclair Lewis and Ernest Hemingway. When he could feel the hard edge of the words, when the writing ran uncompromisingly against the grain, he identified with it.

Hank came across novels and short stories that mirrored his own thinking. Emotional drive coupled with lucidity, for example, in Lewis's *Main Street*, D.H. Lawrence's writings, and Upton Sinclair's *The Jungle*, appealed to him. Unlike Henry Miller, whose first heroes were the boys of his Fourteenth Ward neighborhood in Brooklyn, Hank had no such romanticized heroes. The writers he read made up for the lack of a soul mate in the real world. The bonds he held with his friends could not compare to what he felt for these writers, and when he mentioned the authors to his friends they were mostly unappreciative. He did things with Frank Sullivan and Baldy, but they could not go the distance on the ideas percolating in his mind. Most of his other classmates were pint-size versions of the constricted adult mentality he rejected. These first writers made his sense of solitude all the more acute, and strangely, easier to handle—at last he found others who valued truth. More than fifty years later he talked of that early encounter with books in the library on La Brea: "Here was some guy feeding me blood, beauty. And I feeling like a trapped creature beaten by my father. Then here's this man filling me with words."

Main Street particularly held Hank's interest. He was attracted by the stripping bare of pretenses as the writer roamed through Sauk Centre. He wanted to do the same thing in his own territory. *The Jungle* intrigued him because of the injustices that the writer exposed. "I would say, 'This guy is right. This is the way it is, everywhere.'"

There were others, like Carson McCullers, who blended the real and the magical together. Hank could feel the hot, humid nights in the South that she sketched, and touch the odd characters populating her books. "Jesus," Hank would say. "You people are my friends"—referring to the characters in the novels.

Ernest Hemingway's prose enchanted Hank when he read *The Sun Also Rises* and the Nick Adams stories. For the first time he found a writer who expressed with clear images life and the undercurrent of human character. There was no sentimentality. He felt spurred on to read more Hemingway, and did.

Hank, now fifteen, considered being a writer. Writing offered a defense against the mundane world. While he dived into books, nothing could touch him. The books he read taught him that he had not given in to the norms of society, and was not diminished by his father's cruelty.

By Hank's junior year in high school, his father's domination had ended, physically at least, but not financially. Hank had rejected his father's vision of the world. The idea of having a lifelong profession seemed so foreign to him, a form of enslavement. As a child and adolescent he never fantasized about being a doctor, a lawyer, or a businessman. His rebellious nature belied that kind of thinking. When his father advised him that he wanted Hank to become an engineer because they made a lot of money, Hank scoffed at the idea. What he learned in the library, coupled with the trauma of acne, helped hone his rebellion down to a sharp point.

As in all high schools the upcoming senior prom was a primary topic among graduating seniors—except for Hank, who had convinced himself that no girl would want to be seen with him. The prom was one rite of passage he would have to pass up, but he did plan on attending the graduation ceremonies. The thought of having to put on a robe, however, and to put up with the principal's dreary speech, and then stand in line to await the awarding of his diploma, filled him with loathing.

The graduating seniors made big plans for prom night. Many of the boys would be picking up their dates for the festivities in cars. All Hank had was a bicycle. He listened to the excited talk with an increasing sense of alienation. His feeling of being on the outside was growing ever more acute, especially since he now bore permanent scars on his face. The lack of self-esteem that had emerged when the acne first appeared still governed many of his actions. An inner revolt had taken hold of him, ideas that would later surface in his writing, about how the entire structure of society was populated by smooth-talking phonies.

Henry Bukowski did not view his son's graduation with pride. Rather than delivering a speech to Hank in which he saw a future filled with opportunity, he portrayed a bleak landscape of poverty and unfulfilled ambition. He kept mentioning "normal" kids, asking his son why he couldn't be more like them. Whenever he could, he drew verbal tableaus of failure, summoning up images of furnished rooms on skid row. "You want to end a bum? That's what will happen if you don't get some direction in life," he said.

Boy and girl paired off for prom night at the high school—a ritual played out, of course, all across the country. Talk of the prom grew more intense as the day approached. Girls huddled together in the hallways or on the school grounds discussing their plans, ogling certain young men. The guys huddled together to brag about their intended sexual conquests.

The night of the prom, Hank left Longwood Avenue and walked over to the girls' gym, where the prom was being held. Arriving at the entrance, he heard live music and animated conversation. Laughter, applause, joyful shouts, all intermingled. He stood so near to the wondrous scene within, and yet he stood across an unbridgeable gulf. No matter how he intellectually defined himself as being different, a nonconformist, he yearned to be there with the other young people. He stayed hidden away and looked inside through a wire-mesh window. Every one of the girls had been transformed into an adult. They were so mature-looking in their long, flowing formal gowns. Their gestures seemed grown-up. The boys in tuxedos were equally impressive. Couples danced with ease and grace, or stood in small groups conversing. What further astonished the lonely onlooker was the sight of some of the other class outsiders. There they were, secure, well dressed, joining in with the more well-known campus personalities.

Hank peered in at the scene with his nose pressed to the wire screen. The obligatory punch bowl sat at the center of a decorated table. Young men gallantly led their dates onto the dance floor. Nearby, a good-looking girl stood with a glass of punch in hand, watching the orchestra and whispering something into the ear of her date.

Hank remained in the darkness, observing, celebrating, and cursing his solitude. He began to feel like an animal, some kind of beast, as he compared himself to his self-assured classmates. (In later years, when he often signed his letters "Beastbuk," perhaps he thought back on the night of the prom he didn't attend.) He thought of the girls, wondering how it would feel to touch one, holding her in his arms, embracing her, kissing her. Yet the mere thought of talking to some of the more stately, beautiful girls filled him with terror. Surely they would laugh or run away in horror if he made advances of any kind.

Whenever the band played, the overhead lights cast varying shades of red, gold, blue, and green on the dancing couples. "I really did begin to hate them," Hank says, "all of them . . . as they danced so flawlessly. They had easy, untroubled lives. They had rich parents, most of them did." Again, as when he first entered high school, he focused on the more economically privileged kids, rather than those who, like himself, came from working-class homes—and there were plenty of those in attendance on prom night.

He had never seen any romantic exchanges between his mother and father, nor any other family members. At the movies he attended with his parents, and later on with friends, there were plenty of love scenes, those obligatory moments when man and woman stand together under a pale moon, kissing, or embracing in a half-lit room. All of this filled his head as he stood on the outside.

The experience further exacerbated his sense of being different from the crowd. His friends could not see that there was virtue in being different, but this didn't bother him; he knew that his isolation would become his strength. "Despite how I felt looking into the gymnasium, which had been transformed for the prom," he says, "I knew that things were not so good as they seemed to be." As he stood there, still gazing into the gym, he realized that he hated these happy kids for whom the Depression had only been something they read about in the newspaper, and for whom the future meant a college education and a good job. "Like I said in *Ham on Rye* I knew that someday my dance would begin." Such was the faith that began to take hold of him and sustain him.

Suddenly, his thoughts were interrupted by a school janitor who demanded that he leave. When he protested that he was a member of the graduating class, the janitor brandished a flashlight in his face, took one look at his scars and said, "You've got to be at least twenty-two. Now get the hell out of here." Back home, the young graduate lay in bed, staring at the ceiling, unable to sleep, and telling himself that he would indeed someday have his dance.

Hank went to his graduation obsessed with two thoughts. The first was that he could see nothing good in his future, nothing tangible anyway. And the second was that he had not yet gone to bed with a woman. He listened impatiently to the speech given by the school.

principal, an overweight, bald-headed old-timer. His speech was filled with the usual platitudes concerning the future. He pointed out that the class of 1939 was full of hope, more so than any previous class at Los Angeles High School. Quite a few of Hank's classmates went on to Stanford, USC, UC-Berkeley, UCLA and other leading universities. Ironically, the high school yearbook for the graduating class, summer 1939, offered an innocuous listing for the rambunctious Henry C. Bukowski, Jr. It was noted that in the ROTC he held the rank of Cadet Sergeant, Company A—which hardly conveyed Hank's total disdain for ROTC, all the people in it, and the philosophy of obedience that its leaders espoused.

The sun beamed down on the principal as he spoke. The students smiled with pride, listening intently. Not Hank. He and Jimmy Haddox sat next to each other and commented on some of their fellow students as they passed by on their way to receive their diplomas. One overachiever whom Hank hated they dubbed an "accountant." When Hank was called up, he looked back at Haddox and whispered, "Public Servant." (Little did he know how accurate that prediction would be: he later spent twelve straight years working for the postal service.) He ambled toward the principal, glancing at the teachers, most of whom he despised, took his diploma, and looked down at his parents: his mother, small, dressed very well but plainly, her hair neatly done up, and next to her his father with a sneer on his face. He walked off the stage rubbing his right palm on his graduation robe to get off the sweat left there by the principal's handshake.

After the ceremony, people began milling around. "How are you ever going to make it? I've never seen you look at a school book, let alone inside of one," Hank's father said to him.

Hank retorted: "Some books are dull."

His father fired back that it had cost thousands of dollars to feed and clothe him. "Suppose I left you here on the street? Then what would you do?" Mr. Bukowski said. "Tell me, what would you do?" his father repeated.

Hank snapped back: "Catch butterflies."

Katherine began to cry. Henry took her by the arms and pulled her away, down to where their beat-up car was parked.

Filled with rage, Hank climbed into the back seat of the car. They drove home in silence, as Hank silently recalled the indignities of school and home. His father's reaction to the graduation ceremonies didn't surprise Hank. That loud, unsympathetic voice of the old man's had never shown understanding or compassion. It wasn't enough that Hank felt embarrassed walking around with scars on his face; he had to have a father who was a source of perpetual trouble.

Jane Mary Ball (Eckland), who graduated along with Hank and went on to write two novels and two textbooks, says she doesn't remember him at all. She continues, "We graduated in an aura of innocence. A lot of our class went into the military. The innocence was soon shattered by the war." She and several other students, including Ray Bradbury and Elma Bakker (author of *An Island Called California*), were part of an informal writer's group. Hank didn't even know the group existed, but he says that if he had he would have avoided it. His friends Baldy and Jimmy were the only two guys he really related to well and spent time with.

Hank had already applied for a job at the Sears Roebuck on Olympic Boulevard, one of the company's oldest and largest outlets, and was surprised when they called him to report to work. He had no illusions concerning the job, only hoping it might offer him some liberty from his father's domination. He received fifty-five cents an hour, not a bad wage in those post-depression days. Yet he knew that the other kids from his school were going off to USC, a few miles southeast of the high school and one of the most prominent universities in the country.

Suppressing the image his father had berated him with, spending a lifetime at a low-class, dead-end job, he had put in applications all over L.A. for employment. The thought of being a professional writer was becoming increasingly important. He didn't think of being famous or honored, but of being able to survive on his own terms. Meanwhile, Sears would have to do. "The real reason I put in job applications," he says, "was in the hope of getting away from my parents."

He planned on renting a room in downtown L.A. on Bunker Hill, the neighborhood John Fante described in *Ask the Dust*, which Hank had read by that time. And like Fante, he could picture himself struggling to get into print and earn money with his writing. Also, he would be closer to the L.A. Public Library, where he continued to read books voraciously. He liked the feel of life downtown: it held a sense of freedom that he couldn't find in the suburban neighborhoods.

Hank had grown more independent in another way, too: he envisioned himself as "the singular self," forging his own destiny. His view of his father became a blueprint for his view of society. "The oppressive factor remains like a shadow overhead. I mean, there is always a father trying to press down and annihilate you." What he found in Fante's character in *Ask the Dust* was a man who hated his bosses, recognized his own talents, and would advance regardless of the consequences.

Fante's novel had much of the same spirit behind it as did Saroyan's short story, "The Daring Young Man on the Flying Trapeze." In both, a young person struggles against overwhelming odds to define himself. What Bukowski liked in Fante's book was the presence of the writer himself; the book read like autobiography rather than a fictional account. Hank was really excited that somebody could write like this right in his own city. This was not some distant, ancient voice, but a man not much older than himself surrounded by the noise and crowds of a major city. In other words, the miracle of writing a book and seeing it in print was not such a miracle at all if one worked hard enough and had a little luck.

Fante even describes the public library, that pink-stucco monument to mid-twenties exuberance, where Hank continued the reading that he had begun at the smaller library near his home. Fante rhapsodized over "the big boys in the shelves," Theodore Dreiser and H. L. Mencken. Hank identified with Fante's character, the unknown writer Arturo Bandini, who yearned to be the author of one of those big American books.

When Hank arrived for work at Sears Roebuck, he was confronted by the supervisor, who told him that he had come five minutes late. Hank explained that he had been delayed because he had come across a starving dog on the way to work and had to do something for him. The supervisor looked at his new charge with shock in his eyes. Bukowski remembers him as a tall, thin man with an ungainly belly dropping out, and tiny gray pupils "centered in otherwise colorless eyes." The man's answer to the reason he had just heard—a truthful one—was that in his thirty-five years of service he had never heard such a lousy excuse.

After warning Hank to not come in late again, the supervisor told Hank to find his employee card and punch in. He walked over to the time clock with his card and stood there not knowing what to do. The supervisor said, "You are now six minutes late."

Finally, the man showed him how to punch in. It took some time to explain the process, at the end of which the supervisor told the hapless young man before him that his word was law. He went on to say that it was in his power to kick an employee right back onto the streets for any reason whatsoever, whether or not it related directly to the job.

Hank became aware that Sears demanded employees who were content to spend their entire lives on the job. "This would be one of my first lessons. They expected people to give their entire lives, and all their loyalty, to some shit job. I would see it again and again, in L.A., New Orleans, Philadelphia, wherever I traveled."

How he found this truth was simple: he met his fellow employees. In *Ham on Rye* they are described in detail:

> Four men and three women. They were all old. They seemed to have salivary problems. Little clumps of spittle had formed at the corners of their mouths; the spittle had dried and turned white and then been coated by new wet spittle. Some of them were too thin, others too fat. Some were nearsighted; others trembled. One old fellow in a brightly colored shirt had a hump on his back. They all smiled and coughed, puffing at cigarettes.

[43]

His job consisted of making deliveries from the stock room to the various sales sections of the store. "Here I was, the tough guy, Hank Bukowski. I kept wondering what the guys from school would say if they saw me working with this crew of misfits."

Around the time that Hank took the job at Sears, the *Los Angeles Times* proclaimed in a headline, GERMAN ARMY INVADES POLAND. Talk of possible American involvement circulated everywhere. Hank heard patriotic talk at work, on the streets, at home. It amused him to observe how easily people fell into line, adopting a "God is on our side" attitude.

As soon as Hank began working, he realized that he would not last long at the job. It was a pattern of behavior that followed him through a succession of jobs over the years, until he finally went to work for the post office in the mid-fifties. The uncompromising attitude toward authority figures that was forged in school showed through even when he tried to mask it. He couldn't help commenting on the smallness of rules and regulations. When the supervisor explained the time-clock routine, Hank grimaced and made sarcastic remarks.

During his first days at work, he thought of the rich kids he had gone to school with and how pampered their lives were in comparison to his. There seemed to be little else to do but succumb to his pedestrian life. He imagined what it might be like giving in to the system, staying on at the department store until retirement, being as loyal to his job as his father had been to his, or as the supervisor seemed to be to his. He saw himself as superior to the people around him. He could see that few of them ever entered a library, ever read a book, or ever tried to figure out the meaning of their existence. They were dead, zero, the underclass who took their orders with shit-eating grins, never complaining, always subservient, and glad to be so. "I will never be like them," he told himself over and over again. He bided his time. But it didn't take him long to find out that, whatever his attitude, he was at the bottom of the Sears hierarchy. On his first day he found himself the object of scorn from a sales clerk to whom he had made a late delivery.

Bukowski's primary complaint against society, found throughout his writing, is that people are frightened by social and economic conditions into accepting humiliation and defeat. They accept positions in life that rob them of their individuality and gradually accept, even embrace, their subservience to others in more powerful positions. They lose their ability to think for themselves.

The descriptions in *Ham on Rye* of his job at Sears, somewhat reminiscent of Louis Ferdinance Céline's story of working in a department store in *Death on the Installment Plan*, portray a microcosm of the pretensions, petty meanness, and class consciousness of society at large. Bukowski as stock boy is pitted against smug and arrogant clerks, such as the fictional one he calls Justin Phillips, Jr., only a few years older than himself and already in charge of the men's department. "He stood very straight, had dark hair, dark eyes, brooding lips." And then a typically Bukowski twist is added: "There was an unfortunate absence of cheekbone but it was hardly noticeable." The only thing he ever said to Hank was, "It's a shame, isn't it, those rather ugly scars on your face?"

His father, in contrast, labored proudly at his museum job, boasting that he was the best worker—a one-man booster for the American work ethic, as in years past. A few days into the job at Sears, Hank knew that he would not last. When the inevitable came, and he was fired, his father said, "So, you couldn't hold a job for more than a week."

Reluctantly, Hank decided to enroll at Los Angeles City College on Western Avenue. His mother said his going on to college showed that he had initiative; his father, as usual, believed that it would be another thing that ended badly. But he also understood that it was better to have his son attending college than unemployed. If nothing else, it would look good to the neighbors.

In September 1940, Hank signed up for several journalism courses, two drama classes, and a few academic subjects such as English and history. He believed that formal education meant another kind of enslavement, yet he held a vague idea of somehow using it to his advantage. Maybe journalism would give him a chance to make a living, and it *was* a form of writing. One instructor told the students to turn in one essay a week. Hank handed in ten to twelve each week, sometimes more, on all kinds of subjects. "Your papers are well written," she told Hank at the end of the term. "You should have an 'A,' but I'll have to give you a 'B' because of your bad attitude." According to Hank, this was caused by sarcasm aimed at his classmates.

The school newspaper seemed like a good place to begin publishing. Hank walked in there one morning, talked to the editor, looked around at the students busily at work on the next week's edition of the paper, then turned to walk out. As he retreated to the door he snarled, "Oh shit!" then walked into the hall, relieved to be out there. In Hank's mind those students were snobs. He would never admit it, but possibly some of the animosity he felt toward them was due to a fear of rejection or simply a matter of his chronic alienation when in a group.

At City College he met Robert Stanton Baume, a young man whose father worked as a journalist in Minneapolis. Baume had come out to California on his own and lived at a place on West 11th Street and barely managed to get by working as a bicycle messenger for Western Union. Hank admired Baume's independence; he didn't have a father and mother looking over his shoulder half the time. Baume's intellect attracted Hank, and he admired his short stories. They were somewhat derivative of Thomas Wolfe's *Look Homeward, Angel* and didn't have the touch of madness Hank liked to encounter in writing, but there was still something there. "Maybe there was a little too much contentment in Baume's work, and yet I could feel something in it, the presence of somebody. He might have developed into a very good writer."

Baume had another quality that Hank admired. He was a fearless young man, ready to fight anyone who crossed him. Soon after they met he told Hank that he wanted to be a reporter in Washington because it was at the center of government, the place where important decisions were being made. He would describe how he imagined life

[46]

in the nation's capital would be for a daring young reporter: meeting senators, exposing corruption, and what not. Bukowski's response to this kind of talk was usually sardonic. One time Baume became very angry when Bukowski told him that Washington, D.C., was the center of nothing.

Hank hung around with a friend of Baume's named Robert Knox, who remembers Bukowski as shy and withdrawn, not the fiery literary character of later years. Knox's memory of Bukowski's father confirms his son's own picture of him. "His father was very strict. Very straitlaced. He was a perfectionist. Everything had to be done a certain way. I knew that they didn't get along and that his father disapproved of many of Hank's activities. I guess he was from the old school of discipline." Knox's wife, whom he married in 1941, remembers Katherine Bukowski: "She was small, petite, elegant. You'd think she was really a French type. She was always very nice to us. She asked me once why Henry didn't find a nice girl and get married, settle down, and have children. It was obvious that she was afraid of her husband. She wouldn't talk much in front of him." The Knoxes recall being told by both of Hank's parents that Mrs. Bukowski came from France. This bit of information was probably intended to protect her from any negative feelings due to the rise of Nazism in Germany. "I remember she had an accent," Knox says. "I always thought it was French. They made it clear to me that she had been born in France."

When the Knoxes had their first child, after Hank had left college, they took him over to visit at the Bukowskis' home. Katherine became excited over the thought that maybe Hank would take the example of this young couple, find a woman, and get married. Such thoughts were far from her son's mind, however, as he still saw himself as scarred and untouchable for life.

Knox notes that Los Angeles City College had earned a reputation as "the little red college," due to the large number of faculty members with left-leaning sympathies: "They had these speakers come and talk on campus, espousing communism. News people were there with their cameras before we even knew about the speeches. I wrote an essay for my teacher concerning people worrying about the Germans and how communism would eventually be a greater menace. The professor gave me an 'F'. " Sharing Knox's disapproval of the doctrinaire left-wing attitudes of the faculty members, Hank became a gadfly. He didn't believe in any manner of ideological slavery, whether on the right or the left.

Hank didn't put much effort into his studies. Just getting by satisfied him, as he already knew that the academic life was not to his liking. In fact, he despised most of the professors, largely due to their politics. Hank found them self-centered, self-satisfied, and boring. Occasionally, just to stir things up, he pretended to sympathize with the Nazis. Apparently, word got around, and he was approached by a school administrator who told of his own Nazi sympathies. Hank was so disgusted that he didn't bother trying to set the man straight.

Hank, Baume, and Knox sat in cafés, drinking coffee and discussing everything except political issues. Mostly they talked about school and literature. Hank told of his aspiration to be a full-time writer and said that he wanted to go someplace far from L.A. and get a job writing for a newspaper. He rarely mentioned girls, and showed little interest in them even on campus.

Just as on graduation day at L.A. High School, Hank suspected that skid row lay in his future. The only salvation from a life of toil and failure, he felt, lay in the act of writing. That was the one area of human activity where he knew how to be a worker, instinctively. He knew that some of his stories needed tightening, and that many of them were murky and incomplete, but he kept on working, sure of his talent.

Hank attempted to find a new job and failed. His father saw this as laziness and self-imposed defeat: "I work and other people work. The whole damned world is working and you can't get yourself one lousy job. Don't think I'm going to support you forever." Hank would certainly not work in a department store again, not after the tedium of Sears Roebuck, but he did look other places, and he drank heavily. At least when he drank, he could wipe his father cleanly off the map of his mind for a while, along with his inability to find employment. For Henry Bukowski as long as his son was attending college and planned to be a journalist someday, he wouldn't kick Hank out of the house.

One afternoon Hank was on his way home from City College when his mother suddenly appeared before him. "Henry! You can't go home. Your father is furious. He will kill you."

Hank was taken completely by surprise. He said, "How is he going to hurt me? I can whip his ass."

Katherine Bukowski explained that the old man had found Hank's short stories. "He read them, Henry, all of them."

She described in detail how he had come across them in a drawer and sat down to read them. "He told me he was going to kill you," Katherine exclaimed once again, and related to her son how his father had thrown all of the stories, along with his clothing and type-writer, on the lawn. When Hank heard that, he became furious and could hardly wait for a confrontation. His mother tried to stop him, holding onto the back of his shirt as he kept on going.

When they came to the house on Longwood Avenue, a few blocks away, Hank saw his writings scattered everywhere, across the same lawn that had caused him so much hell as a child. He stood there amidst the dirty laundry, the loose papers and bric-a-brac of his life, and yelled for his father to come out of the house so that he could beat him up. He waited. When his father did not come forward, he began picking up his manuscripts and then his typewriter. He walked to the "W" streetcar, paid, took a transfer, and headed down-town to Temple Street, where he found inexpensive lodgings in a district filled with Filipino immigrants. The rent came to $1.50 per week for a cramped room on the second floor. Little did he know that his newfound quarters foreshadowed hundreds of more rooms roughly the same size, and equally shabby. Far from feeling down in the mouth, however, Hank took to his new environment—especially when he found a bar almost directly downstairs, a place mostly fre-quented by Filipinos, whose slick, gangsterlike appearance appealed to him.

Because he could think of nothing else to do, Hank remained at City College, choosing those courses that interested him at the expense of planning for advanced studies at another institution. In his final semester, which ended early in 1941, he took four art classes and one period of physical education. Gradually, Hank saw that the best class of all, for him at least, lay right before him, on the streets. The rote manner in which the art teachers presented their lessons and the mechanical approach of the journalism classes were doing nothing for him. At the same time, he feared being totally out on his own without school as a safety net.

Hank familiarized himself with the business hub of Los Angeles. In the sixties he used to talk about his adventures there, bopping in and out of bars, lurking around Bunker Hill, Angel's Flight (a funicular railway going up and down the hill), and Pershing Square, a gathering place for itinerant preachers, left-wing orators, and colorful soapbox speakers. He became a regular at many of the bars and occasionally wandered into the skid row area where he believed his future lay. Many times later in life, he talked about the men on the row and how he had gone down there in his college years wondering what kind of people lived there. He often thought he would find a hidden genius, but, as he puts it, he encountered only failure. "You know, I had this feeling that maybe there would be a touch of brilliance there, but I was young, maybe a bit romantic. Yet the people on the row only seemed a little more beaten than those living ordinary, average lives. So I felt all the more like an outcast."

Downtown L.A. in those days was primarily an Anglo-Saxon world. Massive department stores like Bullock's and the May Company were filled with merchandise, smiling clerks, self-important floor managers. The small shops populating the area—hundreds of them— had their own refined traditions of shopping excellence. Between them and behind them were alleyways where tough, sinister characters hammered one another into the ground. There was the Pacific Electric terminal, hub of an electric railways empire. Near to Olvera Street, a block-long miracle of old adobe buildings left over from the days of the Mexican dons, stood Union Station, built in a style evocative of the Spanish missions. It symbolized the American Empire stretching from Atlantic to Pacific, crossing Rockies and Sierras, embracing Great Basin and Great Plains. In the station there were porters dressed in immaculately pressed uniforms, conductors proud of their shiny brass badges. Out on the tracks stood the powerful trains of the famous railroads: Union Pacific, Santa Fe, and Southern Pacific. Steam hissed out of their bowels, billowing around the luggage standing on big green carts waiting to be loaded and travelers rushing to and fro. There was also the amazing Bradbury Building with its offices arranged around a cavernous central courtyard, and wrought-iron elevators rising and falling, exposed on all sides. The Hearst-owned *Herald Examiner* was housed in a Mission-style building, while the *Los Angeles Times* was in a contemporary one across from city hall. There was a thriving Chinatown, a prosperous "Little Tokyo," and many homegrown banking institutions with their own downtown palaces, such as the Security Trust and Savings Bank of Los Angeles and Coast Federal Savings. Years later, the atmosphere of old L.A. would become a vital part of Bukowski's writing. Echoes of his experiences downtown are strongly felt in his short stories.

THREE

ONE afternoon, while Hank sat in his room on Temple Street listening to the radio and writing, Robert Baume showed up. He had left City College a semester before Hank did, and they had lost touch. Either through the Bukowskis or the college, Baume found his friend. He wore a marine corps uniform, and told Hank that he had left his Western Union job.

Baume still aspired to become a famous writer. "Someday my books will be found everywhere," he said. "They'll be reading them all over the world. Like Thomas Wolfe. Everyone reads *Look Homeward, Angel*. That's the kind of book I'd like to write."

"It's overwritten," Hank replied. "And it sounds inflated."

"Who is good, then?" Baume asked.

"James Thurber. He pointed out that everybody was crazy."

Baume began pontificating about writing in general, telling Hank that there were certain standards of literature and that he would learn them. "Only assholes talk about writing," Hank said.

Insulted, Baume asked if he should leave. Hank said he was sorry to speak so abruptly, and added that they were still buddies.

Then: "A man might get himself killed wearing a uniform."

This made the patriotic Baume angry. Young people were eager to

serve their country (there had not yet been a major antiwar movement like the one that later came about during the sixties.) He told
Hank to stop hiding from reality, that he was being unrealistic about
life and hurting his chances to be a true writer. Hank insisted that
good writers hide from reality. "They make their own." When Baume accused Hank of speaking nonsense, their discussion turned into
a heated argument. Within moments fists were flying. Hank landed
a powerful punch. Baume staggered across the room. Hank hit him
another time, just as effectively.

"You win," Baume said.

"Come on, let's have a drink," Hank suggested.

Baume smiled and said, "Yeah, sure."

Hank poured two glasses of wine. They drank until their glasses
were empty. Satisfied with their scuffle and drink, Hank said, "No
hard feelings," to which Baume replied, "Hell no, buddy." He put his
glass down, then punched Hank in the stomach, precipitating a new
round of fighting. The eager young marine knocked his surly friend
unconscious.

When he woke up, Hank found his furniture scattered all over the
room. He lifted himself up from the floor, staggered to the table, and
reached for a cigarette. "That son of a bitch," he muttered. A few cars
passed as he looked out of his window. Two or three men sauntered
down the sidewalk. A knock at the door disturbed his reverie. "Mr.
Bukowski, oh Mr. Bukowski?" It was his landlady's familiar whine.
She used the excuse that she had to change the bedding. In truth, her
curiosity about the overheard fight with Baume drew her there.

"Go away!"

Exasperated, the landlady left. Perspiration covered Hank's forehead and dripped down his cheeks. His heart beat loudly and rapidly,
and he ached all over from Baume's heavy blows. Hank staggered
across the floor and walked into the hallway, where he was surprised
to find a Filipino man who worked for the landlady pounding nails
into the rug. The man glanced at him suspiciously, then resumed
his work. Hank figured the hammer was intended for use against
him. Retreating to his room, he knew that he had to pack up and

leave—not much of a task as he owned almost nothing. He left his room again, carrying his suitcase and portable typewriter. Without warning, the Filipino sprang to his feet and placed himself in Hank's path.

"Where are you going?" he asked.

Hank slammed the typewriter against the man's head. "It was horrible. I mean the impact was so great, you know, and I heard this sound. So I thought, well, Jesus, I must have killed this guy. I ran down the street and got into a cab."

Bunker Hill flashed through his mind as a safe refuge. Once the finest neighborhood in the city, it was crammed with Victorian and Queen Anne-style mansions rented out as rooming houses. Plenty of fugitive types lived there, as well as old dogs of the underworld. When the cab pulled by a place with a vacancy sign he asked the cabbie to stop. He paid quickly, jumped from the cab, and rang the bell. The landlady showed him to a dingy, dark room. "I'll take it," he said. If others could write great stories and novels in rooms like the one he had just paid a week's rent on, so could he, Hank reasoned, while arranging his few belongings.

Gradually, Hank transformed himself into a lone figure, living only for the short story and the next drink, and it is the stories alone that bear witness to this period. But the difficulty of day-by-day survival became all too real no matter how much he wrote or how euphoric his stories made him feel. His pockets were empty. When he made money at one odd job or another it went for liquor and cheap meals. Sometimes he didn't even have the five-cent fare necessary for a ride on Angel's Flight. Securely hidden away in his room, he composed short stories in which he described and explored his desperation. When his typewriter went into hock, he wrote in notebooks. Far from being forlorn, though, he celebrated his freedom.

He tried to imagine that seeing a young couple parading by on the street didn't mean anything, but it affected him. The opposite sex remained a mystery. He could not accept the idea that a woman might love him. He gazed in amazement at empty-faced men locked arm in arm with beautiful women; he felt the rift between these men's sexual nonchalance and his own hypersensitivity and vulnerability. All the more he turned to the typewriter and to the ephemeral glories of intoxication. "Probably, I could have ended up not liking myself," he says, "but I was lucky. There was nothing wrong with me. It was other people who fell short, who didn't have true humanity."

On one of his forays downtown, he walked past a penny arcade and saw Robert Baume, eager as ever to help save his country and dreaming of future literary success. They laughed about the fight they had been in, and went off to a couple of bars. In the last bar they entered, music blared out of a small radio. While they drank and talked about their dreams and ambitions, the music suddenly stopped. An announcer reported that the Japanese had just attacked Pearl Harbor.

Hank looked into Baume's eyes. The marine turned white, and gravely said, "Well, that's it."

Hank nodded. Baume suggested that he sign up right away. "Things are different now," he said. "You're needed."

"No. I'm not getting on the bus with those damn fools."

They walked to the Greyhound depot, where Baume bought a ticket for his base. He asked Hank one more time to join him. When he didn't respond, Baume asked if he had any advice. Hank said he could think of nothing to offer. "It wasn't cruelty. I just didn't know what to say. He was going off to the war and I knew that he might not come home, but I didn't want to say it." Two years later Hank found out that Baume had been killed in the Pacific.

The day after Hank heard the news of the attack on Pearl Harbor, the *Los Angeles Times* ran the headline JAPS OPEN WAR ON U.S. WITH BOMBING OF ALLIES. Beneath those ominous words was a subheading, CITY SPRINGS TO ATTENTION, followed by the announcement that the people of L.A. had promptly risen to the task of defending the country. Hank glanced briefly at the front page—the news left him cold. Three days later the Axis powers declared war on the United States. Hank remembers feeling only revulsion. He didn't see it as *his* battle. By the end of December, he knew that he had to leave the city. His parents, especially his father's constant prattle about the duty of a young man to serve his country, were insufferable. He yearned to stand alone, and to forge himself into a smoothly running writing machine. (Over the ensuing years he would return to his parents' home on several occasions, purely for economic reasons. "Let me assure you that there was no feeling of family love," he says. "I had run out of luck, jobs, and money, and so I would return to Los Angeles.")

In order to make enough money for his first trip, he worked through the winter of 1941–42 at the Southern Pacific yards, scrubbing the sides of boxcars with oakite and using a steam gun to wash the mud off of passenger cars. The men he worked with were mostly younger ones like himself. A few talked of their own wanderings across the country. Some of them had bummed around during the depression years. Almost all were alienated from their families.

Hank drew one of the highest draft numbers in history—near 63,000,000, he says—and since he never gave any thought to volunteering, he didn't have to worry about being shipped overseas. When asked why he wasn't in the service once the country went to war, he simply held up his draft card. He never bothered reading any of the war reports, which had begun to come in on a regular basis. The war remained a distant thing, almost unreal.

When Hank had saved enough money and the day came to leave Los Angeles, he went to the Trailways bus station in downtown L.A. He mulled over what his father had told him so many times in the past months, that while the country was at war every fit young man should serve, no matter how high his draft number. "Other young people will make their parents proud. They don't run from their responsibilities," Henry said. "You'll bring shame on us, nothing but shame." His father's words had rolled off Hank easily; he was too exhilarated to argue. After purchasing a ticket to New Orleans, he went to the Trailways waiting room, where he heard two girls talking. One said to the other, "Look at that man. Look at him, he's beautiful," and the other said, "Yeah, he is." Hank scanned the room.

[57]

Finding no one else there, he understood that he had to be the object of their attention.

While on the bus, he kept to himself, occasionally taking a nip from the half pint of whiskey he had brought along. The hours passed quickly, eventually becoming one vast blur. He didn't feel sad, nor alone. The freedom that grew from within became a celebration. More than anything, he wanted to define himself without compromise, to make his own way—not to be lost in a cheap room somewhere.

Not long after the bus left L.A., it made an unscheduled stop and a handful of soldiers came on, acting very businesslike, with firm, grim expressions. They interviewed people on either side of the aisle, asking where they were born. As they worked their way toward Hank, he wondered what he should say. Telling them that his birthplace was Andernach, Germany, would not leave a very good impression. "Pasadena, California," he calmly said to the soldier who came up to him. Further on, an older man refused to answer. "I don't think it's any of your business." he said. The soldiers unceremoniously yanked him from his seat and took him from the bus, leaving his luggage behind. Hank wasn't shocked by what he saw. With his low opinion of authority, he was surprised that this kind of harassment didn't take place more often.

Somewhere along the line a young redheaded woman got on the bus and started talking to Hank. Her enthusiasm affected him. He let down his guard, probably because of his new and strange surroundings. Perhaps he had been infected by that magic feeling one often experiences while traveling, in which a stranger may easily become someone with whom one shares intimate secrets. Their conversation took a sensual turn as the miles rolled on, and they were openly affectionate, enough so that the other passengers were very much aware of the two young travelers. A few made no secret of their curiosity. When Hank told her that he wrote short stories, she said that she composed poetry. She even took out some paper and a pencil and began doing drawings of him.

The young woman, named Dulcey Ditmore, left the bus in Fort Worth. She asked Hank to come with her. "It's such a beautiful town," she said. He told her that he had to go on, that he must wander around on his own.

"You'll love it here," she said. "It's a beautiful place." She spoke passionately, unable to hide the tears welling up in her eyes and falling down her pink cheeks. Still Hank resisted. Exasperated, the young woman got off the bus. As the bus pulled out, Hank's fellow passengers expressed themselves openly about his failure to join her. Even the driver stared critically at him through the rearview mirror. He laughed inwardly—he could hardly believe this communal judgment that he had somehow failed the young woman. The ride turned so uncomfortable that he left the bus in Dallas, received the first shave of his life and took a shower, all in anticipation—though with some misgivings—of returning to the bus station in Fort Worth from where he would search for Dulcey.

Upon his arrival in Fort Worth, he paid for a room in a hotel that turned out to be a local brothel. He was propositioned as he walked through the halls. "How about a nice girl?" a cleaning woman asked as she busily scrubbed the floor. "Jesus, even the cleaning women?" Hank asked himself. But to her he said that he was too damned tired because he had just been on a long bus ride. "Yeah, but a good piece of ass is just what you need," she said. "It's only five dollars," she added. When Hank inquired as to who the girl was, the cleaning woman got up off of her knees and said, "I'm the girl." While he still resisted, she said it would only cost two dollars. "No, I'm sorry," he replied and went to his room.

Hank settled into his room and spent the night there, and the next morning began his search for Dulcey. She had told him that her mother ran a photography store and so he leafed through the phone directory and took down their addresses. Armed with his list, he wandered through the city, beginning in the downtown area, visiting each of the places on his list. In one of them an older woman said, "*I'm Dulcey Ditmore.*" She wanted to close down the store and take Hank to the nearest hotel room. He quickly left and continued his search. In another store he explained his situation to the clerk who said that she knew a columnist for a local newspaper who specialized in feature writing. "He's the kind of guy who might want to help out," she said. She called the writer and arranged a meeting. When Hank explained why he had come to Fort Worth, the man found the story interesting and said he would get to work on it right away. He composed a column—embellishing it as a human interest story—saying that an established writer and world traveler from Los Angeles named Henry C. Bukowski had met a young woman named Dulcey Ditmore from Fort Worth on an airplane. When the plane landed they somehow lost each other, and now he had come to reclaim his airborne love. Mr. Bukowski would be staying in town until they could meet again.

A day later, Dulcey surfaced. Not knowing what to expect, Hank went to see the young woman at her mother's house. Mrs. Ditmore met him at the door and invited him inside. Dulcey stood in the living room waiting, and he entered. She rushed toward Hank. "I've been thinking about you," she said. She took him to her room. When they were alone Dulcey asked Hank why he wasn't in the war fighting against Hitler. "I would rather that somebody else do it," he replied, adding that he wasn't really afraid of dying—he just didn't like the idea of sleeping in a barracks with a bunch of other men who were snoring. "Plus, I have this very sensitive skin. An army uniform would drive me crazy." Obviously bothered by what he was telling her, Dulcey interrupted to explain that her little brother had been very ill several years earlier, and had been saved through prayer. She described how religious she and her family had become since then, and how powerful prayer was, and how God listened to people in need. "You'd still believe in God even if your brother died," Hank told her. Dulcey said that she was engaged to an ensign in the navy. That settled matters. The girl had religion and a boyfriend, a hell of a combination. "Good-bye, baby," Hank said.

Before leaving town he called the editor to inform him of what had happened. With his meager belongings stuffed into a small suitcase he went to the bus station, ticket in hand, partly disappointed that nothing had come of his reunion with the young Dallas woman, but also relieved to be on his own again.

He arrived in New Orleans at five A.M., worn out from the exhausting trip, his body shaken up by the bumpy roads and the constant lurching of the bus. He ambled along aimlessly, feeling ludicrous with his pathetic-looking suitcase, which had lost one of its hinges and threatened to spill its pitiful holding on the streets. Rain began to fall, one of those hard tropical downpours, drenching him and further damaging the cardboard suitcase. At some point, he figured, he would probably ask somebody where the room-and-board places were. Meanwhile, he found himself in a black neighborhood. A woman called to him, "Hey, poor white trash!" He set his suitcase down and she called out again. He wanted to respond. The looming figure of a large, tough-looking man in the background discouraged him.

One of the first things that hit him when he arrived in New Orleans was the Jim Crow laws. He got on a streetcar one day and walked to the back, where he took a seat, as he used to do in L.A. The conductor looked back and yelled, "You can't do that . . . You just don't sit in the back." Hank asked why not, explaining that he liked sitting in the back of the bus. The conductor asked, "You're not from the South . . .You're not from here, are you?" Bukowski said no. Then the conductor told him to come up and sit in the front, which he did.

Hank found a rental inexpensive enough that even he could afford it. With a roof over his head everything else would fall into place, he reasoned. His only solace came from writing. His stories were still fantasies for the most part, yet they always bore reference to his own experiences. Some of the editors whom he sent the stories to told him that he wrote poetically.

Soon after settling in, he wrote to Dulcey Ditmore. He doesn't quite remember what compelled him to write; probably it was his solitude in the strange Southern city. Despite his disappointment on hearing of her engagement, at least she had shown interest in him. They wrote back and forth, until Dulcey sent Hank a sampling of her poetry. Hank was less than impressed, and he stopped writing.

Even when he had been on the bus to Fort Worth, anticipating meeting Dulcey again, part of him rebelled against it. He was certain that no woman would want him because of his scars. He loathed the idea of meeting someone, marrying her, and having children. He also questioned how a young person like Dulcey, good-looking and with no physical handicaps, or at least none that he could see, would be interested in a guy like him, a man with a flawed face. It didn't make any sense. Beyond all that, he was convinced that he needed to be alone in order to write.

Hank found work at a magazine distribution outfit checking orders to see that they agreed with the invoices. He signed the invoice and packed the orders for shipment or set them aside for local delivery—rote, dull work. Each day he wondered if this was going to be the pattern for the rest of his life. It didn't take more than a few hours to distance himself from the other workers. His fellow employees constantly worried about their jobs, whether or not they would keep them and if there might be a chance for advancement. Two women got into an argument concerning the work. Hank said, "These damn books aren't worth shit. So why argue?" One of the women shot back, "We know you think you're too good for this job."

The job lasted less than a week, coming to an end when he called his boss and asked for a raise. Though he had been working for only a few days, it made sense to him to ask for one. He didn't want to be anybody's patsy and he knew that for the work he did deserve more money. When the man said no, he quit. He saw a want ad for a typesetter in the composing room of a small newspaper on the verge of bankruptcy—it also lasted only a few days.

Life on the road didn't seem quite as adventurous to Hank as he'd thought it would, when he was back home. His thoughts turned to L.A., familiar ground. The drabness of his daily life, the dead-end jobs, were all just too much. But it wasn't a total loss—his time on the road had at least given him a new sense that he could return home stronger, a feeling that living in L.A. was his choice. So he left New Orleans, joining a railroad track crew with Sacramento as its ultimate destination.

On the train, Hank encountered trouble with the other young men. He sat way in back of the railway car, and wouldn't mix with them. When any of the others guys looked his way, he threw a surly glance.

They had marked him as different, and he didn't want to let them down. One of them came to Hank's seat, snuggled underneath it and blew dust in his face. He threatened his attacker in a Bogart-like drawl. The troublemaker retreated to the far end of the railroad car and told his friends to come to his aid if that madman in back attacked him.

The train stopped off in El Paso, Texas. Rather than go with the other crew members to a designated hotel for the night, Hank decided to sleep outside. He walked into the city park and sat down on a green park bench, near a few other men. They were down on their luck, just like he was—but they were trying to scrape up enough coins to go buy some wine. He gave them a few pennies and decided to go into the little red-brick library nearby. The place made him think of the hours he had spent in the L.A. Public Library and in the smaller library near his home. He walked inside, and his sadness fell away, as if a weight had been taken off of him. He didn't think of his poverty, or of his angry father back home—sure to look on him with stern glares of condemnation—as he scanned the shelves looking for a title that interested him. There it was: *Notes from the Underground* by Fyodor Dostoyevski. "I had read some of the Russians, Turgenev and Tolstoi, but this guy I didn't know. I couldn't even pronounce his name properly." He sat down to read. The words marched into him like lightning. He said to himself, *This guy has got it. This guy has got it.*

The irascible character portrayed in this short novel, which pre-dated Dostoyevski's *Crime and Punishment* by two years, is a document of personal suffering and outrage at "respectability." The nameless hero of Notes does not take a fixed position as he examines ideas of good and evil. He rejects the idea that the supposed nobility of man and the search for well-being are paramount. Instead, he concludes, man must search for an ultimate authenticity, no matter how unpalatable or contrary to social norms and codes of propriety. The hero mocks not only the codes men live by, but the idea of the average man and his "common" aspirations. Bukowski identified with Dostoyevski's mistrust of the average man, and with *Notes's* obsession with suffering.

After reading the book in one sitting, and identifying so closely with this alienated character, Hank walked back to the park. As he sat on the bench, a violent sandstorm blew through suddenly, and it was not long before he was covered with sand. With that for a blanket, he fell asleep.

In the morning, he woke to a sharp pain running through his feet and up his legs—a policeman loomed over him, rapping his feet with a nightstick. It was a horrible feeling; the pain was intense. He thought of the hero of *Notes* and how much he had despised authority: here stood the most common authority figure of all, a police officer in full uniform, angrily rapping his feet. He rose from the bench, bent down to get his shoes as the pain registered in every part of his body. Then he shook the sand off his clothing as best he could, and walked away.

On his way out of the park, he met a young couple. They had a nickel between them and wondered where they could get food. They were thin and drawn and had a strangely soft, animal look to their eyes, and seemed as if they might blow away with the next big wind. They had some vague idea of journeying off together.

Hank liked this young man and woman, both near to his own age. He almost walked away with them. He had believed, for a few moments at least, that maybe it would be better to team up with some others, to lessen the pain of getting by each day. In the end, however, he walked away. "I almost weakened. I almost lost my individuality … but I decided to remain on my own," he says of the incident.

Back on the train, Hank's brooding, aloof attitude caused more travail. The other young men barely disguised their animosity. When they arrived in L.A. for a scheduled stopover, they got off the train and began walking to a nearby bar with chits that the crew boss had given them.

Being home emboldened him to take some action: he approached two of the men and asked, "Hey, do you think something is wrong with me? Do you guys have a problem with me?"

Although these same guys had joined the others in taunting him on the train, one of them stepped forward and said, "No. We don't have a problem with you." Hank then walked into the bar with them, and found that the thirteen or more men who had signed onto the road crew were there. At first, he feared that there might be trouble. Instead, they greeted him like a long-lost brother. He had already decided not to complete the trip to Sacramento, and so he bowed out. Exhausted, sore, and penniless, there was nowhere to go but home.

The house on Longwood Avenue looked painfully unchanged, with its immaculate lawn and flawlessly trimmed hedges. Hank knew that his father would judge his return home as nothing less than an admission of failure. Hesitating for a moment, he almost wished he was back in the South again. "What the hell," he told himself as he walked up to the front door and knocked. He heard footsteps. His mother opened the door and screamed out. "Oh my son! Have you really come home?" His answer: "I need sleep." She told him that his bedroom was always waiting. Little else was said between them, and he went off to nap.

A few hours later, his mother awakened him to say that his father had come home. Hank walked into the dining room and sat down for dinner. Without welcoming him home, without asking him what he had seen or accomplished on his trip, Henry told his son that he planned on charging him room and board, plus laundry fee. Hank looked up and saw that his father had become much older in the relatively short time he had been away. There was no sign of fatherly love in the old man's face—nor in his voice.

Hank stayed around the house for a few days, sleeping mostly, but the pressure mounted to get a job. Even his mother had taken a job again, cleaning houses. He leafed through the want ads hoping to find something.

One night he wandered into a bar and drank until he fell asleep. When he woke up he looked at the clock—it read 3:15 A.M. He stayed, drinking up to closing time, 5 A.M. After they kicked him out, he began to stumble home quietly. A police patrol began to follow him, and a heavyset officer leaned out of the car and asked him to stop. They questioned Hank a while and, satisfied that he had broken no law, drove him home. His parents greeted him in their pajamas and robes. Henry laid it on hard, telling Hank he was a no-good drunken bum. Henry's hair stood up in wild tufts. His eyebrows were arched, his face swollen and flushed from a mix of sleep and anger. To Hank, his father looked ridiculous. "You act as if I had murdered someone. All I did was have a few drinks."

"You'll kill us all," his father responded. "After all we've done for you and this is what we get."

"Yes, Henry," his mother said. "You listen to your father. He knows best."

Hank eventually found work at an auto parts warehouse, staying until he decided to move to San Francisco. He caught the bus north and found quarters in a boarding house run by an elderly Italian woman. He took a job with the Red Cross, helping to set up temporary blood banks in various churches around the city. He carried folding beds into the churches, put them together, and then rolled out the bottles five days a week—which didn't leave much time for writing. He managed, though, to establish a routine that allowed some time for writing in the evenings. He came home each night after working at the Red Cross job to a large bucket of ice loaded with bottles of beer, courtesy of his landlady, who had taken a motherly interest in him. This, and the Victrola that she had brought him, made his time in San Francisco much more pleasant than the trip to New Orleans had been. "I used to go into these record stores where you bought three records, and then you would turn two back in later, something like that. I was able to hear a lot of the great composers."

When he'd had enough of the hard, boring work and quit his job, the landlady became even more solicitous, asking if he had enough food to eat. He stayed in the city a few months, hoping to find acceptance for his fiction in a national magazine. Before leaving San Francisco for St. Louis, probably in 1942 (to the best of Hank's recollection), he sent a letter to his father telling him to think of something to tell the neighbors because he didn't plan on ever going into the military. This was one of the few letters he ever wrote home. But the fact that he wrote it, and that he still occasionally needed his parents because of economic hardship, kept him from becoming completely estranged from them.

He wrote mostly fantasies. One concerned a bird sitting outside of his window. "I was drinking. So I wrote about this bird sitting there on the wire. I went on and on about it. Why was the wire there? And the bird? And why did it make me feel so strange? Then the bird has flown away and the wire is there. I go on and on. I thought it was great. And I went down on the streets. Well, I wasn't eating much. I was truly enjoying this. I was drunk so much … a lot of what I wrote was not logical."

He goes on to say, "Maybe the writing was crap, but it gave me something. I wasn't eating much, but I was truly enjoying the way writing was taking me. Even starving to write . . . it was worth everything." He spent hours jotting down his words, never stopping to outline a story or work out a plot. Long hours sitting in dark barrooms and in furnished rooms guzzling whiskey, getting into fights with the locals, yearning for female companionship—it was all there before him: "I just didn't see it then. Years later I found out this made for good stories," he says, "but I didn't know it at the time."

Hank moved from city to city, coming home to L.A. infrequently. When he did come home he treated his parents to a taste of his increasing alcoholic madness and listened to Henry's impassioned defense of the war effort. One time he arrived home, knocked on the door, and his father answered: "What are you doing here?" The old man turned white. "What's wrong?" Hank asked as his mother frantically motioned him inside. "We told the neighbors that you went off to the war and got killed," Katherine explained. As she talked to Hank, Henry yanked the star off the window that designated a family member killed in combat. "Well, what are we going to do now?" his father asked. Hank said that he would leave if they gave him ten dollars. Henry handed the money over and Hank took a hotel room downtown.

One evening in 1943 he visited Robert and Beverly Knox, who recall that Hank was his usual quiet, polite self, not anything like the half-crazed person he wrote about many years later in his poems and stories. Knox worked for a paper company in L.A. He joined the navy a year later. He was glad to see Hank, as it brought back good memories of his time at L.A. City College. They talked until about three in the morning and became so drunk that Knox never touched liquor again. But even drunk, Knox recalls, Hank remained soft-spoken and well mannered. Several hours after Hank left their house on 62nd Street, Knox discovered that Hank had taken his portable Corona Zephyr typewriter. He heard from Hank's mother that he had gone to Philadelphia. Katherine Bukowski wrote Hank, asking that he send the typewriter back, which he did.

He stayed in Philadelphia twice. "I can't be real positive on the dates," he says. "You know, I was drunk on my ass all the time and getting into fights. I hardly even knew the war was going on. People would talk about some battle in Europe or the Pacific and I didn't know what the fuck they were talking about." Despite his high draft number, Hank was obligated to report to the draft board, but he had fallen into the habit of not responding to the notices he received from them asking that he send his current address. Rather than doing that, he merely left his forwarding address at the post office, thinking that sufficient. He had received a notice from the Selective Service in St. Louis to report there for his draft examination, but wrote back to say he had moved on and wanted to appear at the board in Philadelphia. He never received a response. One night late in 1942, while writing in a Philadelphia rooming house, there was a knock on his door. He thought it either had to be the landlord or one of the people living on his floor. He buttoned his shirt, walked to the door and opened it. Two well-dressed men stood before him. He had been drinking on and off most of the afternoon and evening, and in his semi-feverish condition he thought that these men had come to offer him a Pulitzer Prize. (Considering that he had not published anything yet, that would have been quite some achievement.) One of them asked if he was Henry C. Bukowski.

"Yeah," he said.

"Come with us," the man responded, "and bring your coat along." He added that he and his partner were FBI agents. Perplexed, Hank went back into the room for his coat, turned off the radio, and went with them downstairs. They led him to a waiting car where two other men sat. He got in the car with them and they drove off. One of the men commented that Hank was acting pretty cool about being taken from his room by FBI agents. "Most people would be asking what they had done wrong, and a lot of other questions," the man continued. Hank remained listless. He was entertaining thoughts of suicide during this period of his life, working as little as possible, and wondering, feeling already defeated, if he would have made it writing stories had circumstances been different. Nothing these men said or did could affect him much. The agents became so aggravated by his coolness that they began hassling him in minor ways. "Sit up," a gruff-voiced man said. Another mentioned that they hadn't hit him yet, and perhaps they should.

"We haven't struck you, have we?" the agent repeated.

"Not yet," Hank answered. He was ordered to keep his hands on his knees. Just before they turned into the facility where he would be held for one night, he reached up to scratch his nose. "Okay! Watch that hand," he was warned.

After one night in a holding tank, he was taken to Moyemensing Prison, a large detention center built in a neo-Egyptian style in 1836 and closed in 1963. Described as a huge urban jail by a former guard, the facility once held Edgar Allen Poe as a prisoner in the debtor's wing. The other section, where Hank would be detained, looked like a medieval castle with turrets and brick walls. It consisted of a pair of three-story cell blocks housing over twelve hundred inmates. It had originally been a facility for hardened criminals, but now housed a population of inmates interred for a variety of petty offenses. As he entered the prison, a huge door swung open. It seemed over thirty feet wide and easily as high. Hank imagined himself entering a castle on the Rhine. Instead of feeling downcast, he felt honored and in awe.

[69]

He landed in a cell with a swindler we'll call John Jones, who Hank claims held the distinction of being Public Enemy Number One (although the term has always been loosely applied). Jones was heavy-set and balding, not a particularly menacing-looking fellow—but, as Hank found out, neither did he have a good disposition.

When Hank told him he had been arrested for draft dodging, Jones became exceedingly self-righteous, saying that he and the other inmates didn't like draft dodgers or indecent exposure cases, to which Hank snapped back, "Oh, I see. It's honor among thieves, right? You just keep the country strong so you can rob it."

"We still don't like draft dodgers," Jones said.

Hank explained to his cellmate how he had been moving around the country and simply forgot to mail in his current address to the draft board. "I gave my forwarding address to the post office," he said. "It's not like I was really running away."

Jones said that sounded like the usual bullshit that everyone gives out.

Despite the verbal abuse for alleged draft dodging he received from some of his fellow prisoners, Hank had a relatively easy time while incarcerated. He did well with the dice while in the prison yard. He made much more money than he earned on the outside, and was soon ordering special food. After the lights went out the cook brought steaks, baked potatoes, pie, cake, ice cream, and coffee. This earned him the admiration of John Jones, with whom he shared the bounty. Jones and he became noticeably fat eating the food. Once, the FBI men came by (and saw how comfortable and well fed he was) and very pleasantly asked Hank how he was doing. He just smiled and engaged in small talk. Life seemed so much easier on the inside than it had been out on the street. The agents commented that Hank didn't look like a man who was suffering: "You kind of like it here, don't you?" one of them asked.

"I don't mind it."

The cell was so full of bedbugs that it had to be fumigated. After he and Jones complained often enough, they were put in separate cells so that the fumigators could do their work. "I ended up with a madman," Hank says. All this man did from morning until night was repeat the words, "Tara Bubba eat, tara bubba sheet." Hank returned from the exercise yard after his first day with the new cellmate to find that the old man had torn his bed sheets into strips in order to make a clothesline on which to hang his socks and shorts. Hank snarled at him, telling the man he was in for murder. The man answered, "Tara bubba eat, tara bubba sheet."

Finally, he was released. It had been found that he didn't intentionally deceive the draft board. When told he would have to appear at the local induction center, Hank resigned himself to fate. Perhaps, after all, he would have to serve in the army and fight in a war he didn't care about.

When it came time for his physical, he found his way to a crowded building in downtown Philadelphia; the men there with him were mostly young and desperate-looking. Hank himself was thin, disheveled, and generally weakened by heavy bouts of drinking. Others were frightened and bewildered. He went through his physical and passed. Then they sent him to see the psychiatrist, a middle-aged man with a kindly face. The authorities had confiscated several of Hank's manuscripts when they had arrested him and handed them over to the psychiatrist, who probably passed Hank off as unstable when he read lines like "My mother's heart is dead."

The doctor briefly shuffled through some papers, then looked up at Hank and asked, "Do you believe in the war?"

"No," Hank answered.

The psychiatrist then put this question to him: "Are you willing to go fight the war?"

This time Hank said that he would go if called on to do so. As unbelievable as it may sound, the psychiatrist said, "I can see that you are a very intelligent man. We're having a party over at my place next Wednesday. There will be doctors, lawyers, scientists, artists, and writers. Will you come to my party?" Hank said "No." Rather than being offended, he was told, "All right, you don't have to go."

"Where?" Hank asked.

"To the war," the psychiatrist said.

As Hank got up to leave, the doctor said, "You didn't think we would understand, did you?" Hank gave his last negative answer and walked from the office with a paper on which his examiner had written, "hides extreme sensitivity under a poker face." One last official looked at his papers and motioned for him to go.

He made his way back to his room, thinking how beautiful everything looked, even the dirty sidewalks. "Everything seemed bigger," he recalls. "I mean as if the world had been bathed in a special light." He returned to the shipping clerk's job he had landed a few weeks earlier, explaining to the boss that he had been picked up for draft dodging. Four days later, the FBI arrested him all over again. This time they took him to their office. He was asked about his Uncle John, long since dead. At first he thought that the agent was referring to some kind of gun. Hank stood there looking perplexed. "Your uncle, John Bukowski," the man finally said.

"What do you want to know?" Hank asked.

"We want to know where he is." Hank explained that his uncle had died back in the thirties.

"Jesus. No wonder we can't find him," the agent said. From then on, the government left Hank alone.

In Philadelphia, at the age of twenty-three, Hank had sex for the first time. While sitting in a bar near where he lived, an extremely fat woman of indeterminate age walked in. He sat beside her and ordered several rounds of drinks. Because he was drunk, he could speak openly, saying that he could offer her something she would never forget. She seemed amused, and this encouraged him to go on in that vein, which he did, telling her all the delightful things he was going to do once they were alone. The woman laughed, and suggested they go up to his place. "We stayed until closing time. Then we walked to my place. She must have weighed three hundred pounds. I wrote a story about her." In his recounting of the story, published in the underground newspaper *Open City* during the sixties, and included in his book *Notes of a Dirty Old Man*, he wrote:

then she really started to bounce and whirl. I hung on and tried to find the rhythm: she rotated pretty good, but it was rotate and then up and down and then back to rotate. I got the rhythm of the rotate, but on the up and down I got thrown out of the saddle several times. I mean the deck would be coming up as I hit it, which is all right under ordinary conditions, but with her as I hit the deck coming on it simply caromed me completely out of the saddle and oftentimes almost out of the bed onto the floor …

In the morning he and the woman woke up to find that the bed had totally collapsed during their escapades. Hank didn't know what would happen when the landlady saw it. He offered the fat lady some money, but she told him that she could not accept it—he was the first man in years to make her feel good. When he came home from his job the following evening he passed the landlady and the cleaning woman, who made some comments about the bed. Hank walked into his room and saw that they had replaced his old wooden bed with a steel-framed one. The landlady said, "Let's see what you can do with this one."

The writing kept flowing. Hank traveled often now, frequently pawning his typewriter for food money, which forced him to write in longhand. He hand-printed more than fifty stories in ink, and sent them out. Not unlike other young writers, he amassed a huge collection of rejection slips. His life at that time resembled that of Martin Eden, Jack London's fictional character who nearly starved to death trying to break into the popular magazines. Unaware of Martin's travails, Hank had enough of his own to contend with.

Wherever Hank went, he traveled light, usually having one suitcase in which he could fit a cheap radio, an extra pair of work shoes, shorts, socks, a comb, razor and razor blades, and a few towels. At each new place, he wrote. Most of the pieces were without strong story lines.

Inevitably, his work came back. Whit Burnett of *Story*, the legendary magazine that had originally published William Saroyan and many other well-known authors, wrote personalized rejection slips, offering encouragement and suggestions. Hank started to feel he knew Burnett. The rejections, at least those in which the editor said more than a cursory "Sorry, these won't do," became important to him. They helped him keep his confidence and the belief that somehow, someday, he would have a story in print, and that would be a day to celebrate.

In 1944 Hank stayed in St. Louis, where he landed a job as a packer in the warehouse of a dress shop. Just before he left work for home one day, his boss summoned him into his office. The officious-looking older man sat behind his deck puffing on a fat cigar. A friend sat near him in an overstuffed chair. They were both vigorous-looking, energetic men. The boss introduced his friend as a writer. After having worked a full day for next to nothing, Hank felt mortified in the presence of these two very satisfied men. They sat in silence for a while, until the boss finally said that his friend had many books out and that he earned a considerable sum of money from them. Hank had put down on his application form that he was a writer, as a convenient way to explain the gaps in his employment record. It was obvious to Hank that the boss had called him in to humiliate him. Not knowing what to say, he just stood there, observing the two men, neither of whom had motioned for him to sit down. A few more minutes passed. Finally, he asked if it would be okay for him to leave. "Yes. That's fine," his boss said.

Walking home from the encounter with his boss, he fantasized that someday he would be sitting behind a desk, smoking fancy cigars: Lord of the realm, able to hire and fire with ease. If he couldn't be master over factories, there were banks and service stations to rob. He kept on walking. The bare branches of the trees reached into the approaching darkness of early evening. What a bad time he had suffered in that office.

Hank surveyed the ragged clothing he wore, and his bleak surroundings. His face burned from the humiliation suffered in the boss's office. As he looked around the room, he saw an overstuffed manila envelope lying on the rug. He went over to the windowsill, took the bottle of wine that had been chilled by the wind, and had a drink before picking the envelope up and opening it. Inside he found yet another rejected work of short fiction from *Story*. Included with it, however, was a note informing him that "Aftermath of a Lengthy Rejection Slip" would appear in the March–April 1944 issue. This bit of good news from Whit Burnett hardly seemed believable. Hank poured himself a drink, read the note again, and imagined that he had now been set on the road to literary success. He gazed out the window. A rush of cool air refreshed the world, images of Hemingway and Saroyan passed through him. Burnett must truly be a very great man, a man of impeccable taste. He savored each word in Burnett's note:

> Dear Mr. Bukowski,
>   We are sorry but this one didn't quite do. But we very much liked "Aftermath of a Lengthy Rejection Slip" and we will run it in our March–April issue …

Hank used his own name and included Burnett himself as a character in "Aftermath," which surely must have amused the editor and swayed him to finally publish this strange, unknown young man who kept sending wild stories about sleazy bars, down-and-out people of the streets, and crazed nights in solitude. This earliest surviving work of Bukowski's begins with an actual note from the editor that offers a pretty good idea of the kind of work he was writing in the early and mid-forties:

> Dear Mr. Bukowski,
>   Again, this is a conglomeration of extremely good stuff and other stuff full of idolized prostitutes, morning-after-vomiting scenes, misanthropy, praise for suicide etc. that is not quite for a magazine of any circulation at all. This is, however, pretty much a saga of a certain type of person and in it I think you've done an honest job. Possibly we will print you sometime, but I

don't know exactly when. That depends on you. Sincerely yours,
Whit Burnett

Oh, I knew the signature: the long "h" that twisted into the end of the "W," and the beginning of the "B" which dropped half-way down the page.

I put the slip back in my pocket and walked on down the street. I felt pretty good.

Here I had only been writing two years. Two short years. It took Hemingway ten years. And Sherwood Anderson, he was forty before he was published.

I guess I would have to give up drinking and women of ill-fame, though. Whiskey was hard to get anyhow and wine was ruining my stomach. Millie though—Millie, that would be hard-er, much harder.

… But Millie, Millie, we must remember art. Dostoyevsky, Gorki, for Russia, and now America wants an Eastern-Europe-an. America is tired of Browns and Smiths. The Browns and the Smiths are good writers but there are too many of them and they all write alike. America wants the fuzzy blackness, imprac-tical meditations and repressed desires of an Eastern-European.

Hank remembers many of his stories of this period as having been "impractical meditations," but they contained plenty of humor as well. He learned from James Thurber and John Fante how powerful hu-mor can be in revealing the human condition. Primarily from Fante he learned to appreciate the value of writing about the life immedi-ately before him. To use his own name, and to include Whit Burnett in a fictional piece, foreshadows the kind of autobiographical fiction that later became his stock-in-trade.

The story goes on to describe his interactions with Millie, a fiction-al name for a woman he knew at the time. Later, a man appears at his door whom Bukowski mistakes for Whit Burnett. He falls all over himself to please him, even letting him spend some time alone with Millie. While Millie cozies up to the man thought to be Mr. Burnett,

Bukowski excuses himself and goes into the kitchen:

> It was hard enough sharing Millie's love with the cheese sales-
> man and the welder. Millie with the figure right down to the
> hips. Damn, damn.

He takes a chair at the kitchen table and begins reading his rejection slip. This provokes the memory of an incident from his days
at L.A. City College. Picking up the theme of "fuzzy blackness"
he had mentioned in relation to the Eastern European sensibility,
he wrote:

> In college, even, I was drawn to fuzzy blackness. The short
> story instructress took me to dinner and a show one night and
> lectured me on the beauties of life. I had given her a story
> I had written in which I, as the main character, had gone
> down to the beach one night on the sand and began med-
> itating on the meaning of Christ, on the meaning in death,
> on the meaning and fullness and rhythm in all things. Then,
> in the middle of my meditations, along walks a bleary-eyed
> tramp kicking sand in my face. I talk to him, buy him a bot-
> tle and we drink. We get sick. Afterward we go to a house of
> ill-fame.
>
> After the dinner the short story instructress opened up her
> purse and brought forth my story of the beach. She opened it
> up halfway down to the entrance of the bleary-eyed tramp and
> the exit of meaning in Christ.
>
> "Up to here," she said, "Up to here, this was very good, in fact,
> beautiful."
>
> Then she glared at me and with that glare that only the artifi-
> cially intelligent who have somehow fallen into money and po-
> sition can have. "But pardon me, pardon me very much," she
> tapped at the bottom of my story, "just what the hell is this stuff
> doing in here?"

After he relates this, Bukowski rushes back into the living room where Millie and the supposed editor are embracing. As they talk, he discovers that the man is not the editor of the prestigious *Story* magazine, but an insurance agent:

> "Pardon me," he said, "Why do you keep calling me Mr. Burnett?"
> "Well, aren't you?"
> "I'm Hoffman, Joseph Hoffman. I'm from Curtis Life Insurance Company. I came in response to your postcard."
> "But I didn't send a postcard."
> "We received one from you."
> "I never sent any."
> "Aren't you Andrew Spickwich?"
> "Who?"
> "Spickwich. Andrew Spickwich. 3631 Taylor Street."
>
> . . . I ran like hell toward my room hoping there would be some wine left in that huge jug on the table. I didn't think I'd be that lucky, though, because I am too much a saga of a certain type of person: fuzzy blackness, impractical meditations, repressed desires.

By the time his piece appeared in *Story*, Hank had gone by bus to New York, hoping that a new and glorious chapter would soon open in his life. One story! It made all the difference. Success lay before him, he thought as he walked the city streets: all of his hard work and tough living had not been in vain. Passing through Greenwich Village he saw his name on the cover of *Story*. He purchased the magazine and imagined that people would notice him. Charles Bukowski, writer. Seeing his name there, he was glad that he had dropped "Henry," as he felt it wasn't literary enough.

The twenty-five dollars he received in payment meant a lot, not merely because it was the first money he had ever received for his writing, but because he had so little money at the time. (Just a few days earlier he had left his room and bought a bag of popcorn for five cents, his first food in two or three days. Although it tasted salty and greasy, every kernel that he devoured seemed like a steak dinner.)

Hank's excitement over his first publication did not last long. Alone in his room, already weary of New York, the thought arose that Burnett had taken his story only because it was a curiosity piece. Burnett had placed it in the end notes, rather than in the main part of the magazine. Nothing deterred Hank from a self-deprecating view of the whole process that led him to being in *Story*. Making it as a major writer and appearing regularly in the *Atlantic Monthly* and *Harper's* no longer seemed important. He wrote occasionally, but the old drive had gone. Added to this he decided that he needed more life experience. The writing still meant something, but he wanted to learn more about the world. He never wrote to Burnett again, and rarely submitted manuscripts over the next ten years. In the back of his mind, however, he knew that he would return to writing again.

Just after the war ended, Hank landed in Philadelphia for a second time. He stayed there until mid–1946. He found a hangout where the morning bartender opened the door for him at 5:30 A.M. and served him drinks on the house until the customers arrived at 7:00 A.M. During the day Hank delivered sandwiches and newspapers for the customers of the bar. When not working, he drank whiskey at the bar, usually until closing time. In general, he walked around in a half-stupor, not quite knowing how he managed to survive. He had suicidal thoughts quite often, and continually got into fights. Tommy McGilligan, a bartender Hank used to fight regularly, was a fairly big guy who fancied himself a ladies' man. McGilligan won most of the fights, mainly because Hank's strength waned as he went without much food for long periods and remained drunk for days at a time. Yet amidst the craziness of his life, and the seediness of his environment, he still found some time to sit alone in his room and write. His second published work of fiction, "Twenty Tanks from Kasseldown," appeared in Caresse Crosby's *Portfolio: An International Review.*

She wrote and inquired, "Who are you?" Hank replied,

> Dear Mrs. Crosby,
>   I don't know who I am.
>   Sincerely yours,
>   Charles Bukowski

There was a gangster bar in Philadelphia where Hank wanted to go to precisely because he was warned to stay away.

"You can't go in there, Hank," one of his barroom buddies said, "those sons of bitches will kill you."

"Oh fuck, nothing will happen to me," he answered and proceeded to go to the bar. He ordered a drink, saw an attractive woman sitting alone and walked over to her. "What are you drinking, baby?" he asked. While awaiting a reply, he noticed that the mood of the bar changed dramatically. The bartender stood there, frozen-faced, and the customers stopped talking to one another. A big guy approached Hank and said, "You're talking to the boss's daughter. You know what that means?"

"Yeah, go away, man." And then he asked the woman what she would like to drink. There was no response, so Hank dropped some money in the juke box and then went to the restroom. Two men followed him. One of them produced a blackjack and hit Hank over the head. He fell against the wall, then staggered back into the bar. Everyone was muttering in amazement as Hank sauntered up to the bar and demanded a drink. The boss arrived with a couple of his men. Hank expected trouble as the bartender explained his actions in some detail. Rather than being angry, the well-dressed gangster asked Hank outside and invited him to join his gang. Hank inquired why—to the amazement of the head man and his associates, who looked at one another dumbfounded.

"Because you've got guts, man."

"I'm sorry," Hank replied, "it's not my kind of thing."

FOUR

L ATE in 1946, Hank's wandering around the country came to an
    end. Even though he liked the bar scene in Philadelphia, Los
Angeles was home territory. He continued drinking as heavily as
during the war years and wrote an occasional short story. One of the
bars he frequented, the Glenview on Alvarado Street, became like a
second home. On a hot summer night, walking along Alvarado one
could easily deliriously mix palm trees and half-dilapidated store-
fronts with the humidity and the dark, long dream of Los Angeles.

One evening, in the dim light of the Glenview, Hank saw an older
woman sitting by herself. He glanced at her, turned away, jingled
the change in his pockets, and found himself looking back again,
noting her blond hair and mournful blue eyes with the slightest hint
of pouches forming under them, and a way of gesturing that told
him she had once been a very classy person. *She must have been
a real beauty*, he told himself. A sense of lost glamour and an aura
of good things long gone radiated from her. Oddly enough, no one
had approached her. One old guy sloshed the whiskey around in his
shot glass while two veterans of the L.A. night huddled in drunk-
en conversation. Normally, one or another would have introduced
themselves to an unescorted female. Curiosity led Hank to ask the
bartender why no one talked to her. "Because she's crazy," he said.
Hank ordered a drink and moved over to the unoccupied stool next

to her. The woman looked straight ahead, not acknowledging Hank's presence. He stared into his drink, then at the mirrored wall, and back to his drink.

"I hate people. Don't you?" she said, without making eye contact with him.

Not missing a beat, he told her that it wasn't so much hatred as his not wanting to be around them.

Hank ordered two scotch and waters.

"Listen," he said. "What do you do?"

"I drink."

Hank smiled. She had verve and was either a realist or a humorist, maybe a bit of both. They sat there a while, finishing their drinks.

"I'm out of money," Hank said.

"You really don't have any money?"

"No money, no job . . ."

"Come with me," she said, motioning toward the exit.

They walked from the bar to a liquor store across the street where she ordered two fifths of scotch, beer, some cigars, and a few miscellaneous items. Hank watched passively as the clerk matter-of-factly informed her he had to make a call. "Sure," she said. He dialed a number, mumbled into the phone, returned to the counter, "Yeah. He okayed your purchase."

When they left the store, she explained that she had it put on the tab of a successful real estate broker who loved her. They proceeded to Hank's apartment and began drinking.

He lit a cigar, "Listen, baby, I know this isn't much," Hank said of his shabby quarters with its bed that sagged in the middle, a naked light bulb that emanated a sickly yellow glow, and a wobbly kitchen table that looked as if it would fall if anyone breathed near it.

She poured two drinks and lit a cigarette. "It'll do," she said as she brushed her hair from her forehead. "Let's just forget about everything and get drunk."

"Remember, I don't have any money," Hank said. "I mean I don't have any money at all."

"I know. What the hell does it matter?"

Jane Cooney Baker's history was soon revealed to Hank. She came from Carlsbad, New Mexico and was ten years older than Hank. Her well-to-do mother had been too busy with her social life to be burdened with caring for her child. At an early age, she found herself in an orphanage operated by an order of nuns. While there, she and the other girls would jump out of the dormitory windows at night and run to the vegetable garden to dig up radishes because they were served very little food. She had no friends to speak of, but when she was eighteen, Jane met a wealthy young man from Connecticut by the name of Baker. Hank doesn't know the circumstances of how they met, but believes it must have been in a cocktail lounge. They married, had two children, and lived a life of luxury for several years. Hank seems to recall hearing Jane say that her husband was an attorney with a flourishing practice, at least in the beginning. Unfortunately, he turned into an alcoholic, and brought Jane along with him. Their storybook marriage turned into one doomed for failure. They were divorced, and right after they split up, Baker died in an automobile crash while drunk. Broken by her bad luck and the death of her husband, whom she still loved, Jane settled in California. Her children moved in with her husband's family and she lost touch with them.

"Losing my kids, that was the most painful thing," Jane told Hank. "I can't even tell you how it makes me feel."

The two loners began living together, not planning it, just letting it happen. They loved and fought passionately. Jane threw things and hurled curses. Hank shouted back at least as many. They battled so ferociously that they were often evicted from one furnished room, only to move into another. Yet they had plenty of good times: singing, drinking, and sharing a great dislike for the average man. After their arguments, in which Jane threw anything and everything at Hank and at the walls, they usually made love.

An intuitive understanding of life seemed to pass between them. Jane joined him in commiserating about prying landlords, fat-assed bosses who ruled like dictators in dimly lit warehouses and in the shipping rooms of department stores. Hank talked to her in a way that he had not been able to with others. Their conversations were rarely on an intellectual plane, largely because of Jane's drinking. She often lapsed into a semi-alcoholic stupor and did not want to talk about anything at all. Hank drank a lot, but she drank more. There were days when he simply had to desist from even looking at alcohol—not so with Jane. The first rays of sunlight were like signals for her to spring out of bed and search out the next bottle or the nearest cocktail lounge.

A series of part-time jobs Hank had (most lasting two or three days until he lost them because of drinking, fighting, or not following orders) kept them at least partially afloat. Whenever Jane scolded Hank, he said that he didn't care where life took him. "I don't give a fuck," he would say. "I'll quit my goddamned job and get the hell out of here." During those times he worked, he asked Jane to please be home when he returned, knowing she would probably head for one of the nearby bars. "Oh sure," she would say, "don't worry about me. I'll be home." There was one time Hank was coming from work and he knew which bar she was in. "Jane was acting very hoity-toity at the time. So I walked in there. She saw me coming. Her eyes got real big." Everyone in the bar understood Hank's intentions as he approached Jane. First he slapped her across the face, and then he yelled, "You fucking whore! I tried to make a woman out of you, but you're just a whore!" Jane sat quietly, whimpering. Someone had shut off the music. A moment of dead silence hung over the room until Hank turned to the crowd lined up at the bar and said, "Now, if there is anyone here who doesn't like what they saw . . ." Nobody said anything. No one did anything. The moment he hit the streets, Hank heard an explosion of voices from inside.

Once they were sitting in a cocktail lounge that had a large window. Jane kept looking at it as they sat drinking scotch, seemingly fascinated. She turned to Hank and said, "I bet you don't have the guts to break this window." He said, "Yeah, I do, but it wouldn't make any sense." Thinking that was the end of it, he called out to the bartender, Marty, for another drink. The bartender motioned toward Jane, who was just about to throw her glass at the window. Hank stopped her in time. "Look, baby, have another drink," he said. They began drinking whiskey. Hank tried steering the conversation away from the window, but Jane brought it back. She fixated on it. "Well, we got drunker and drunker until finally I took a beer bottle and smashed the window. For some reason, all the lights went out. We both started running out of the rear of the bar and ran up the alley." They came to a small fruit market, and pretended to shop for fruit. He picked up a banana and looked at it with interest. Jane perused the oranges. They stayed there a while, listening to the sirens of the police cars arriving at the bar. After a half hour or so, they walked to the front of the bar, got into their car, and drove off. "Jane had goaded me into doing it. I guess when I saw her getting ready to smash it herself, it put it into my mind."

As for Hank's parents and Jane, there was little communication between them. Hank recalls: "My parents met Jane sometime in 1954 or '55, shortly before we broke up, which means we must have been together about ten years. You know, she had a pot belly from all the drinking. They thought she was pregnant. So we went on this picnic together and they treated us nicely, even my father."

At 3 A.M. one morning Hank stood on the dirty rug in their room, facing Jane as she sat on a wobbly chair braced against a far wall. They were both far gone on cheap red wine that they had been drinking for the past fifteen hours. Silence hung between them for a moment. A slight breeze came in the half-opened window.

"I'm a genius and nobody knows it but me!" Hank yelled.

"Shit! You're a fucking asshole," Jane said in a mocking tone.

"You don't know anything, you whore!" he rejoined, as he threw a shard of broken glass into the air, almost hitting her.

"Fuck you!" she said.

The telephone rang. Before the caller could announce his name, Hank screeched into the phone, *"I'm a genius and nobody knows it but me."*

It was the desk clerk warning Hank that he and Jane were keeping the guests up.

"Guests? You mean those fucking winos?" Hank said.

Jane grabbed the phone and yelled into the clerk's ears: *"I'm a fucking genius too and I'm the only whore who knows it."*

Knowing what might happen next—because it had in the past—Hank secured the chain on the door to their room. The two of them then propped a sofa against the door, turned the lights out, climbed into bed and awaited the inevitable.

"Open up! Los Angeles Police Department! Open up in there!"

In a poem called "40 Years Ago in That Hotel Room," Hank recounts the story almost verbatim, ending it with the policemen finally giving up. Hank and Jane remain in the room,

> *. . . sipping at our*
> *wine.*
> *there was nothing to do*
> *but watch two neon signs*
> *through the window to the*
> *east*
> *one was near the library*
> *and said in red:*
> *JESUS SAVES*
> *the other sign was more*
> *interesting:*
> *it was a large red bird*
> *which flapped its wings*
> *seven times*
> *and then a sign lit up*
> *below it advertising*
> *advertising*
> *SIGNAL GASOLINE.*
>
> *it was as good a life*
> *as we could*
> *afford.*

Another near miss with the law came when Jane and Hank were walking home from a bar. She saw rows of corn growing on a hill-top near to where they lived. "I want some of that. I want to cook some corn," she pleaded. Hank said nothing. She climbed the hill, which was private property, of course, and joyfully began ripping off ears of corn and stuffing them into her bag. As she came down toward Hank a police patrol pulled up. "Jesus. Let's get the fuck out of here," Hank said. They ran to their apartment building as the policemen called over their loudspeaker warning them to halt or they would start shooting. "We just went on inside," Hank remembers. "We knew they would never find us once we were safely upstairs."

During the last few years they were together, Jane's frenzied drinking bouts worsened. There were times when she hardly seemed aware of her surroundings. Hank at least held on to the hope, however buried it might be, that someday he was going to sit down and write again. Jane, on the other hand, never freed herself from the anguish of her past: she had been forced into a corner. Hank had chosen his way of life, chosen not to accept the day-to-day grind that turned men's faces into hamburger and their hearts into stone.

Jane's lack of inhibitions earned Hank's admiration. When they first met she had inquired about his complexion, wondering what had happened. He asked if it really mattered and she told him that he looked beautiful. The fact that she loved the rest of his body as well only fulfilled him all the more. After the sexual drought of his youth, and the years he would either pay for women or have one-night stands, he could not resist Jane's enthusiasm. Due to her morning demands for sex, Hank lost a good job at a bicycle company. The boss gave him a man-to-man talk, telling him what a good clerk he had been. "But we can't have guys coming in late all the time," he said. When he asked what was the matter, Hank told him that he had just gotten married, that he was on his honeymoon. Despite the picture he painted of a young married couple at the beginning of their relationship, the boss simply replied that he would have the severance pay readied.

For a period of time, Jane worked as a typist for the Eastern Furniture Company, a downtown furniture store housed in a large blue-green building.

"Hank, if I can keep this job, it can mean a lot for us," she told him after a week of work.

"Sure, baby. All you have to do is hold on."

"It's so hard, Hank. The people are so stupid. They can't think."

"That's normal," Hank said.

Becoming a househusband may have been out of character for Hank, but he learned to adapt. He saw Jane off in the morning, accompanying her to the bus stop on the corner, and shopped for the evening meal (which he later prepared), kept their place reasonably clean, and took the dog they had for a while on long walks. Then he either went to a bar or stayed at home, maybe drinking a little. Later he would return to the bus stop to meet her. From the moment Jane alighted from the bus, she complained that her high heels were killing her and started talking about various problems at the office; it reminded Hank of how his father used to complain about the milk company job. He would have hot water in the bathtub waiting for her, and while she sat in the tub, he would bring her a glass of wine and prepare dinner. Things were going well. He even wrote a poem or short story now and then, but never consistently.

In 1952, hearing that the postal service needed temporary help for the Christmas rush, and that they were lax in their hiring policies, Hank applied, thinking that a month or two of such work wouldn't be a bad idea. The short-term employment turned out to be a three-year run in which he got more than his fair share of the working man's plight. As a mail carrier, his biggest problem centered on the people he had to deal with, including an army of zombielike employees who disgusted Hank with their subservience to postal rules and regulations. An even bigger problem came in the form of the supervisors, or "sups," as they were called, who lorded it over their underlings. They had pegged Hank as a troublemaker. It took him three years to attain "regular" status—that is, to become a full-time employee.

During most of this time, Jane didn't work. "Most of my money went toward liquor," Hank recalls. "I couldn't even buy a decent pair of work shoes. Jane drank all the time, of course, and I tried keeping up with her, even though I held down a job." So his time was spent working hard on the job and then carousing with Jane. Not even the enormous hangovers he suffered could keep him from this routine. He kept throwing his empty bottles through the apartment window. Several times he took the window frame down to a nearby hardware store so that new glass could be installed.

One day while Hank was casing mail, the man working alongside him said he looked ill and should go home. Hank had felt sick all morning, but shrugged it off. Suddenly, he was assigned to unload a mail truck. As he unloaded the heavy bags he realized that he really shouldn't be on the job and needed to go home and rest. He immediately signed off from work and took a bus to his neighborhood. Jane was sitting at the kitchen table drinking when he arrived. He told her to go to the grocery store and buy ice cream, thinking that would make him feel better. Jane obliged. He began eating, but then he started vomiting. Somehow he got through the night, but toward morning he began vomiting blood. He awoke with blood coming both from his mouth and rectum. He asked Jane to call a doctor. When the man examined Hank he said that he needed to go to a hospital or he would die. Jane called an ambulance.

When an ambulance arrived, the attendants said that Hank was too big to carry down the stairs. So he walked down, feeling as if he might collapse at any moment. Once on the sidewalk he got on the stretcher and they put him in the ambulance. "We were packed in there," Hank remembers. "It was like death itself. They got me up on the third tier of bunks and left me there. Blood still came pouring from my mouth, dripping on the person in the bunk below me. I was ready to die." But Hank made it to the charity ward at the county hospital. He had never saved any money. On the way there, he thought, "Okay, Papa, death has caught up to me. Mother of Christ. This is the way it goes." At the hospital he was put through a battery of questions: birthplace, date of birth, financial status, marital status, and so on. He was then whisked away to an elevator and taken down to a large, dark room. A pair of indifferent attendants rolled him into the room and placed him on a bed. After taking a pill given him by an orderly who had come out of nowhere, he looked around him and saw that the room was filled with several other men. Hank did not feel comfortable. The room remained dark and cold. The man in the bed next to him lay face up spinning a mad tale about chickens. Hank lay silently, listening for a while, and then spit out a mouthful of blood.

After an uncomfortable night, a nurse finally appeared. Hank was taken for an X-ray. A mad scene ensued in which he was too weak to stand upright for the technician. After two attempts at getting a proper X-ray the technician told the nurse to take Hank away—he had just wasted two negatives. He told Hank that the film cost a lot of money and he didn't want to waste any more. All through this, Hank's pain intensified. Surrendering to the situation seemed like the best course to take, but when he was taken into a new ward, he rebelled against the nurses, who seemed oblivious that he was suffering. Hank kept spitting up blood, much of it on the floor because he could not always make it to the bathroom in time. A nurse finally came to his bed and yelled at him for making her job difficult. Hank responded with a nasty comment, after which the nurse lifted his head and slapped him across the face a couple of times. "Florence Nightingale, I love you," he told her. One of the nurses told him that they could not give him any blood because he didn't have any blood credits. "You have a bleeding ulcer," she said, "and it is very serious." The nurse then asked if he wanted to see a priest (he had told the admissions clerk that he was a Catholic).

Hank remembered his father boasting about giving blood to the county's blood bank. So Hank gave the nurse his father's name and phone number. Two days later Hank was given a massive blood transfusion. "It was a mad scene . . . I really thought I was dying. But my gracious father decided to spare my life." After the transfusion, a priest visited Hank's bedside. Hank informed the priest that his services were not needed, not because Hank thought he would pull through, but because he had no faith in God.

Jane came to the hospital with Hank's father. Henry Bukowski stood off to one side smiling as Jane stumbled, drunken, across the room to Hank. "Lover, oh lover boy," she said.

Hank accused his father of deliberately getting Jane drunk before coming for the visit.

"I know what you've done," Hank said. "It was on purpose—to prove a point."

"Lover, don't you want to see me?" Jane continued.

Henry, showing no sympathy for his son, said, "I told you she was no good." Hank answered, "You son of a bitch. One more word out of you and I'm going to take this needle out of my arm and get up and whip the shit out of you."

Then Hank told them both to leave.

The next morning he was released from the hospital. A nurse gave him a list of foods to eat, and a doctor told him he would die if he drank. Just before Hank left, another doctor recommended an operation. "You're out of your mind," Hank said.

Home from the hospital, Hank found it difficult to return to his post office routine. He couldn't take it anymore. For years he had been persecuted by a supervisor whose every word and deed could be found in the postal regulations. Hank stood out as the rebel, the man to break. But when he didn't knuckle under, this "company man" began writing him up with increasing regularity and sending him out on the most difficult assignments. Finally Hank went down to the federal building, a huge blocklike structure only a short distance from the Temple Street flophouses he used to live in. He did something a full-time post office employee rarely does: he resigned.

Soon afterward, Hank sat down at his typewriter, long unused, and began typing out poems. He didn't know where they came from, but believed they probably were spurred on by his near brush with death. "It was some kind of madness. I didn't even think about what I was going to write. It was just automatic." This unexpected, totally unplanned reaffirmation of his writing excited Hank. For a moment he thought of writing stories again. This didn't happen—the poetry came too fast, and each one made such a complete, final statement that he no longer had the desire to venture into prose.

At the same time that the poetry burst forth, Jane introduced him to the racetrack, in the belief that it would take his mind off liquor. When she mentioned going to Hollywood Park, he didn't even know what horse racing was. She explained the track to him, talked about betting, even told a few stories of people who had made fortunes betting.

"Is there one open now?" he asked, intrigued by the idea, but also convinced that he would find the crowds annoying.

"I think Hollywood Park is open," she said.

"Let's make it," he replied.

They drove south to Inglewood in their battered-up car, which had cost them almost nothing; having arrived late, they parked in a residential area nearly a mile from the track and made their way to the entrance. Just as Hank expected, the crowds annoyed him. And yet he sensed a thrill growing within him as he and Jane went up into the stands with a racing form in hand that Jane had just purchased. All around him were people of every size and description. Rich and poor intermingled; men obviously down on their luck sat next to people to whom life had been one continuous wheel of fortune.

"What do you think?" Jane asked as they found seats in the stands.

"Jesus. It sounds kind of stupid to me. All these people, mindless masses of people, hovering together, watching these animals go around the track. I don't quite get it. Maybe something is wrong with me."

He amused himself by secretly concocting stories about some of the people he observed, especially the ones who studied their racing forms, oblivious to the crowd, unaffected by the carnival atmosphere around them. Their detachment fascinated him. They weren't alone in a crowd—they were free from the crowd. He knew instinctively that these were the true scientists of the race track, the ones who were serious enough to really try to win.

When he found out that beer was available he relaxed more, and then he and Jane began pouring over the racing form after she explained that it gave you a record of what each horse had been doing. She went on to talk about the entire betting process, throwing out terms like, *win, show, place, longshot,* and *across-the-board betting.* Hank never understood how Jane knew so much about the horses, but surmised she might have gone there with her late husband.

Hank picked three winners on this first trip to the race track. One of them paid fifty dollars. It all seemed so easy to him. He went home and, against the advice of the doctors who had told him that the next drink would kill him, he mixed wine and milk. He drank one glass, then poured another, this time with less milk. Later in the evening he began drinking straight wine. The true test came when he woke up the next morning and didn't hemorrhage. He moved around like his old self again and decided to go to the track. The second visit brought more victory and only made him want to return. As the weeks went on he became acquainted with the names and histories of the top jockeys, and it didn't take him long to begin experimenting with his own systems of play. He enjoyed the inventiveness, the utter privacy of his mind working with the racing form. The track itself, the excitement of gambling, and the study that went along with it, together with the pressing in of the crowd, spurred on his drinking. With a beer in hand, he felt more capable of making the right moves. For a while, he hit on a winning streak, which helped to increase his daily intake of liquor. Jane brought port to the track, and they ordered plenty of beer while they were there. During their winning streaks, they drank hard liquor, usually scotch and water, at the track bar. "As soon as I quit my job, the winning streak began. I was lucky." When their first big winning streak came to an end, they were down to cheap port and muscatel.

One day Jane returned from her job and accused Hank of making love with a woman who lived in the back apartment. He explained that she had come over with the intention of going to bed with him, but that nothing had happened. "Hell, she's just a fat slob," Hank protested. "I love you, baby," he assured Jane.

[93]

It was true he had no interest in the woman. The neighbor had knocked on their door several times before with the sole purpose of enticing Hank. She lifted her dress up, showing her legs, but he didn't respond. Jane refused to believe him no matter how he tried convincing her otherwise.

Moreover, Jane's daughter had just shown up pregnant; Jane told Hank that he would have to move out so she could devote her time to helping her daughter.

Hank turned more vigorously to his newfound work as a poet. Somehow, without giving it much thought, he knew that his strength lay in illuminating the sleazy bars, littered alleyways, furnished rooms, and lunchpail compatriots with whom he had rubbed shoulders most of his life. As he wrote those first poems, Disneyland opened its doors, as did Marineland on the Palos Verdes Peninsula. In Hollywood, the Capitol Records Tower, designed by Welton Becket, became an instant monument to Hollywood glitter. Buried beneath all of this, Hank laid aside whatever had held him back from the typewriter and went at it with a vengeance. One of the earliest poems was "Layover."

> Making love in the sun, in the morning sun
> in a hotel room
> above the alley
> where poor men poke for bottles;
> making love in the sun
> making love by a carpet redder than our blood,
> making love while the boys sell headlines
> and Cadillacs,
> making love by a photograph of Paris
> and an open pack of Chesterfields,
> making love while other men—poor fools—
> work . . .

The clear language of this poem reflects Bukowski's insistence that his lines be true to his own speech. It was summed up later by a critic who described his work as "the spoken word nailed to paper." The common speech of Bukowski echoes all the way back to Walt Whitman and his prefaces to *Leaves of Grass* which call for an indigenous language coming up from the people, a poetry of the streets.

Not knowing where to send his work, Bukowski purchased a magazine called *Trace*, edited in Los Angeles by James Boyer May. Each issue contained an updated list of little magazines and poetry journals. He brought the magazine home, closed his eyes and ran his fingers down the list, and landed on a magazine in Texas called *Harlequin*. Judging by the title, he imagined a little old woman who kept canaries editing the magazine from a small wooden frame house on a tranquil side street and specializing in rhyming poems. "But I said 'Fuck it' and mailed my poems off. Then this letter came back." The editor, a woman named Barbara Frye, wrote to tell the poet that she had never read work like his and that he was a genius. He was doing better than the first round of short story submissions he had sent during his early twenties.

The letters exchanged between the small Texas town where Frye lived and the poet's Los Angeles became increasingly frequent. Frye soon launched into topics having little to do with poetry. Hank sensed that she was a lonely, eccentric woman, and probably looking for a husband. As things heated up and the correspondence became personal, Barbara cautioned him, "No man will ever marry me. I can't turn my neck from shoulder to shoulder." Hank wrote that he had a scarred face, and compared himself to a tiger. "We will march through the world together," he wrote. She sent him a few photographs, and he thought she looked pretty. In letter after letter Frye kept referring to the hopelessness of her situation. One night, while in a drunken state, Hank wrote, "For Christ's sake, I'll marry you."

He sent the marriage proposal to Barbara, laughing it off as words torn from the craziness of a wild night. The recipient of his offer, however, took it as a serious proposal. She sent more photos. Feeling like a martyr, Hank thought that at least he would be able to make her happy, and resigned himself to his fate. As he thought over what he had done he reasoned that if you can bring happiness to one other person in the world then life is worthwhile.

Hank and Barbara decided that she should take a bus to Los Angeles and they would go to Las Vegas to be married in a quick civil ceremony. When the bus from Texas arrived at the station, Hank watched closely as the passengers filed off one by one. Finally, he saw this cute, vivacious blonde who radiated sex and didn't seem much older than twenty.

"Are you Barbara?" he asked.

"Yes," she said. "I guess you're Bukowski?"

"I guess I am. Shall we go?"

"All right."

As they drove to his place, she told him that she had almost gotten off the bus and returned home. "It's kind of scary," she said.

"I know," he answered. "We'll just take it day by day."

Hank stopped off for beer and whiskey, after which they drove to his place and drank. "Listen, let's go to bed," he said late in the evening. "Not until we're married," she answered. The next morning they drove to Las Vegas, as planned. The trip across the desert was one of the quickest Hank ever took. "I just wanted to get there, sign the fucking papers, say what had to be said, and get the hell back home. It was eight hours going and eight coming back, through all that desert. And it was worth it. We must have stayed in bed about fifteen hours." Barbara turned out to be about as far from Hank's image of a little old lady editor as possible. The truth is, she demanded so much sex that it nearly drove him crazy. Although it turned out that she really couldn't turn her neck, it never interfered with their sex life.

After they had settled into a routine, Barbara decided that she wanted to take Hank to see Wheeler, Texas. He quit his job as a shipping clerk and they left for her hometown; according to Hank, Barbara's grandfather Tobe Frye practically owned the small town and had even given Barbara her own small house.

While they lived in Wheeler, Hank was a marked man. He was supposed to be the guy who had married all this money, the gold digger. Everywhere he went in town, people perceived him as the cool city slicker who had gotten the money. He deliberately affected certain characteristics, such as walking around with a swagger in his gait and smoking big cigars.

The irony was that Barbara's family wasn't all that rich. Tom Frye, Barbara's cousin, a retired airline pilot who lives in the Wheeler area, recalls that the family members were not millionaires. "There was one working oil well on Tobe's place, but it didn't bring in much money. Barbara's father owned a crop dusting business and, at one time, had seventy planes. He was probably wealthier than his father." Another of her cousins, Sunny Thomas, who lives in L.A., said that the Frye ranch had originally been thirteen square miles but had been broken up over the years. "The family were real pioneers. When Tobe Frye died, he left Barbara a house and some land. But anyone who thinks she was wealthy would be crazy." Barbara's father refused to meet his son-in-law. The one time he visited his daughter's house, she and Hank were in bed. Mr. Frye opened the door to her bedroom, saw them lying there, and asked Hank, "What do you do for a living?" Hank looked at him and said, "Nothing," whereupon the old man stormed out of the room and slammed the front door shut behind him.

Grandfather Frye was different. He lifted a few glasses of whiskey with Hank every so often. One day the family was driving outside of town and the old man asked him if he wanted to see some buffalo. The big-city man answered that he thought all the buffalo had been killed. "Oh, no . . ." the old man said. They drove out to a fenced-in area along with Barbara and her grandmother.

"Just climb over the fence and walk out a ways," the old man said. Hank did so, overwhelmed with curiosity. He yelled out, "*Well, where are the buffalo?*" Then, out of nowhere, the beasts appeared, three of them. They were not moving slowly. Instead, they headed toward him at what he surmised to be full speed. He turned quickly, with only one thought in mind: to get over the fence before the buffalo reached him. Somehow he managed to do just that. Meanwhile, Tobe Frye and his granddaughter couldn't stop laughing. It was a real Texas plains baptism by fire. In his novel *Post Office*

Hank sketches his life in Wheeler. He calls Barbara "Joyce" and doesn't name the town:

> Joyce had a little house in town and we laid around and screwed and ate. She fed me well, fattened me up and weakened me at the same time. She couldn't get enough. Joyce, my wife, was a nymph.
>
> I took little walks through the town alone, to get away from her, teeth marks all over my chest, neck and shoulders, and somewhere else that worried me more and was quite painful. She was eating me alive.
>
> I limped through the town and they stared at me, knowing about Joyce, her sex drive, and also that her father and grandfather had more money, land, lakes, hunting preserves than all of them.

They left Wheeler because Hank couldn't stand the place after living there three months. He drank there, but not enough to keep him from feeling trapped. There just weren't enough sidewalks, alleyways, bars, and people to satisfy Hank, who, after all, was used to city life. Also Barbara, a strange, stubborn girl who, according to Sunny, kept her distance from others, wanted to prove that she could live without her family. "I want to show my father that I can make it on my own," she said, and sketched out plans as to how they would move back to Los Angeles and earn their own money. Hank reasoned that they already had plenty of money from her family. "Baby, we don't have to work," he said. She wouldn't listen. "No," she replied, "We have to be independent. That's one thing I'm sure of." No amount of arguing could change her mind.

In Los Angeles, Barbara insisted that Hank take a job. "But, Baby, I mean, we don't have to do this," he protested.

"No, I won't have it any other way."

With money her family had given her, Barbara bought a brand-new 1957 Plymouth. The purchase of the car left a considerable dent in her bank account, so Hank came up with the idea that she take an exam for a county job. Before he knew it, she had a job with the sheriff's department. Hank quit the shipping clerk position he held, telling Barbara that he had been fired.

One day, while typing his poems, Hank received a call from his father, informing him that his mother was ill and was in a nursing home. He drove to see her and found out that she had been operated on for cancer. "Well, I'll get better," his mother told him. "I just had an operation." Hank was perplexed that he hadn't been told earlier, but considering his relationship with his father he should not have been too surprised. He visited her two more times. On the second visit, his mother motioned Hank over to her side and, in a voice filled with emotion, said, "You were right, Henry. Your father is a horrible man."

On the third visit, he found a wreath on the door. That was how he knew she had died. The funeral was held two days later. His father played the part of the bereaved husband, but Hank knew that he had looked upon his wife more as a possession than a companion. He thought back to a few years earlier when his mother had run off from Henry and taken a small room in a boarding house. She had contacted Hank and told him how much she enjoyed her freedom. It was so out of character for her to rebel that Hank could hardly believe the news. She had run from Henry's tyranny, which had only increased over the years. Hank believes she returned home after months largely out of financial need. "Beyond this, I don't know anything," Hank says. "It was her one great rebellion. But this is all I know about it."

In 1957, Barbara published eight of Bukowski's poems in *Harlequin*. He was the magazine's co-editor at the time. One of the poems, "Death Wants More Death," begins:

> *death wants more death, and its webs are full:*
> *I remember my father's garage, how child-like*
> *I would brush the corpses of flies*
> *from the windows they had thought were escape—*
> *their sticky, ugly, vibrant bodies*
> *shouting like dumb crazy dogs against the glass*

only to spin and flit
in that second larger than hell or heaven
onto the edge of the ledge . . .

Probing poetically into his father's garage, Bukowski focused on particular, concrete images. From his earliest work on, he avoided the purely abstract. He had learned from the prose writers how to observe. He hinged philosophical and meditative writing on things discernible in the real world. "Dumb crazy dogs" is typical of the kind of direct, common imagery that marks his poetry.

A rented cottage on a hilltop on the outskirts of downtown became Hank and Barbara's home. With Barbara working, Hank concentrated on the racetrack, his writing, and drinking. He didn't love Barbara, and often he chuckled inwardly at how he had plunged headlong into this mail-marriage. They did a lot of things together, such as attending art classes at Los Angeles City College, and editing *Harlequin*, but Hank grew restless. As it turned out, so did Barbara. More and more, on coming home from her clerical job at the sheriff's department, she would tell Hank about this suave, sophisticated man she had met. Barbara became obsessed with the man, portraying him as "a real gentleman." She told Hank how her friend had suffered, caring for a sick wife who finally died.

"Listen, Barbara," Hank said one evening. "I've bummed all over the country. You know, people play games in offices. They're out of their minds with boredom. You know, whatever you feel for this man doesn't mean a thing."

A week or so later, at 7:00 A.M., Hank was awakened by a man who served him divorce papers. He took them, read them over, and went into the bedroom where he awakened Barbara. "I'm sorry, Hank," she said. He told her that she shouldn't have gone to the trouble of serving papers. He would have agreed right away to a divorce. They made love one last time, then Hank took his suitcase of belongings, drove off in the Plymouth, which Barbara gave to him, and began looking for a vacancy sign.

Hank and Barbara Frye received a divorce decree on March 18, 1958. Their marriage had lasted two years, four months, and twenty days. The decree included the following: "The 1957 Plymouth automobile will be awarded to the defendant, conditional to his paying the balance due on same." Hank kept the car well into the sixties. On rare occasions, he heard from Barbara, who ended up marrying an Eskimo and moving to Alaska.

In 1959, Frye became the subject of several Bukowski poems. One, "The Day I Kicked Away a Bankroll," appeared in the small journal *Quicksilver* in the summer of 1959. Here, Bukowski adopts a tone of both indignation and humor to explain the end of his marriage. Nothing is spared. Less lyrical than many of his other poems from the period, it is one of the tough-guy poems that would gain him a wide audience among readers who had never before paid much attention to poetry. It begins with a catalogue:

> *and I said, you can take your rich aunts and uncles*
> *and grandfathers and fathers*
> *and all their lousy oil*
> *and their seven lakes*
> *and their wild turkey*
> *and buffalo*
> *and the whole state of Texas . . .*
>
>   . . .
>
> *and your famous tornadoes,*
> *and your filthy floods*
> *and all your yowling cats*
> *and your subscription to Time,*
> *and shove them, baby,*
> *shove them.*

He goes on to say he can return to ordinary work and still pick up twenty-five dollars for a four-round boxing match. "Sure, I'm 38 / but a little dye can pinch the gray / out of my hair . . ." This dimension of the purely autobiographical added a bold element to Bukowski's developing oeuvre. Even more than Whitman, he exposed himself, right down to the most private trials and tribulations of daily existence. This was not rare in prose, but certainly so in poetry.

Henry Bukowski, Sr., passed away nine months after Hank's divorce, while he was in his kitchen reaching for a glass of water on the morning of December 4, 1958. His death was completely unexpected, since he had had no major medical problems. He was not too many years away from retirement. The old man's girlfriend had come to his house in Temple City, not far from the Santa Anita Race Track, knocked on the door, and heard no answer. Standing on the porch a few minutes, she heard the sound of running water inside. She knocked again, then, sensing something might be wrong, she ran to a neighbor for help. They managed to get into the house, where they found him lying on the floor, glass in hand, kitchen sink overflowing. She called Hank immediately to inform him that his father had died.

A feeling of relief swept over Hank when he heard of his father's death. He had been freed of a great burden. He busied himself with funeral arrangements, notifying his father's friends. Then, he went to his father's house in Temple City, a place he had passed close to on his way to Santa Anita, but rarely visited.

It was an odd moment for him. He began sorting through his father's things. He went outside and watered the lawn and shrubbery. The neighbors came by, tentatively at first, and then unabashedly. One by one, he gave various household objects to them, from paintings to garden tools. As he later put it in a story: "They left me the garden hose, the bed, the refrigerator and stove, and a roll of toilet paper."

He inherited the house in Temple City, a tidy and compact suburb just east of Los Angeles. He later described it as a substantial place with large rooms and a big yard. He had no interest in keeping it, preferring to continue living in the cheap rooms he was used to in East Hollywood. He sold the house for $16,000, and gambled and drank the money away as quickly as he could, partly as a protest against all that his father had stood for: seeking wealth, owning several homes, and being finally secure.

He had not seen much of his father or his mother before they died. Early in his marriage to Barbara Frye, his parents came by one Christmas Eve. Henry Senior complained about things: the Christmas tree lights weren't put on right, his son did not have a well-paying job. Unable to restrain himself, Hank told his father, "Get your ass out of the house." He told him to leave before he threw him out. His mother protested, saying, "You can't talk to your father that way," but the old man had already stormed out to his car and was sitting there. Katherine Bukowski demanded that her son go out and apologize to his father. "You can't just leave him sitting there," she said. Hank didn't respond. His mother repeated that he should tell his father he was sorry.

"Sorry for what?" he asked.

"But he's all alone there," she said.

"I think it's time for you to leave too."

FIVE

As the fifties ended, occasionally Hank looked in the newspaper and skimmed over the events of the world. Eisenhower still ruled, his eyes almost gentle as they stared at the poet from the front page of the *Los Angeles Times*. A revolutionary Cuba captured the world's attention. A young senator from Massachusetts named John F. Kennedy had tossed his hat in the ring for president. Little of it, except for a mention of Castro, made it into Hank's poetry.

The racetrack provided much of the color and atmosphere of his poems. The horses energized him. As he balanced life at the track with the realities of eking out a living, the real work at home, writing poetry, became sharper for him. Images came into focus. He spent hours at a time writing and sending the work out, sometimes in big batches. He liked the idea that readers of the little magazines, mostly writers themselves, were taking notice of him, a man who lived in a darkened room with a big crack in the wall, drinking beer and wondering if he would ever find a woman again.

One day late in 1958 Hank ran into Jane. Whatever had been smart and attractive about her in the past no longer existed. Her body was flabby and her face looked much older. There had always been a vagueness about her; now she seemed almost invisible.

"I saw you with that woman," Jane said, referring to Barbara. "She's not your type."

"Yeah? Well she's gone now."

Jane told him that she had lost touch with her daughter. She didn't say exactly why, but Hank figured it must have been her drinking.

"I'm all alone, Hank. I don't have anybody." Mainly out of pity, Hank began to see her on a regular basis, spending the night in her furnished room in an apartment building at Beverly and Vermont. She drank more than ever, still going on about how hopeless people were—but the fire had gone. She evoked strong feelings of lost love, pity, and guilt in her former boyfriend. He wanted to help her, but when she brought up the idea that they try living together again, he couldn't go for it. She carried with her a sense of overwhelming sadness, which made Hank uncomfortable, and nostalgic for their vanished life together. He had enough bad feelings to deal with. The burden of another person's crippled emotions was too much for him to handle. Left with no other alternative, Hank stopped seeing her.

This older woman with mournful eyes once was his muse—not for love poems, but his lines were definitely informed by the years that they had been together. His aspirations to live and to express the profane sacredness of the commonplace had been hammered into his consciousness, in part, by Jane's companionship. People could be happy together without being consumed by greed or enslaved by middle-class values.

After leaving Jane, Hank returned to the postal service, beginning a twelve-year run sorting mail that ended in 1970. Low pay and horrible working conditions were a reality, but he desperately needed a regular paycheck. Nearing forty and having not fulfilled his dream of being a money-making writer, he saw skid row looming ahead. Thinking of all the years he had spent with Jane, and of the death of his parents, he suffered bouts of depression aggravated by the back-breaking work at the post office. A saving grace lay in not having to do any deep thinking while on the job. His rote assignments helped conserve his mental energies for the poem and the racetrack.

As with other aspects of his life, he tended to glorify his depressive moods, writing to editors and poets, telling them about having the blues, suffering under the weight of his job, and losing at the track. In truth, he handled his mood swings fairly well. Those who saw him as a disorderly poet—through his writings and later through the legend that grew up around him—did not know that he dressed immaculately (albeit in inexpensive clothing), that he kept to a tight schedule, and that even his drinking remained under control. He drank every day, and sometimes went on binges that lasted three or four days, but that didn't keep him from work, from the track, or from his poetry.

Discipline became one of his bywords. He set aside a portion of each day for poetry. He knew by now that writing required a place apart to clear his mind. A radio tuned to classical music, a six-pack of beer, a stack of typing paper, and his typewriter were his stalwart companions. On the typewriter he sang in a voice strengthened by a sense of having served a long, silent apprenticeship, and by an intimate knowledge of himself forged from fighting his demons in solitude. Hank forged on ahead as if the deck had been cleared: Katherine and Henry lay buried behind him, and L.A. lay before him, a vast network of memories and present-day images that had become integral to his growing body of work.

It was his writing that saved him when he heard that Jane had been hospitalized for excessive drinking. Her landlady had given her a job cleaning up the rooms when she couldn't pay the rent. The tasks were not that difficult, but Jane had long ago lost the ability to do any kind of work: her hands shook, her back hurt, she had trouble going up and down stairs. For reasons unknown to Hank, the realtor who had helped her in past years was now out of her life. The little money she received went for liquor. Even so, the news of her hospitalization and imminent death shocked him. They had spent nearly a decade together and he didn't want to believe that this woman who had gone through so much pain was dying at the age of forty-nine.

He entered Jane's hospital room to find her semicomatose. "It was so clean in there, and quiet. I saw her lying in bed, unaware that I was there." He walked up to her quietly, bent over, kissed her lips, and whispered her name over and over again. Jane opened her eyes and said, "I knew it would be you."

The several hours he sat at her bedside deeply affected him. When it came time to leave, he bent over and kissed her forehead, then drove to her apartment and found several unopened bottles of liquor given as Christmas gifts by the people whose rooms she cleaned— enough, had she not been hospitalized, to have killed her.

When Jane died in 1962, Hank contacted her son who lived in Texas and made plenty of money in business, though he never sent any to his mother. He came to L.A. while Hank continued making arrangements for the funeral, even paying for it himself, thinking that Jane's son would take care of buying the headstone. Hank ordered a heart-shaped floral wreath for which he paid fifteen dollars, quite a sum in those days. The men who brought it leaned the wreath up against a tree, since the stilts it came with did not work properly. While the casket was being lowered, the wreath fell forward on the ground. Jane's son, a cold and impersonal character, never came through with a headstone. Hank wrote a poem "For Jane: With All the Love I Had, Which Was Not Enough":

> *I pick up the skirt,*
> *I pick up the sparkling beads*
> *in black, this thing that moved once*
> *around flesh, and I call God a liar,*
> *I say anything that moved*
> *like that*
> *or knew*
> *my name*
> *could never die*
> *in the common verity of dying.*

. . .

I lean upon this,
I lean on all of this
and I know:
her dress upon my arm:
but
they will not
give her back to me.

He surprised himself one evening when he sat down and wrote a poem about another death, that of his father. "It was not about my father as he was, but about as he should be," he said many years later. There are tender moments as the son tries on his father's coat and finds that it fits. "I guess the poem has some of that feeling of kinship. I mean, after all, he was my father despite everything, although you shouldn't get the idea that I was overcome with sadness." Written in 1959, and published that year in a San Francisco magazine, *The Galley Sail Review*, "The Twins" received a considerable amount of notice, the poem expressing a rare vulnerability, yet the poet's strong personality prevails. It reads:

he hinted at times that I was a bastard and I told him to listen to
Brahms, and I told him to learn to paint and drink and not be domi-
nated by women and dollars
but he screamed at me, For Christ's sake remember your mother,
remember your country,
you'll kill us all! . . .
I move through my father's house (on which he owes $8,000 after
20 years on the same job) and look at his dead shoes
the way his feet curled the leather as if he were angry planting roses,
and he was, and I look at his dead cigarette, his last cigarette
and the last bed he slept in that night, and I feel I should remake it
but I can't, for a father is always your master even when he's gone;
I guess these things have happened time and again but I can't help
thinking

[109]

to die on a kitchen floor at 7 o'clock in the morning
while other people are frying eggs
is not so rough
unless it happens to you

. . .

inside, I try on a light blue suit
much better than anything I have ever worn
and I flap the arms like a scarecrow in the wind
but it's no good;
I can't keep him alive
no matter how much we hated each other.

we looked exactly alike, we could have been twins
the old man and I: that's what they
said. he had his bulbs on the screen
ready for planting
while I was lying with a whore from 3rd street.

very well, grant us this moment: standing before a mirror
in my dead father's suit
waiting also
to die.

Infernal Henry Senior, sentinel of hatred and beacon of oppression, never opened up to his son. Now, after the old man had died, Hank could really come home and finally have the last word. His words are not bitter, rather they are filled with remorse, a feeling for the hopelessness of the human condition, and a genuine struggle to understand the relationship between himself and his father. There was nothing about him that Hank admired, and yet he understood that there was no way to escape the fact that the old man had helped shape him into the person he had become. Henry Senior never wavered from his belief in middle-class values, and his obstinacy and endurance became Hank's creed: he didn't veer from his role as an outsider. Unwittingly, Henry helped shape his son into the arm of the opposition. Hank never knuckled under to his father's belief system, in which a person must achieve material wealth in order to succeed.

Hank's poetry began to bring him a readership. At first, there had been a few letters from other small-magazine poets. By the late fifties, Hank had become an important voice in the underground poetry scene, sought by important small-magazine editors who coveted his name for the contributor lists. For some of the more staid publications, printing a poem by Bukowski meant the loss of subscribers and angry letters of protest to the editor. Upon receiving contributor's copies in the mail he sometimes found himself included with writers who only wrote rhyming poems. "It was amusing," he recalls. "You'd see this tough guy, Bukowski, alongside someone writing a sonnet to the moon or the stars."

Rumors abounded about his life in L.A. Where did this man who lived and wrote on the edge come from? Had anyone else written poems dedicated to Willie Shoemaker, a jockey? Was it true that he drank ten beers a day? Much of this was propagated by Hank himself in his ever-growing correspondence with editors and poets. He often referred to his past, telling his correspondents that he had been educated on the streets, that he had not served in the war, and that he despised the general tenor of the literary scene. The theme of the perennial outsider who avoids popular causes and mainstream opinion, which dominated much of his poetry, also ran through his letters, furthering the mythic image of Bukowski as literary maverick.

Of the magazines Hank published in, most were poorly funded, and disappeared after the first issue. In lieu of royalties, they paid in contributor's copies. However, from the ranks of these little magazines many well-known poets emerged, and became permanent fixtures in the literary landscape. Thomas McGrath, Robert Bly, Diane Wakoski all began in the same little magazines Hank knew, and they too went on to publish with major presses.

Hank had not been concentrating on fame, unlike in the forties when he believed himself a new Hemingway or Saroyan. In his fantasies he sometimes played out romantic literary stories in which he had achieved success. Now he simply enjoyed the act of writing without such images crossing his mind. When news came from E.V. Griffith, the editor of a magazine called *Hearse*, that he wanted to publish a collection of Hank's poems, Hank began to believe that maybe there really was a chance for him, after all.

To publish a first book of poems, even when it is only fourteen pages in length, is momentous news for any poet. Hank plunged into the project and began exchanging letters with Griffith, in which he said he wanted to leave the selection of poems up to the editor. And so *Flower, Fist and Bestial Wail* began to take shape.

Not having experienced book publication before, Hank soon became impatient with Griffith's delays, wondering if his book would ever really be printed. Out of nervousness and paranoia, he wrote to Griffith in September 1960:

> Are you still alive?
> Everything that's happening to me is banal or venal, and perhaps a more flowerly and poesy versification—right now drab and bare as the old-lady in the shoe's panties. I don't know, there's one hell of a lot of frustration and fakery in this poetry business, the forming of groups, soul-handshaking. I'll print you if you print me, and wouldn't you care to read before a small select group of homosexuals?
> I pick up a poetry magazine, flip the pages, count the stars, moons and frustrations, yawn, piss out my beer and pick up the want-ads.
> I am sitting in a cheap Hollywood apartment pretending to be a poet but sick and dull and the clouds are coming over the fake paper mountains and I peck away at these stupid keys, it's 12 degrees in Moscow and it's snowing; a boil is forming between my eyes and somewhere between Pedro and Palo Alto I lost the will to fight: The liquor store man knows me like a cousin; he cracks the paper bag and looks like a photograph of Francis Thompson.

Hank rushed to the post office one day not long after this letter and claimed a package that had arrived from Eureka, California.

Unable to contain himself, he opened it on the street. Inside he found his book: the cover in red on a white background, fourteen pages, offset edition. *Hearse* chapbook number five. A modest beginning. He stared at the cover and then knelt down on the sidewalk as traffic and people flowed past.

He went home and typed a letter to his editor, dated October 14, 1960:

> I went down to the post office this morning with card left in my box yesterday—and *yowl!*—there it was, set of HEARSE chapbooks by one Charles Bukowski. I opened the package right in the street, sunlight coming down, and there it was: FLOWER, FIST AND BEASTIAL WAIL, never a baby born in more pain, but finally brought through by the good Doctor Griffith—a beautiful job, beautiful! The first collected poems of a man of 40, who began writing late.
>
> Griff, this was an event! Right in the middle of the street between the post office and a new car agency. But then the qualms came on and the fear and the shame. I remembered my last letter to you when I finally cracked, scratching and blaming and cursing, and the sickness came.
>
> I DON'T KNOW HOW IN THE HELL TO APOLOGIZE E.V., BUT JESUS I ASK FOR FORGIVENESS. That's all I can say. It's a beautiful job, clean and pure, poem arrangement perfect. I'm mailing out copies to some people who think I am alive, but first off with this letter to you.
>
> I hope I can live down any disgust I have caused you.

Living in a furnished apartment at 1626 North Mariposa Street, Hank only wished that Jane were alive to see his book and that he had a woman to celebrate his fortieth birthday with in August 1960. On his birthday, he had gone out alone, first to a strip joint where he consumed nearly twelve beers and then on to a series of bars.

One poet who knew him at that time, Jory Sherman, published alongside him in the magazine *Epos*. In 1958 he and Hank had started writing to one another at the suggestion of that magazine's editor, Evelyn Thorne. In 1959, Sherman had moved to San Francisco, where he was visited by Jon Edgar Webb, Jr. Jon Webb, Sr., who became an important friend in Hank's later life, lived in New Orleans and was planning a major poetry journal to be called *The Outsider*. Having read Sherman's poetry, Webb Senior had sent his son to invite the poet to be his West Coast editor. Webb Junior carried a list of people that his father wanted to publish and Bukowski was one of them. Just after his birthday, on August 17, 1960, Hank wrote to Sherman:

> It's all over, I'm 40, over the hill, down the other side . . . made the rounds Sunday nite . . . alone . . . sat in strip joints, watched them shake and wiggle like something going on . . . bored . . . $1.25 for beer, but drank em like water, water hell. I don't drink much water. Place after place . . . faces sitting there empty as jugs. shit. shit. oh, I got a lovely buncha coconuts! nothing woke up with cracked toe, blood, couldn't walk . . .
>
> old girlfriend sent over huge buncha flowers, all kinds, quite nicea her, like a funeral, like a beautiful funeral, buried at forty . . .
>
> sick today.
>
> Thanks for all the info on the mags. OUTSIDER hasn't accepted anything for #2, but said he will from large bunch I sent him. . . .
>
> Do you mind if I sign myself Charles? Its an old habit. when I write or when somebody writes me I am Charles. When they talk to me in a room I am Hank. This, my solidification. A chunk of 40 stones.

Late in 1960, Sherman paid the first of many visits to Hank, accompanied by Norman Winski, editor of *Breakthru*, a small magazine of philosophy and literature in Los Angeles. Hank's second-floor apartment on Mariposa was a nondescript place, typical digs for a single man who worked at a low-paying job. There was a table on which the typewriter sat, a stack of envelopes, a few manuscripts, some books, and a small red radio. When Sherman and Winski entered the apartment they heard Haydn on the FM station.

Hank's innate dignity caused him to dislike the infighting, currying of favors and back-stabbing that went on in the poetry community. Through his letters and with visitors, however, he sometimes engaged in literary infighting. He also could become incredibly combative, to the point of striking back in a poem or short story against enemies, real or imagined. When he drank excessively he was often transformed into a loud, angry figure, denigrating the editors and poets who made up the little-magazine scene. He and Sherman ended many of their evenings together in mad rages, arguing over one or another poet's merit or about a particular social or political issue. Sober, though, Hank was gentle, and withdrawn. He told Sherman how much he disliked the antics of the Beat poets and of his distrust of the literary world in general: "I like to keep the shades drawn," he said.

Friends invited him to readings and poetry workshops, all to no avail. He did not hold back his opinions of the writings he appreciated. In a letter to Sherman, he singled out Robinson Jeffers:

> Jeffers, I suppose, is my god—the only man since Shakey to write the long narrative poem that does not put one to sleep. And Pound of course. And then Conrad Aiken is so truly a poet, but Jeffers is stronger, darker, more exploratively modern and mad.

Hank continued to foster the public image of himself as a hard-drinking man near to madness. He read Allen Ginsberg's *Howl* and Gregory Corso's poetry, like many other poets writing for the small poetry journals, or "littles," as he called them, but he was unimpressed. What annoyed him the most about the Beat poets was their engagement in social and political issues. He believed this hampered their poetry, that a true poet had greater concerns than tampering with current affairs. At the same time, Hank condemned the short-circuiting of an individual's full humanity by the social structure. Unlike the Beat poets he is not the self-conscious bard, deliberately striving to instruct the reader. He is teaching himself rather than others. He has proceeded from the standpoint that the artist is responsible only to himself. He once said to an activist friend, "I don't know why you go to those campus demonstrations against the war. Don't you realize that a poet's job is to write? Why must you go with the crowd for any popular cause, like Allen Ginsberg, responding to any call for his name. What may seem good now could become bad later."

Hank appreciated the little-magazine scene because it provided an open field for quick publication and did not impose any political or social test. The cottage-industry sensibility that pervaded the little-magazine world did not repel but rather attracted him. He commented in praiseworthy terms, both in poems and letters, on the fact that many of the editors were half-mad (like himself) and barely able to hold on. He wrote hundreds of poems, sending them out quickly, usually not bothering with photostats or records of where he sent his work. Enough poems were accepted to satisfy his expectations, yet in that cynical and skeptical manner of his, he let it be known to Sherman that "politics and association finally get to these new mags and they go the way of rot." And on the same wry note: "It's much easier to place in new magazines before the backslappers and partysitters arrive. I hate to seem like a crank, but it seems everything goes."

Epos gathered together thirteen of Hank's poems, along with four illustrations, and released *Poems and Drawings*. Not long afterward, Evelyn Thorne became impatient with Bukowski when she began receiving wilder and wilder letters from him. Luckily, there were plenty of editors who wanted precisely the kind of communication with the L.A. original that Thorne had come to dislike.

One such editor was poet Carl Larsen, who published Bukowski's *Longshot Pomes for Broke Players* in 1962. Larsen's own poetry appeared frequently in the poetry journals. He developed a concept he called "organic poetry," which involved writing the middle of a poem first, and then working one's way around it, going down the page from the end or up from the beginning, as intuition demanded. The straight-forward, concrete imagery he strove for was already embodied in Bukowski's work.

Longshot Pomes ranges over a wide variety of themes. There are poems on the racetrack ("Hello Willie Shoemaker"), mind-maps of the poet's dead-end jobs ("Poem for Personnel Managers"), sardonic appraisals of his fellow writers ("Letter from the North"), and poems reflecting his knowledge of classical music ("The Life of Borodin"). Bukowski deliberately distorted the spelling of "poem" in the title, hoping to loosen up the seriousness surrounding the poetry scene— a choice that suited Larsen, who strongly condemned the solemn tone of mainstream American literature and whose own book was entitled *The Popular Mechanics Book of Poetry*.

The cover for *Longshot Pomes* was done by Hank himself. It shows four men, three of them smoking cigars, one with a beard and glasses, playing cards around a table on which stands a bottle of wine and wine glasses. They are intently focused on the game while in front of the table lies a woman in bed, also drinking. She's big-breasted, a real Bukowski type, smoking a cigarette, her long dark hair falling across her shoulders. She seems oblivious to the men and their games, a portrait of the separation of the sexes. The poet had been inspired to draw by James Thurber. Of this and other drawings Bukowski recalls, "I always had this idea that I should paint. Hell, Henry Miller did. Eventually I would. But it was Thurber's cartoons that really got me into drawing. It was like writing a poem, you know, with a story in it."

Bukowski wrote an autobiographical note for the book, one that he dashed off at his Mariposa Street apartment one evening after returning from work. "I was sitting there, not quite knowing what to do and then, of course, I thought of my dear sweet father and so I wrote about the time he gave me the Indian suit because the other kids on the block had cowboy suits. I thought that would really interest my readership, such as it was at the time." He writes of his wanderings, mentioning New Orleans, Philadelphia, Miami Beach, Chicago, and elsewhere. References to this period in his life would later resonate in the film script for "*Barfly*": "Ran errands for sandwiches and let the bartender beat me up. . . when I felt like it." He then listed the many odd jobs he had taken during the forties and early fifties: "dog biscuit factory, coconut man in a cake factory, shipping clerk, truck driver, stock boy for Sears Roebuck, mailman, janitor, night watchman, dock hand. . ." Inevitably, Hank got around to offering his sardonic overview of the poetry scene. It's interesting that here, as elsewhere in his earlier musings, he ignores the Beat writers. It's as if they weren't on the map for him. Instead, he concentrated on the little-magazine scene, then jumped to talk of his literary heroes. After a few disparaging remarks on poetry in general, he continues, "If I have a god it is Robinson Jeffers, although I realize that I don't write as he does."

Gazing out onto Mariposa Street from his shabby front room, Hank wrote "The State of World Affairs From a Third Floor Window." His writing desk faced the window and as he stared outside long enough to gather an image, ". . . a girl dressed in a light green sweater, blue shorts, long black stocking. . ." appeared. So far, so good, but he notes that "her breasts are too short, poor thing. . ." She has a dirty white dog and there is also a half dead pigeon circling overhead. It was a sad scene and the observer himself fits right in as he was, "upstairs in my underwear, 3 day beard, pouring a beer and waiting for something literary or symphonic to happen." But, of course, nothing does and the poet notes that, "there are piles and piles of H-and-A-bombs, enough to blow up fifty worlds and Mars thrown in." Still, he informs us that things will go on much the same as before and, "the bombs will never go off."

The response to *Longshot Pomes* was enthusiastic among the handful of people who read books from the small presses. Readers were generally swept away by Bukowski's second collection of poems. As Sherman says, "Hank's humor, street diction, and tough persona were all mixed together here, and the book generated a lot of excitement."

Next came *Run With The Hunted* from Midwest Press, also in 1962. His publisher, R. R. Cuscaden, who supported himself as an insurance underwriter and as an editor of trade magazines, admired Hank's independence. He thought of Bukowski as some kind of crazy expatriate from Germany, and admired him for being non-Beat and nonacademic, and for living in California as if on the edge of doom. Cuscaden received numerous letters from Bukowski. "They told about his drinking and going to the racetrack, and he did all these incredible drawings," Cuscaden recalls.

In *Midwest*, a magazine of poetry and criticism, Cuscaden's aim was "to find a legitimate response to the Corso/Ginsberg/Ferlinghetti syndrome (and imitators) on one side and the tea-cozy *POETRY* mag gang on the other side. Buk obviously was the answer." The editor recalls a poem by Bukowski that he published in the summer of 1961, called "no title at all . . .," which expressed the simplicity of style that was so innovative:

> . . . *I know a man who once spoke to Picasso,*
> *he lives in 309,*
> *his rugs are full of paint,*
> *there's even paint in the john.*

>   *but he can't paint worth a damn,*
> *Pablo.*

Run With The Hunted, an unpretentious looking chapbook with an illustration of a potted tree on the cover, continued to enhance Hank's poetic autobiography. He sensed this in his growing oeuvre scattered through hundreds of magazines: "My work was bound to be a kind of autobiographical statement. I was writing about myself, mostly, and it was almost always true. Some of my readers thought I was inventing, but, like, 'A Literary Romance,' that really happened, man. This woman was insistent. It was as if she was asking to be put into a poem. I don't remember when I wrote it, but there it was and Cuscaden put it in the book. So people asked if I was making it all up, and I had to tell them, hell no. They thought I was some kind of sex machine the way I went on."

The poem is typically humorous. Hank had been corresponding with a woman who wrote poetry. He tells us that she sent, "very sexy poems about rape and lust," and yet came off as somewhat intellectual. When he finally met her, she told him she had a secret to confess. Before she could tell it, he drops, "I know: you are a virgin 35 years old." She goes on to show him a few poems, a life's work. "And I tried to be kind but they were very bad and I took her somewhere, the boxing matches, and she coughed in the smoke. . ." Still, they saw one another a few more times and had some fun together, but Hank's final appraisal was unsparing, "I think that when a woman has kept her legs closed for 35 years it's too late either for love or poetry."As with many Bukowski poems, the story element, the pure narrative, sustains the work, and what he had learned as a short story writer helped him in that regard. He was simply reporting, directly, what was happening around him, the common daily occurrences of his life.

"Hooray Say the Roses," however, stands in sharp contrast to the more narrative poems of this period. It's about as close to the purely lyric as Bukowski gets:

> *hooray say the roses, darkness comes*
> *all at once, like lights gone out,*
> *the sun leaves dark continents*
> *and rows of stone.*

Cuscaden recalls that it was really the narrative drive that attracted him and his fellow *Midwest* editors to Bukowski's poems. They sensed the connection between the great American novelists of past generations and Bukowski's tough, yet humorous story poems. It is what finally convinced them to take the risk and publish a book of his poetry.

Cuscaden wrote the first major essay on Bukowski in Satis (Spring–Summer 1962). "Charles Bukowski: Poet in a Ruined Landscape" was a seminal introduction to the poet and his work, comparing him to Charles Baudelaire, whose isolation in a barren world represented a writing tradition the Cuscaden saw in *Flower, Fist and Longshot Pomes*.

This critical introduction to the poet helped to foster Bukowski's mythic presence. For the editors who published him, and the poets who read his work, his was a highly original voice, rebellious without appearing experimental and, at the same time, richly American in tone and temperament. Cuscaden's description of Bukowski as a man in permanent opposition was echoed in "Charles Bukowski and the Savage Surfaces," by John William Corrington (*NorthWest Review*, 1963) and "Jeremiah in Motly: Charles Bukowski," written by John Z. Bennett for the fall 1963 issue of *Descent*.

Bukowski sent a copy of the Cuscaden review to Ann Menebroker, a poet in Sacramento with whom he had been corresponding, and wrote:

> It is a good damned thing I do not wear a hat or I could not get it around my head after reading these reviews.
>
> Darling, this is the trap: BELIEVE YOU'RE GOOD WHEN THEY TELL YOU YOU ARE GOOD AND YOU ARE THEREBY DEAD, DEAD, DEAD. dead forever. Art is a day by day game of living and dying and if you live a little more than you die you are going to continue to create some pretty fair stuff, but if you die a little more than you live, you know the answer.
>
> Creation, the carving of the thing, the good creation is a sign that the god that runs you there inside still has his eyes open. Creation is not the end-all but it is a pretty big part. End of lecture #3789.
>
> I must run to the track now.

A few weeks later he wrote to her:

> Ann, I think you know this—I am not primarily a poet, I hate god damned people poets messing the smear so their lives against the sniveling world, and poets are bad and the world is

bad and we are here, ya. What I am trying to say is that poetry, what I write, is only one tenth of myself—the other 9/ to
hell tenths are looking over the edge of a cliff down into the sea
of rock and wringing swirl and cheap damnation. I wish that I
only could suffer in the classic style and carve out of great mar-
ble that would last centuries beyond this dog's bark I now hear
outside my 1963 window, but I am damned and slapped and
chippyed and wasted down to the nothingnesses of my arms
and eyes and fingers and this letter tonight, May first or second,
1963, after hearing your voice on the phone.

I deserve to die. I wait upon death like a plumed falcon with
beak and song and talon for my caged blood. This may sound
pretty god damned pretty but it is not. The poetry part of me,
the seeming actuality of what I write, is dung and dross and sali-
va and old battleships sinking.

It is important to note that the accolades Hank received, and the
fanfare surrounding him, were limited to a small circle of literary
people. The magazines he published in, and the books that bore his
name, rarely went beyond a circulation of three or four hundred.
In the popular mind, poetry hardly existed at all, and when it did,
people thought either of traditional icons such as Robert Frost or
Carl Sandburg or, due to their notoriety, the poets of the Beat generation: Allen Ginsberg, Lawrence Ferlinghetti, and Gregory Corso.
There were better known journals in New York City, Chicago, and
San Francisco that served as "house organs" for the Beat rebellion in
poetry. Bukowski remained largely unknown in these major literary
centers.

Not long after the publication of the Seven Poets Press book, Hank
came to San Bernadino to see Jory Sherman, who had moved to
southern California from San Francisco. Sherman had appeared at
the home of Sam and Clare Cherry, owners of a local bookstore and
art gallery, looking depressed and shouting that sometimes life wasn't
worth the struggle.

The Cherrys decided to call Bukowski in Los Angeles and ask if he would come out and talk to Sherman. At first, his response was, "Oh shit, man! Don't pay any attention to his histrionics. This isn't the first time, you know." Sam Cherry continued describing the state Sherman was in, and Hank finally relented, saying Norman Winski would drive him over.

Cherry informed Sherman that Bukowski would be there in an hour. At first this quieted him down, but gradually Sherman's emotions welled up again, and he became even more agitated. The Cherrys finally persuaded him to sit down and talk to them about his troubles. While he poured out his tale of the hard road a poet like him has to travel, especially when burdened with a wife and children, the screech of brakes could be heard outside. Unintentionally, Hank and Norman Winski had announced their arrival.

Norman Winski, a tall, blond-haired man, flashed his smile and introduced himself to the Cherrys and said he had brought Bukowski because he had a flashy sports car and could make the trip faster than the poet could in his old jalopy. Hank held himself off to one side as Winski spouted off about his own writing. Hank maintained a wry, enigmatic grin and kept silent. Winski bragged that he wrote books on philosophy while Hank began talking to Sherman, telling him that everything would be all right. "Look, kid," he said. "We all go through some rough times."

"You guys care. You really care," Sherman finally said.

They all sat around in the Cherrys' living room talking for an hour or more. Hank just sat back in an armchair like a king on his throne, occasionally making comments. To Sherman's complaints about his rough life, Hank said, "Hell, you don't know what rough is, man. I've worked in slaughterhouses. I've heard the dying bulls. I've been jailed so many times I don't even remember"—most of which was pure hyperbole. Hank engaged in it often, especially when drinking, and when a group of people were present.

It was easy to see that Hank had become bored with mere talk. He told Sherman that he wanted to speak with him in private and took him into the bedroom. After a few minutes he called Winski in and said, "Hey, man, Jory just called you a bastard and said you wrote nothing but bullshit. He said when he sees you the next time he's going to blast the shit out of you." Winski became furious. He socked Sherman in the stomach. They came back into the living room and continued to spar with one another. Hank stood off to one side, laughing. "That's it, boys, go for the jugular," he said. As they continued fighting, he added, "The lions are at one another's throat. The mad lions are going for the kill."

Sam Cherry intervened, then turned to Hank and accused him of instigating the fight. Hank said they were lucky that he only instigated it and hadn't participated in it. He said, "You know, if I had been fighting, you both would be dead." He then turned to Cherry and said, "You know, Sam, I've killed men and don't forget, I used to work in the slaughterhouse and butchered the limbs off those carcasses. And I know death!"—again, playing up his image as the tough guy. But Cherry detected a smile as the poet continued in that vein.

By this time, it was 2 A.M. Clare Cherry went into the kitchen to whip up a predawn breakfast. Sherman and Winski had both settled down and were talking civilly once again. Hank slowly moved into the kitchen. He came up to Clare Cherry, whom he had met for the first time only hours earlier, placed a hand on her arm, nuzzled his chin into the back of her neck and said in a disarming, soft, gentle voice, "Hey, Clare. That Sam isn't worth a damn. Come and let's you and me skip this joint and start a new life together."

Mrs. Cherry was shocked, not by the suggestion, but by the softness and small size of his unlabored hands, and by the gentleness of his voice. She turned to him and said, "Come off it, Bukowski. You're acting like an adolescent."

"You've got my number, Clare," Hank replied.

SIX

H<small>ANK</small> deliberately sidestepped historical analysis and hints of epic. When he told himself that his writing would be the poetic equivalent of some of those gutsy novels, such as *U.S.A.* by John Dos Passos and James T. Farrell's *Studs Lonigan,* he committed himself to an empathy that nailed him down in his own neighborhood. He writes in "the kings are gone":

> *to say great things of kings and life*
> *to give equations like a math genius,*
> *I sat in on a play by Shakespeare*
> *but the grandeur did not come through;*
> *I do not claim to have a good ear*
> *or a good soul, but most of Shakespeare*
> *laid me dry, I confess,*
> *and I went into a bar*
> *where a man with hands like red crabs*
> *laid his sick life before me through the fumes,*
> *and I grew drunk,*
> *mirror upon myself. . .*

Another man who had also bummed around a lot and, in the manner of Bukowski, lived outside of mainstream America, had plans for the poet—Jon Edgar Webb, editor of *The Outsider*. The relationship that grew between poet and editor went beyond the business of putting a book together. They corresponded, eventually met, and became friends. Even before Webb brought out the first issue of the magazine, he and Hank had exchanged letters. Sitting in his apartment in East Hollywood, the poet thought of Webb and his wife, Louise, also known as Gypsy Lou, sweating it out in New Orleans's French Quarter amid the old iron-railed buildings and the living remnants of old-time blues. Unlike many of Hank's editors, Webb was an older man and had a long, colorful history behind him. He had worked for some of the great newspapers of his day, in an era when the smell of printer's ink permeated the newsrooms.

Early in his life, Webb taught grammar school and then worked as a police reporter for the *Cleveland Plain Dealer*. All through his days as a journalist, he kept up an interest in literature, befriending Ernest Hemingway, Sherwood Anderson, and other literary figures, and writing short stories. In 1930 he was arrested for armed robbery of a jewelry store in Cleveland and sent to Mansfield Reformatory for three years, where he ran a prison paper called *The New Day*. He wrote, edited, and printed it with the help of his cellmate. The incongruity here, of hard-working Jon Webb, a literary man, being involved in a robbery, has always perplexed those who knew his work. In 1939 Webb married Louise (his second marriage). They eventually moved to New Orleans, where he wrote short stories and a novel primarily dealing with crime and the lives of desperate men and women in low-life conditions.

The first issue of *The Outsider* appeared in the fall of 1961. Webb spared no expense. Over two years in the making, it showed a breathtaking level of care and was a triumph of quality printing as well as an editorial masterwork. Poems by Gregory Corso, Gary Snyder, Allen Ginsberg, and Lawrence Ferlinghetti, along with prose by Henry Miller and William Burroughs, gave the magazine an aura of importance. Webb had gone beyond the little-magazine ghetto, seeking contributions from the well-known Beat poets, whom he very much admired, along with plenty of work from less-er-known writers. Miller was one of his heroes, and like the old master, he avoided academic literature. Webb found a renegade quality in Bukowski, who, of all the writers he published, excited him the most. Just how much he liked the work of the poet from L.A. is demonstrated by "A Charles Bukowski Album," *The Outsider*'s centerpiece, which began in the gatefold and ran for six pages. This portfolio of poems brought Bukowski's work to the attention of the Beats and to the literary critics in New York and San Francisco. Webb had chosen the poems carefully, rejecting many, while adding early Bukowski classics such as "Old Man, Dead in a Room"—a poem that Webb saw as the prime statement of the writer, alone, isolated from society, accepting his state.

> *this thing upon me is not death*
> *but it's as real*
> *and as landlords full of maggots*
> *pound for rent*
> *I eat walnuts in the sheath*
> *of my privacy*
> *and listen for more important*
> *drummers . . .*

The carefully measured tone is maintained throughout, culminating with an ultimate recognition of personal vulnerability:

> *this thing upon me*
> *crawling like a snake,*
> *terrifying my love of commonness,*
> *some call Art*
> *some call Poetry;*
> *it's not death*
> *but dying will solve its power*
> *and as my gray hands*
> *drop a last desperate pen*

in some cheap room
they will find me there
and never know
my name
my meaning
nor the treasure
of my escape.

The second issue (Summer 1962), featured a documentary about the Preservation Hall Jazz Band of the French Quarter. Bukowski is represented with two poems, "Sick Leave" and "To a Lady Who Believes Me Dead." In a profile he wrote on the Webbs, Bukowski discusses the genius of the editor that surfaced through his wise and strong selection of prose and poetry. He wrote that it is difficult to find a decent editor, emphasizing that they are rarer than good writers. It was a prelude to later tributes Hank would write about Jon and Louise Webb.

The third issue of *The Outsider*, published in the spring of 1963, was devoted primarily to Bukowski's poetry. The cover photograph showed a thoughtful Bukowski: eyes wide open, jaws firmly set, the countenance of a man on the verge of national recognition. Webb received an angry letter from a well-known English writer expressing outrage that a magazine dare to place such a disgusting face on the cover—naturally, Webb merely laughed at this.

The Bukowski tribute was a comprehensive overview of the writer to date. Tributes from R. R. Cuscaden, Evelyn Thorne, and E.V. Griffith along with an essay by William Corrington dealing with specific Bukowski poems. Webb even printed an eviction notice from when Hank lived with Jane:

Aragon Apartments, 334 S. Westlake Ave, Los Angeles, California. Apartment occupied by Mr. And Mrs. Bukowski, said apt. to be Vacated for Reasons: Excessive Drinking, Fighting and foul Language. Disturbing other tenants.

Webb introduced Bukowski as recipient of the "Outsider of the Year Award" for 1962. This was followed by a response from the poet himself:

> Then there's W. and there's T. and then there's M, in New Haven and don't forget G. Still, I feel pretty much outside, as about as outside as you can get. The act of creation is still the most important thing, and with all the g.d. photos you wanted I have written less than a snail . . .

After being named Outsider of the Year, Hank was honored with a Loujon Press Award Book. When Webb first suggested doing a volume of selected poems, Hank conjured up the title *Look What the Net Drug Up*. Another possibility was *The Virgins Bathing with a Bear*, his idea being that "bear" meant poems and madness, while "virgins" meant prudes, dilettantes, phonies, and academics. By January 1963 Hank settled on *It Catches My Heart in Its Hands*. Then he began worrying that Random House might not give permission to use it, since it came from "Hellenistics," a poem by Robinson Jeffers.

Confiding to Ann Menebroker, Hank shared his excitement over the Loujon Press and his feeling for the Webbs:

> I write for selfish reasons: I have a book on the press now, Selected Poems 1955–1963, *It Catches My Heart in Its Hands* . . . Loujon Press, 618 Ursulines St. New Orleans, 16, Louisiana. 2 bucks, baby, and an autograph, even. Christ, y've got 2 bucks somewhere haven't you? What I mean is, I don't get any money out of this book at all—as if it mattered—but I am pumping for these people because 2 bucks to them might mean such a simple thing as eating on this day—or not. they eat one meal a day and forward such bastards as I, and I figure I can forget immortality and carefulness and isolation and maybe even myself and go out and ask people to buy the g.d. book. If you think this is slick sales talk, it is not. I have thrown money into the fire. I have thrown my guts into the fire. I know more than this. But

these people are the oddest set of living gods ya ever saw. She sells picture postcards on the sidewalks for meek coin and he stands 14 years, hours a day poking paper into a cheap press he has hustled somewhere. I can't tell you more than this, only that these people are giants in a world of ants. If you can get hold of the OUTSIDER #3 (same address) (as book) perhaps you will understand more of what I mean.

Webb sent pages of the book for Hank's signature. Alone in his room on Mariposa Street, he dutifully affixed his name to the pages which his editor later affixed to the finished book. As he put it to the Webbs in a letter, "my can of beer there, the cigarette smoke going up in the air and signing CHARLES BUKOWSKI, CHARLES BUKOWSKI as if I were Hemingway, drinking the beer down . . ." Webb sent him the dummy of *It Catches* in May 1963, asking for comments. Hank's suggestions primarily had to do with front and back matter for the book. Webb and Hank agreed on everything from typefaces, paper stock, and binding problems to the spacing of the poems.

From June to September 1963, the Webbs printed *It Catches My Heart in Its Hands: New & Selected Poems 1955–1963* at 618 Rue Ursulines, a slave-quarters workshop connected to an old mansion deep in the French Quarter. The setup sounds romantic, but it was far from luxurious. The window opened onto a walled garden, actually a courtyard half-settled into the earth. This jungle of rotting banana trees, giant cockroaches, stinkweed, moths, spiders, snails, bats, rats, ticks, wasps, silverfish, and flies was the outdoor counterpart to the small steamy room in which the editor went about his work. Jon Webb labored like an artist before his palette: a cork cover and paper in nine separate colors.

Seven hundred and seventy-seven copies of the book were printed, "one page at a time," they reported, "hand-fed with 12-point *Garamond Old Style* for the poems, 18-point *Pabst O.S.* for the titles—to an ancient 8 by 12 Chandler and Price letterpress." This information comes at the end of the collection in what is described on the back jacket cover as a "sweet-ending historiography."

This kind of personal note in both his magazine and the books he printed became a Webb trademark. His passion, and that of his wife, is well documented. He often told of his and Louise's travails while they printed *The Outsider*, and of their financial impoverishment caused by running a renegade magazine. These lengthy, interesting descriptions were followed by pleas for money. In the piece written for Bukowski's book, they described how rainwater seeped into their workroom, causing them to have to do many pages over again, and how mischievous rodents had gotten into the typecases, scattering alphabets. Then, adding catastrophe to inconvenience, the press broke down, not once but several times, causing more delays, and "the humidity burst open composition rollers, kept ink from drying on finished runs, and etcetera." Despite it all, they concluded by informing their readership that "the experience was unforgettable, one that could not be bought with gold—nor sold to the devil."

Hank's response to the publication of *It Catches* is expressed in his letter to the Webbs written on November 23, 1963:

> In all libraries in all the cities i have never seen such a book put together in such a way, inventive creativeness and love. Where have the publishers been for centuries? You've done it.

Webb divided *It Catches* into four sections, beginning the first with one of Bukowski's earliest poems, "the tragedy of the leaves," an important piece in the ever-unfolding Bukowski myth. The poem reads like an anthem of Bukowski as Outsider, and is filled with the motifs that are so much a part of his persona, from a woman gone out of his life to a landlady demanding payment of rent:

> *I awakened to dryness and the ferns were dead,*
> *the potted plants yellow as corn;*

my woman was gone
and the empty bottles like bled corpses
surrounded me with their uselessness;
the sun was still good, though,
and my landlady's note cracked in fine and
undemanding yellowness; what was needed now
was a good comedian, ancient style, a jester
with jokes upon absurd pain;
pain is absurd
because it exists, nothing more;
I shaved carefully with an old razor
the man who had once been young and
said to have genius; but
that's the tragedy of the leaves,
the dead ferns, the dead plants;
and I walked into the dark hall
where the landlady stood
execrating and final,
sending me to hell, waving her fat sweaty arms
and screaming
screaming for rent
because the world had failed us
both.

In this stale, stultifying environment, the poet abandoned by his lover amid the recognition of life's uselessness, Bukowski reveals one of the keys to his poetry and to his character: the ability to recognize the humor behind even the most sordid events. The image of the jester, the court clown, gives the poem an added historical dimension, taking us beyond the immediate situation of being terrorized by a landlady. Both nostalgia and the sharp sense of being *almost* overwhelmed by seedy metropolitan surroundings are deftly intermingled. The "man who had once been young and said to have genius" understands that this tragedy is everyone's tragedy, and that his feelings are universal.

Beginning with that poem, this new book added more material to the growing Bukowski mystique. The reader finds a clear voice emerging out of the squalor of Los Angeles, singing a string of working-class melodies and deep blues. The book demands that the poems be taken as a unified whole, and that is how Webb approached it. Moreover, Webb was not against fueling the mystique. In dubbing Bukowski "Outsider of the Year," the editor helped enhance the persona anchored in the poetry. With many of the writers Webb published, he cast the choice of being an outsider as a political one, whereas in Bukowski it was intrinsic to his basic character. "The tragedy of the leaves" is relentless in etching the image of the ultimate outsider, a man with much the same temperament as the character in Dostoyevski's *Notes from the Underground*.

There are a number of purely autobiographical poems in this book. A description of the last few days with Barbara Frye, "sundays kill more men than bombs," is typical of his personal revelations in the poem form:

> and I went back to bed with her and said,
> don't worry, it's all right, and
> she began to cry cry cry,
> I'm sorry, I'm sorry, I'm sorry,
> and I said, please stop,
> remember your heart.

John William Corrington, a writer who then taught at Louisiana State University and was a friend of Webb's, wrote an introduction for *It Catches My Heart in Its Hands*, entitled "Charles Bukowski at Midfight." In it, the poet is held in juxtaposition to the Pound-Eliot-Auden days. Corrington sees these three giants of modernism as stuck in formalism and as having spawned generations of bad imitators who filled their work with affectation and pompous language. Bukowski, on the other hand, is the vanguard of a new poetry freed from literary pretentiousness.

Webb insisted on an introduction. By the time he began working on the book, he knew Hank's history fairly well. He did not want to print the book and forget it. In truth, he hoped to help emblazon the name of Charles Bukowski on the literary consciousness of the land. To do so he wanted to "place" the poet, to offer the reader critical inroads into his work. He had done that in the special Bukowski issue of his magazine and now, with *It Catches*, he had faith that, along with the introductory essay, he was completing his mission.

The Webbs sent along the reviews of *It Catches*. Hank liked the attention, and thrived on the more negative reactions to his work. Much of the latter came from conservative critics who attacked Bukowski's graphic imagery, while others criticized him as being akin to an unschooled barbarian.

It Catches helped make big changes in Hank's life. One of the major topics of discussion between Bukowski and the Webbs after the publication of *It Catches* was a new book of poetry. He told his editors that a new book would be great, but he wondered if they had enough poems. He was referring both to poems left out of *It Catches* and new ones he had sent to them late in 1963. He suggested that they might want to consider a simpler format, and using a less expensive paper and cover stock. He even came up with the idea of helping them financially, but cautioned that this offer depended on how he did at the racetrack.

A woman named Frances Smith who first became aware of Hank when a friend in Los Angeles sent her a Bukowski poem about a cat killing a mockingbird soon became an important presence in his life. Frances recalls that this first Bukowski poem she read ends, "and I would have screamed, but they have places for people who scream." She read it over and over again, deciding that someday she would have to meet this man.

She went to the local bookstore to see about buying his books. They had difficulty tracing down the publishers, all of whom were small presses. Finally they located them, and Frances took home Bukowski's first three collections of poetry. Rather than pause between volumes, she kept on reading. The force of the poems compelled her to write him a letter. She mailed it care of Hearse Press. Not long afterward a letter came back saying "Buy my books. My publishers are starving." Frances kept the letter with his address written on it, but didn't write back until she had moved to California, about a year later.

Frances had attended college in Massachusetts, where she studied literature and poetry. She once sent one of her own poems to William Rose Benet at the *Saturday Review*, who published it in his column, "The Phoenix Nest." During the war she wrote a lot of poetry, but dropped out of college, remembering that she wanted to experience life firsthand. She joined the Woman's Army Corps, looking on the army as an all-embracing "father" that would take care of her. Quickly disillusioned by the regimented life in the service, she became pregnant, got married, and left the army. For fifteen years she remained married, had four daughters, and wrote very little poetry. Finally, though, feeling bored and constrained, she divorced her husband and decided to move to the West Coast. Although her daughters remained behind, she stayed in touch with them.

Arriving in 1962, Frances lived with her mother in Garden Grove, a suburb of Los Angeles. Eventually she wrote Hank a letter from her mother's house, explaining how she felt about his work, and included her phone number, not expecting to hear from him. She felt she understood him through his poetry, and saw him as a person of great inner strength. One night she received a phone call. She knew right away that it was Hank. "You have to get over here," he said. "I need you immediately." He repeated the same thing over and over again, his voice edged with desperation. "I didn't understand what the emergency was, and of course the emergency was that he was all alone and had nobody to talk to . . . He wanted to make human contact."

Frances figured out that she was just a convenient phone number, something near at hand. But she had determined to meet him. The closest bus was in Anaheim and she didn't know the transit schedule. She took his number, walked several miles to Anaheim, caught a bus to Los Angeles and arrived downtown. She called from the station, asking him to come get her. He told her to take a taxi-cab. Frances saw that he was too drunk to drive, so she hailed a cab and hoped that he would have the money to pay. She had no money on her, having forgotten to borrow a few dollars from her mother. "I remember when I first saw Hank in the doorway. He seemed so huge and gave off so much electricity. He was like a giant in a fairy tale. He just stood there so kindly . . . this friendly, kind, benevolent giant. He paid the cab driver and I went in and we sat and talked for hours. I didn't drink, but he was drinking beer."

They talked from two in the morning until the sun came up. Hank told Frances about growing up in L.A., the beatings his father gave him, his problem with acne, his half-drunk years in the rooming houses, all those rejections for his early short stories, going into the hospital in 1955 and nearly dying there. More than anything else he talked about Jane.

As Frances listened she felt the woman come alive. One story in particular, about Jane's strength of character, impressed her. Hank explained that he had become very drunk one night and said to Jane that it was a shame people were made to stand up for the national anthem and the pledge of allegiance. He didn't like this and wanted to remain seated, but didn't have the courage to do so. A few days later he and Jane went to the racetrack and when it came time for the national anthem Jane remained in her seat. Hank, who naturally became nervous, tried to coax her up. Jane didn't move.

Hank endeared himself to Frances with each story he recounted of his life's trials. When he first applied for the post office job, the interviewers tried to discourage him because of his belief that the government interfered too much in people's lives. But when he began to demonstrate a thorough knowledge of the law, they saw that he had a clear understanding of his rights, so they backed down.

When Frances brought his mother up, saying she must have given him a lot of good nurturing for him to have so much self-confidence, he quickly put that notion to rest. His mother, he made it clear, never stood up for him against his father's injustice. It was *despite* his parents that he became strong inside, not because of them, he would say.

They saw each other regularly. In order to be nearer to Hank, Frances moved to a small apartment on Vermont Avenue by the Hollywood Freeway. She now had a more complete picture of the man, not just the poet, finding a strength of character she had not seen in any man before. And, for all his talk of being a loner, she also saw that he needed people from time to time. He frequently told Frances he feared she would get pregnant and tie him down financially. Frances understood this as reasonable caution, not cruelty. "Here was this outsider, and people-hater, who always paid the rent on time, never missed a payment," Frances says. He "had money in the bank which he did not touch, which he put away before he went to the track or on a run for beer. He wasn't careless that way."

As Frances got to know Hank better she saw through his tough-guy manner and recognized a sensitive man who would never let a friend down. "He cares about his friends, and more importantly, he knows what will be of help and what will not be . . . A lot of people look at Bukowski superficially," Frances says. "They cannot understand why so many women flock to him. He has the magical appeal of a very solid person underneath lots of bluster, a father figure. Everybody's father."

Yet the thought of being a father himself, in the literal sense, frightened him. Having a child would mean, he felt (and made clear to Frances), a loss of the freedom from familial constraints that he had worked so hard to attain. His writing would be derailed, he felt, if he were suddenly saddled with a wife and child.

Often, Hank asked Frances to come over and clean his place. He reciprocated by preparing dinner for her. They dated no one else, and though they still lived apart, began acting like a real couple. Eventually Hank and Frances fell into a pattern whereby he would become drunk and abusive, Frances would leave in anger, and then come back on her own or wait for him to call and ask her forgiveness.

Frances became pregnant shortly after the assassination of President Kennedy. She told Hank, hoping that the gentle, sensitive side of him would come to the fore. The father-to-be responded well to the news of Frances's pregnancy and started making plans, saying that they should get married and find a place to live. Frances wondered if he was simply saying what he thought she wanted to hear. Furthermore, she didn't want to get married. She loved Hank, but one marriage had been enough.

On March 1, 1964, Hank wrote to Jon and Lou Webb about Frances while listening to Richard Strauss on his radio:

> Frances pregnant, looks as if I'll have to move from here, looks like marriage (again) and disorder but hoping for more suave luck and grace to help me this time. I would not hope to be cruel to either woman or child, god give me grace for I am weak and sad and do not feel good, but if any disorder happens . . . let it be my life, not theirs . . .
>
> . . . she is a good woman, she gets a little snappish and curlish at times but they all do, and I pretend I am asleep or I do not hear and it soon passes . . . She kind of has this coffeehouse attitude, appears determined to save all mankind . . . the other night she fell asleep reading THE PEOPLE'S WORLD, and then she goes to a writer's workshop . . . I have my racetrack and my beer drinking friends . . .

In mid-March, Hank and Frances began looking for an apartment to rent, staying close to the East Hollywood neighborhoods Hank knew best. In late April, they finally settled on an apartment on De Longpre Street—an upstairs unit in the back—with the understanding they could move into one of the front lower units when one became available. Although not married, they signed the rental agreement as Mr. and Mrs. Charles Bukowski, and that is how they became known to their friends.

On May 4, 1964, the Webbs moved to Santa Fe, New Mexico, but stayed for less than a week. They returned to New Orleans, renting a vest-pocket-size room at 1109 Royal Street in a historic building where Walt Whitman had once lived. Shortly after settling in, they made plans to visit with Hank in Los Angeles. Webb wanted to do Bukowski's next book, but he wanted to meet him first, to get to know him in person. He told Hank, in letters and by phone, that a meeting would give him a better perspective on his poems. They decided to come before the baby was born, knowing things would be too hectic later.

On August 22, the Webbs took a room in the Crown Hill Hotel, what Louise remembers as a flophouse: it had a reputation as a low-life hangout, filled with prostitutes, dishwashers, muggers, and the like. With Frances at his side, Hank went to meet them, so the editor from New Orleans waited on the sidewalk. When Hank pulled up in his battered old car with Frances and a six-pack of beer and a fifth of whiskey, he found a small gray-haired man wearing a white bandanna and a tall white sombrero, nervously pacing back and forth, puffing wildly on a cigarette—about as far from the professional type as a man could get. Gypsy Lou Webb lived up to her name, dressed in a typically bold and wild outfit. Hank's first impression of her was of an Italian woman, a person with a fiery temperament.

Webb walked up to him and asked, "You Bukowski?" Hank answered, "Yeah. And this is my woman, Frances." Webb fired back, "No man can ever call a women his own. We never own 'em. We just borrow them for a while." They walked up a dark, narrow hall painted a drab blue as Webb explained that this was the only place they could find that would accept their two dogs.

Hank and Frances offered them whiskey and beer. The two couples sat around for hours talking about literary matters. Hank did his best to keep the Webbs entertained, which gave him a foretaste of what he would have to do for a growing number of editors and writers who knocked on his door with increasing frequency. Although in awe of Hank, Webb was still feisty. He was quick with the wry remark and fast on rejoinders. They discussed Hemingway, Wolfe, Saroyan, and Miller and then came down on contemporary times. Webb was a good talker, tough and colorful, Hank remembers.

The next day they went to Hank's apartment, where they stayed up talking until just before dawn. Finally, everyone went to sleep, the

Webbs in Hank's bed, Hank on the floor, and Frances on the couch. The Webbs debated whether or not to move to Los Angeles. "We really were gypsies," Lou Webb says, "unable to settle down for long anywhere." They had lived in the Hollywood area many years earlier when Jon Webb was trying to sell a film project, which never got off the ground.

Webb pressed Hank for whatever free time he had available. In the five days they stayed in L.A., several meals were cooked at De Longpre, a few of them by Frances and Lou, and stacks of beer cans grew in Hank's living room.

Webb talked about his days as a police reporter, the jewelry heist he was involved in, and his time in jail. What intrigued Hank was the time that the editor had spent in prison. He especially liked hearing about Webb's black cellmate who helped him edit the prison newspaper, and about other prison characters. Finally, when the day came for the Webbs to leave, August 26, Hank and Frances drove them to Union Station, amid many promises of return visits and pledges of loyalty.

The day after the Webbs left Los Angeles, Hank fired off a letter that reached New Orleans before they did. He told them,

> You two are the real people, the type one hopes to but never meets. I only hope that whatever is driving you back and forth across the country eases a bit. I'll come see you next year—as early as possible—wherever you are.

The Webbs filled a void in Hank's life. Most people really did fall short of his expectations. The Webbs had not disappointed him. *It Catches* had been proof enough of their commitment to his poetry. The visit only confirmed what Hank knew in the first place, that they were honest, hardworking, soulful people. Webb went right back to work on his new project, *Crucifix in a Deathhand*, when he returned to New Orleans. He wrote Hank to let him know that meeting him had been "an honor dream," but that, to his surprise, meeting Hank did not change his feelings about the poems. "Usually meeting an author in the midst of a book is disastrous," he wrote. "I had that fear but it didn't materialize." In fact, Webb's only remorse was that he couldn't keep up with Hank's drinking. He admitted wanting to get totally drunk, but he wrote that he had a big hangover the evening of the second day after they met.

As the expected date of Frances's delivery grew nearer, Hank made a few practice runs down to the hospital. He tried to keep his cool in front of friends, but some of them saw his growing excitement. To Jory Sherman, he expressed both his hopes and anxiety: he worried that he might do the wrong thing with the baby, and hoped that he would be a good father. And on September 6, 1964, they rushed to the hospital; Frances was spirited off to her delivery, and Hank sat in the waiting room reading a copy of Plato's dialogues.

Frances and their baby girl emerged from the delivery room a few hours later, and Hank saw them briefly before going home to rest. When he returned he brought Frances a gift of a small round bowl with what seemed to be white floral patterns etched into the glass, filled with pink roses. Frances discovered that the floral pattern was actually just a plastic doily at the bottom of the bowl. This didn't lessen the gift in her eyes, but Hank felt as if he had let her and the baby down. He was heartbroken and forlorn: he convinced himself, but could not convince Frances, that his gift didn't mean anything. No matter how often she told him it was a beautiful gesture, it was still flawed in his eyes.

When Frances got ready to leave the hospital, the newborn wouldn't stop crying, though the nurse kept rocking her in her arms. She told the proud father that he had a strong little baby. Hank took his daughter in his arms, and held her carefully, rocked her and talked to her, looking into her large blue eyes. They drove back to De Longpre, glad to get out of the hospital, where Frances had had problems registering the infant as Marina Louise Bukowski because the parents were not truly married. She demanded that the nurse call up the county clerk's office to check on the law. The nurse came back and said that in this case they were going to make an exception.

Determined not to repeat his father's mistakes, at home Hank paid a great deal of attention to Marina. Frances saw that he loved the child deeply and saw how intensely he would gaze at her. "It was especially wonderful that he was so natural and direct in his love for her." The counterbalance, irritant at times, to this domestic scene was Hank's busy life as a postal employee and underground literary figure. At work, things remained difficult, and in his literary life he obliged himself to keep up his growing correspondence, especially with Jon Webb over the shaping and direction of his book projects. There were poems to write, envelopes to address, stamps to lick. With two people sharing his life twenty-four hours a day, he began to feel crowded. Frances had diapers to wash and both of their own clothes to clean, although Hank mainly sent his shirts to a Chinese laundry (laundry became a major bone of contention between them). He would sleep in between his job, writing, and the racetrack, and Frances had certain chores she needed to do. His love and devotion for Marina remained as strong as ever, but Frances says he couldn't help feeling oppressed. In many of his letters during this period he expressed the difficulty he felt living with two other people and having them dependent on him.

Frances admired Hank's ability to write so voluminously and still find time for everything else. Often he came home from work with terrible, wrenching pain in his shoulder. When he might have been resting people came over for a drink, to sit at his feet, to argue. Most of the visits ended with the host getting so drunk that he would insult his guests, causing them to leave.

At first Frances found it funny to watch him become increasingly drunk and vociferous, but its repetition began to annoy her; she soon felt as if she had two children on her hands. Relief came when she took Marina to Washington, D.C., on a Greyhound bus for a visit with her other children, who lived there. She wanted to see her kids, whom she missed, and to acquaint them with their baby sister. Hank took them to the bus station, said good-bye, and went back to his routine. Both of them knew that when Frances returned their living arrangement would have to change.

SEVEN

B EFORE the first Loujon Press book, Bukowski's reputation lay primarily with his little-magazine publications and not the individual chapbooks. Once his poetry was in trade-book form, readers could see it more comprehensively—what Jon Webb had hoped for from the beginning. Webb wanted to complete *Crucifix in a Deathhand* as quickly as possible, hoping to establish Bukowski as a major new talent in American letters.

Literary success aside, the post office job continued to go badly for Hank. He suffered almost constant pain in his arms and shoulders due to his twelve-hour stretches sorting mail. While driving home at night, shooting pains ran up and down his arms. Added to this, even at the post office he had to deal with the travails of other writers. Joe Links (not his real name), a man he worked alongside, had been trying to write for years. A short, wiry man with small, intense eyes, he had the kind of attitude toward writing that Hank did his best to avoid: he wanted money. Links had written a novel that publishers kept sending back. Hank told Links that he should write out of his own life experiences, forgetting whether or not his prose would earn him money. "I told him a couple of times to hit the road . . .but he lacked the nerve and I gave up trying."

Because of the demands of having Frances and Marina cooped up with him in a small apartment, Hank had not been able to do his usual amount of work. His poetry output slowed to a trickle and he communicated this to Webb. Whether it was Frances doing the wash or Marina crying, life at home sometimes became overwhelming. Both he and Webb worried about getting enough poems for the planned new collection. After much urging from the Webbs, he planned a trip to New Orleans for March 1965. The thought of a week in another city began to sound better and better as the time to go approached.

On March 4, Hank boarded the Sunset Limited out of Union Station. On his way down to New Orleans, he made the bar car his headquarters and had little use for the scenery he passed through. There were no women aboard to beguile him. To help pass the time, he began thinking of the poems he would write in New Orleans. Most of those he had already sent Webb had a lean, spare quality that separated them from the work in *It Catches*.

The Webbs met Hank at the train station. "He was drunk when he got off the train," Gypsy Lou recalls. "Jon and I hid behind a pillar. We wanted to see what condition he was in before we came out to greet him." Hank wobbled up to them and promised new poems to help complete *Crucifix*, just what Jon Webb wanted to hear. As they made their way to the Webbs' apartment-office—half buried beneath the sidewalk—Hank soon found himself surrounded by the aged, mildewed, picturesque buildings that gave the French Quarter its special character.

"Do you want a beer?" Webb asked. They drank for a while and talked about the train trip, and about the forthcoming book. Webb began to spin a tale of failure and triumph as a publisher, just as he had in the course of his letters, promising that this new volume of poetry would be better looking than the last.

"That's a hard performance to pass," Hank said.

Webb blended in with his surroundings, so different than the world Hank knew in Los Angeles. In L.A., countless architectural styles vied with one another, but here there were the iron railings, long narrow windows, bright colors, and gracefully aging buildings of a compact world unlike any other in the country. The Webbs were enamored of the gentle nobility of the place, and much aware of its importance as a cultural hub of the South. Hank watched the tourists walking through the streets, rushing in and out of the gift shops. He wondered at first how the Webbs could put up with them. It did not take long to see that Jon Webb was too involved in his work, especially *Crucifix*, to worry about the tourists. Jon and Gypsy Lou were survivors, like Hank himself. They had forged ahead on a combination of good luck, boundless energy, and sheer dedication to the task. Hank studied Webb closely, watching him as he pointed out the press and the pages of the projected book. "Don't forget those new poems," Webb said. "That's one of the reasons you're here."

"This is Bukowski you're talking to. Don't worry. I'll get you more poems."

"Well, you'd better."

When Hank saw that almost every available space in the Webbs' apartment-workshop was filled with pages of his poetry, even the bathtub, he felt embarrassed. The scene was surreal. He watched closely as Webb worked on the press, methodically feeding the paper with an air of delicate grace. "Those are my words going into that machine," Hank thought to himself. "Jesus, do I deserve all of this?" He would look carefully around the room, taking slow, calculated steps for fear of tripping over a stack of printed pages.

At one point during his stay, Gypsy Lou began to scream, "*Bukowski, Bukowski, Bukowski! He's everywhere! I hate the son of a bitch. And now he's here in our place drinking beer with his big belly and looking wise!*"

Hank encouraged her outburst: "Hey, Gypsy. Come on, say it, baby."

He admired her ability to say whatever was on her mind regardless of who heard her. Webb presented quite a contrast to his fiery partner. He was the solemn master over the typefaces and the stolid magician of print.

The Webbs arranged for Hank to stay with their close friend, Minnie Segate, a heavyset woman with mournful eyes and rosy cheeks.

[145]

Minnie, who was in her late-middle years, owned a small café called the Cajun Kitchen. She had a much larger house than the Webbs did, right around the corner, and was excited to have Charles Bukowski as her guest. He had his own room there, and she attended to him, cooking for him and doing his washing and ironing. Minnie would come home from work each day complaining that she didn't have enough customers, and then she'd prepare dinner for herself and Hank. She cooked him steaks at night and big breakfasts in the morning. While the food cooked, she would work on stylish hats that she made for wealthy women who would stop by her place to purchase her latest creations. Minnie didn't care about Hank's literary accomplishments; she admired the man himself. But they did have a few stormy arguments, almost as if they were married.

He wrote poems at Minnie's and then headed to the Webbs'. Before letting him in the door, Jon Webb would ask, "Do you have any new poems?" If he did, then the editor quickly turned on a wide grin and let him inside. Webb would set type and feed each new poem into the press—no editing of individual poems, no haggling over words or lines.

On good days Hank handed in ten or fifteen poems at a time. Webb would look at him with a serious expression and ask, "Is that all?" If Hank didn't produce that particular morning, Webb slammed the door shut. On the one hand, it was rather comical, but midway through the trip, despite the charms of Minnie Segate and some good bars like the Bourbon House, Hank became depressed. He drank with numerous visitors the Webbs introduced to him, and as a result found himself the butt of accusations from Webb each morning about his misdeeds while drunk on the previous evening. Webb's harsh grin and pointed finger of accusation were, he felt, like that of a father or girlfriend. Webb continued setting the poems and feeding them into the press, pressuring Hank to write more. Webb's single-mindedness (he was not printing anyone else at the time) made him all the more demanding.

On his own, Hank wandered through some of the haunts where he had spent time more than twenty years previously. "Jesus. It was like I saw myself standing before me. In a sense, I almost yearned to be back there, alone, young, wanting to be the great writer, half out of my mind with it, living on candy bars, luck, and moxie." He saw the building where he had worked for a printer and the place where he had sorted magazines to be delivered. New Orleans wasn't bad, but he began to get restless. He felt his relationship with the Webbs had become too close for comfort. He knew he would be seeing them through the years, and he wanted to keep a certain distance.

The Webbs arranged a meeting between Hank and William Corrington, imagining that a great literary friendship would develop. This was not to be the case. When Corrington and his wife met Hank, introductions were made and photographs were taken—and Hank sized up Corrington as a literary snob. Louise Webb remembers that Hank acted subtly sarcastic while Corrington played the role of a suave professor and literary figure. Hank joined Corrington for a dinner at a Chinese restaurant, where they talked politics. Hank talked offensively about Barry Goldwater, who was one of Corrington's heroes, and the evening dissipated into a disaster. Hank turned increasingly argumentative and Corrington became distant and cold.

Even before their meeting, Hank had been genuinely distressed at some of Corrington's ideas about writing, as well as distrusting his university position. He disliked Corrington's attitude that a novel is a step up from poetry. In a letter, Corrington had told Hank he liked poetry and loved prose. Later on, Hank wrote to Webb, "it looks like he [Corrington] married the wrong one and we can never talk him into divorce."

Hank had already written Webb that Corrington's novel was flawed, explaining that the American novel suffered from predictability, a lack of daring, and that most novelists were held down by a preoccupation with traditional notions of craft. Less than a year later, he would write one of his first extended prose pieces of the sixties for another independent editor, a work that would flow out of his typewriter with the kind of rawness that he believed was necessary for producing great fiction of any kind.

His disdain for Corrington reveals much about Hank's whole approach to life and literature. He had immediately identified the

Southern poet with a kind he had known all his life, institutional types, whether in grammar school or college art classes or on jobs. They usually liked Bukowski at first, then took a fast dislike to him. He believed their turning away had to do with their sensing in him a natural rebellion against the authority that they reveled in and obeyed. He told Webb that the meeting with Corrington was like "beard and no-beard, prof and no prof."

Hank clearly distinguished between what he termed "the clean fingernail boys" and the people he had chosen to be closest to in his formative years, namely bar bums, laborers, and those who learned on the streets. Formal education meant death and decay. When Corrington told him that he wrote poetry to perfect the art of the novel, Hank protested that this was a limited intellectualism, an excuse to go for the big royalty instead of the spontaneous utterances of the heart.

Hank spent some time in New Orleans with a deaf-mute acquainted with the Webbs. They communicated by writing back and forth to one another on paper napkins while carousing in the Bourbon House.

One night the Webbs took Hank to a local cocktail lounge, where the entertainer at the piano bar rose up to announce, "Ladies and gentlemen, we have with us here tonight the great poet Charles Bukowski." The crowd let out a big round of applause and Bukowski waved and then returned to his drink. He later went into the bathroom, where a man accosted him, asking, "Sir, just what is it you have written?"

"Forget it, baby," he answered, and walked back to where the Webbs were sitting.

When it came time for Hank to return to Los Angeles, there were pledges of mutual admiration and love all around. Jon and Gypsy Lou talked of coming to Los Angeles, while Hank expressed his desire to return sometime for another visit. He left them feeling confident that his new poems were in good hands. "I almost felt kind of guilty. These people were surrounded by madness and poverty.

They lived on top of my manuscripts and the pages of the book." Yet he understood that what they were doing amounted to an art form. Their sacrifice paralleled those of the poets they published.

A young New Orleans poet, Marcus Grapes (later known as Jack Grapes), met Jon and Gypsy Lou in the French Quarter when they were first publishing *The Outsider*, and he remembers Webb's dedication when he worked on *Crucifix*. He went there on a rainy night to see how the Webbs were progressing on the book. When he walked inside he was greeted with a room full of stacks and stacks of single, printed pages for Hank's book of poems. There were narrow paths between the stacks that allowed Jon and Gypsy to navigate through the chaos. When Grapes came inside, he found Webb seated at his small desk, a sheet of wood placed over two orange crates, binding the books with a big can of glue and a large paintbrush. "It reminded me of Tom Sawyer," Grapes says. "Webb and his brush." What amused Grapes even more was the machete that Webb used to slice the pages of each copy of the book.

"Jon looked like a very gentle, bald-headed school teacher," Grapes recalls. "He wore a straw cap. It looked something like a baseball cap. He was kind of quiet, and would look at a person with steel eyes. There was something about him, it seemed to me, that liked and appreciated the darker elements in another human being. Whenever I talked to him about the darker side, or said anything off the wall, he got this gleam in his eyes as if he were about to really say something important."

He describes Gypsy much as Hank does, as a quiet person who could suddenly burst into passionate declarations, dominating whomever happened to be near at hand. "You looked at her and she was like a gypsy from the movies. She had black hair and a very angular East European face. You couldn't imagine two more different people than Jon and Gypsy, and yet they had a great relationship."

Grapes offers insight into one of the reasons Webb felt such an affinity with Bukowski's work. Aside from the lyrical qualities of his poetry, and his ability to say things succinctly and with clarity, Webb admired the tough persona Bukowski presented to the world. Grapes recalls how Jon Webb talked enthusiastically about Bukowski's wildness when in New Orleans, his ability to drink huge amounts of beer, and the ease with which he told stories that never even hinted at sentimentality.

Over the course of several months Webb negotiated with independent New York publisher Lyle Stuart to publish *Crucifix*. As a result, he was able to print 3100 copies. He told Hank often enough that the poems deserved a wider audience than the usual small-press run and that having Stuart's imprint meant a wider distribution.

When Hank returned home he complained about an article that appeared in the New Orleans *Billboard*, an entertainment magazine in which Webb said that Hank was six feet, six inches tall, drank a case of beer per day, and wrote thirty poems a week. Hank protested to his friends saying that he was only five feet, eleven and three quarters, and, more seriously, that he didn't like this kind of hype. The magazine described Webb's workshop—apartment on Royal Street as being a "cluttered dungeon," with an antique printing press. Webb is further quoted as saying that he occasionally lifted objectionable words from Bukowski's poems, usually with his permission, but oftentimes without it. Although Webb's distortions annoyed him, Hank accepted them as a necessary and even amusing evil in the creative mania and general oddity of poets and editors. Hank has no recollection of Webb having ever taken words from his poems, although he concedes it might have happened, but rarely.

When *Crucifix in a Deathhand* arrived in his hands. Hank was as awed as he had been with the Webbs' earlier effort. Illustrations for Crucifix were done by New York-born artist Noel Rockmore, and Bukowski wrote a foreword, revealing much about his state of mind in those years when his reputation as a poet began to grow rapidly. It reads in part:

> Note: said that I could not write a foreword and was told to write one simply as a writer, but am not a writer. What I'm afraid of: becoming one, becoming very good, knowing how to

WORK THE BULL . . . It scares me and I no longer trust myself. Fear I am getting out of it, that I cannot any longer see real light with my eyes . . . Loving this book is bad also—we do not trust this loving. It's so bad I walk down the street . . .—and think about it, my luck: another book . . . people (scholars too) are talking about me in groups—as a poet—as a writer of poems, and they know more about Bukowski than he does . . . am crawling into the hole I usually crawl in after a book, forgetting the tote-board sun, forgetting the image, hack or no hack . . .

In the foreword Bukowski mentions Jeffers, that one poet who stayed away from literary power-plays, who deliberately placed himself far from the centers of the literary life. Jeffers had Bug Sur as his fortress. L.A. became Bukowski's fortress. The freeways were like a moat against the outside world. He would wall himself away for months at a time, going only to work and the racetrack.

The title poem, "Crucifix in a Deathhand," is itself a major work, a quintessential L.A. poem, boring directly into the heartbeat of the entire metropolis. It glorifies knowledge of the land and its meanings, delving into the history of place, yet retaining a sense of oneself as somehow independent of one's surroundings. Bukowski gives us a thumbnail biography of the raping of the hillsides and of the open, pastoral lands. He focuses his feelings through a strong Catholic image and a rare, for Bukowski, historical reference:

> this land punched-in, cuffed-out, divided,
> held like a crucifix in a deathhand,
> this land bought, resold, bought again and
> sold again, the wars long over,
> the Spaniards all the way back in Spain
> down in the thimble again . . .

And, in meditative mood, the poet brings us to the familiar scenery of the days when he bummed around:

[151]

. . . and I think too of old men sick of music
sick of everything, and death like suicide
I think is sometimes voluntary, and to get your
hold on the land here it is best to return to the
Grand Central Market, see the old Mexican women,
the poor . . . I am sure you have seen these same
women many years before
arguing
with the same young Japanese clerks . . .

A refined ear and an effortless ability with common language are unified. Bukowski's sympathies lie in a vision anchored far beyond the concerns either of the masters of metropolitan growth and development, or of those who cherish a sense of history. It isn't alienation that distances him from the things around him, but a sense of the ultimate power and enduring quality of the inner landscape, the place of the mind, the place of spontaneous creative thought.

The wellsprings of creative thought were definitely on his mind when he wrote the Crucifix poems. In "Beans with Garlic" he wrote:

this is important enough:
to get your feelings down,
it is better than shaving
or cooking beans with garlic.
it is the little we can do
this small bravery of knowledge,
and there is of course
madness and terror too
in knowing
that something of you
wound up like a clock
can never be wound again
once it stops.

Crucifix is filled with many voyages. The resolute Bukowski hammered away at the idea of everyman's personal crucifixion, and, in "Something for the Touts, the Nuns, the Grocery Clerks and You," he wrote an anthem for the working man, beginning:

> *we have everything and we have nothing*
> *and some men do it in churches*
> *and some men do it by tearing butterflies*
> *in half*
> *and some men do it in Palm Springs*
> *laying it into butterblonds*
> *with cadillac souls,*
> *Cadillacs and butterflies*
> *nothing and everything . . .*
> . . .
> *and nothing, and nothing, the days of*
> *the bosses, yellow men*
> *with bad breath and big feet, men*
> *who look like frogs, hyenas, men who walk*
> *as if melody had never been invented, men*
> *who think it is intelligent to hire and fire and*
> *profit . . .*
> . . .
> *and nothing, getting your last paycheck*
> *at a harbor, at a factory, at a hospital, at an*
> *aircraft plant, at a penny arcade, at a*
> *barbershop, at a job you didn't want*
> *anyway.*
> *income tax, sickness, servility, broken*
> *arms, broken heads—all the stuffing*
> *come out like an old pillow . . .*

Still very much a working man himself, Hank continued writing at breakneck speed after his visit to New Orleans, and even took on new literary projects. When Jay Nash and Ron Offen of *Chicago*

Literary Times and Cyfoeth Publications offered to do a chapbook of his poems, Hank suggested that he personally select work rejected from his previous collections, including outtakes from the Loujon Press books. In a short introduction to *Cold Dogs in the Courtyard*, which became the title for the new book, he wrote:

> the poems in this book have all seen publication in magazines but that is only their non-distinction. What makes them special—to me—is that they have been overlooked (or overlooked and shunned) by those people who for reasons unknown to society, publish collections of poesy. This, I hope, will be the 6th gathering of my work since I began writing at the cobby age of 35, a sad long 9 years back, and these are the poems that the editors didn't want for the earlier books . . . This was their party. I have never selected my own work for collection, feeling—as the formula goes—that a writer is not a very good judge of his own work . . .Very lately, I can tell a good woman when I see one, a good fire, a good whiskey, a good car, a good painting
>   . . . why couldn't I tell a good poem? Even one of my own. So, I went through the magazines looking . . .
> Now, of course, there will be some who think I never should have been collected in book-form or any form at all. this is all right because I think that way about many writers myself.
>   So, here's the book. And I guess that makes me an editor. I never thought I'd be an editor. Next the Atlantic Monthly, Life, Time, or on the staff of The New Yorker. Meanwhile, I'll have another scotch and water. and, man, what's all that *howling* out there? Let them in, let them in. Let there be LIGHT!
>   And Jon, Rob, Carl, E.V., I forgive you, this time.

This last sentence refers to Bukowski's editors, Jon Webb, R. R. Cuscaden, Carl Larsen, and E.V. Griffith.

From June 27 to July 4, 1967, Hank visited Jon and Gypsy Lou in Tucson, Arizona, where they had moved for health reasons. They had just completed Henry Miller's *Order and Chaos chez Hans Reichel* and had begun work on a double issue of *The Outsider* (issue 4/5). For some time Webb had felt that Hank resented the attention that they gave to Miller. While this didn't diminish the poet in Webb's eyes, he did become impatient with Hank's attitude. Perhaps that accounts for a violent argument they had on the last day of Hank's visit. They had gotten onto the topic of rape. Hank jokingly insisted that it was all right to rape girls under twelve years of age, saying that men sometimes need this kind of satisfaction at various times in their lives. Webb, taking him seriously, argued that this was a disgusting proposition. Hank held to his argument even as Webb began shouting loudly that Hank wouldn't stand for the raping of his own daughter.

Webb experienced other difficulties with Hank during this visit. He told him that Gypsy Lou was subject to violent asthmatic attacks when she fried food. "What did Buk do but demand fried foods all during his visit," he wrote to Edwin Blair in New Orleans. He described a poker game they played in which Hank quit the game at once because Webb had drawn four kings, even though Hank was ahead on the money. According to Webb, Bukowski said, "Who the hell can beat a four-king player?" before dropping out.

Webb viewed these personality quirks as indications of Hank's jealousy toward him and Louise for having focused so much attention on Henry Miller. Hank treated the Miller book with indifference, which disappointed Webb's hopes for both the book and for Hank.

In early 1968, while the Webbs were still finishing the double issue of *The Outsider*, Hank phoned Jon and stayed on the line for forty-five minutes. The call consisted primarily of a vintage Bukowski monologue, aggressive and tender at once. Hank explained that he couldn't afford to carry on a long conversation and complained that the editor had somehow compelled him to place the call. This went on for quite a while until Hank finally said he was getting off of the phone. Before he hung up the phone, he told Webb how much he loved him. "You guys went all the way for me," Hank said, "and I can never forget that."

In June of 1971, at age sixty-six, Jon Edgar Webb died at Vanderbilt University Hospital in Nashville, Tennessee. Marvin Malone devoted an issue of *The Wormwood Review* as a tribute to Jon Webb. In it, Hank wrote a memoir of his association with Webb and Gypsy Lou. He said of Webb:

> The miracle of Jon Edgar Webb, x-con, x-writer, x—editor . . . It would seem that now the skies would come down a bit or that the streets would crack and open up, or the mountains waver. But they don't. It's history, history, and the game goes on. A new deck. Another drink. And the sadness. That they built us not to last, and that we waste so much, make so many mistakes. Look, Jon, I see you grinning . . .You knew Buke would write it for you. It's cold now and a white Corvette pulls up outside and a beautiful girl gets out. I don't understand it . . .

EIGHT

L OS ANGELES, that city-as-afterthought in the American imagin-
ation, a place Bukowski chauvinistically held up against a
smoother, well-oiled America, remained the backdrop for his poems
throughout the sixties and in later years. The city served him well with
its plainness and lack of pretension. He did not celebrate the city as
Whitman had done with New York in *Leaves of Grass*, but he brought
the mood of it to people who lived far away, in another America. L.A.
was supposed to be the city without literature—literally without a
voice. It conjured up images of choking freeways and vast parking lots,
of decaying palm trees bristling under a hot summertime sun. There
were plenty of literary imports, some of whom had even written about
L.A. and its environs: Aldous Huxley, Christopher Isherwood, Bertolt
Brecht, even Thomas Mann. William Faulkner came for a while. Robinson Jeffers attended Occidental College. And there was Raymond
Chandler, the dark angel of the city's underbelly. But the writer in L.A.
with whom Bukowski felt a sustaining affinity was John Fante, whose
influence on his own writing he has always acknowledged.

Bukowski chose to wrap himself around L.A.'s mundaneness.
Whereas many poets yearn for the literary cafés and cosmopolitan
culture, their absence is precisely what Bukowski liked about it. Playing himself off against the slow, gentle decay of East Hollywood, he
brought fresh images into American poetry. Rather than looking

toward Europe, as many poets on the East Coast did, influenced by the expatriates Ezra Pound and T. S. Eliot, or toward Asia, as a later generation of West Coast poets such as Kenneth Rexroth and Gary Snyder would do, he gazed down on the sidewalks and cracked pavement of L.A. and wrote in "the new place":

> *I've got to finish this thing*
> *but it's just a poor little neighborhood*
> *not much place for art,*
> *whatever that is, and*
> *I hear sprinklers*
> *there's a shopping basket*
> *a boy on roller skates.*
> *I quit I quit*
>
> *for the miracle of food and*
> *maybe nobody ever angry*
> *again, this place and*
> *all the other places.*

There is almost a perfect logic in Bukowski's influence on a generation of rebellious younger poets who yearned to find a language, and a spiritual topography radically different from that which they encountered in literary journals and college classrooms. In Bukowski's poems these young writers discovered an anarchic sensibility and a consciousness divorced from the usual literature of rebellion. He became a leader for these wild young minds, whose concerns he articulated with an authentic and jarring voice.

In sharp contrast to Jon Webb's commitment to letterpress printing, a number of mimeographed poetry journals were begun in the mid-sixties by several of these restless, younger poets. The poor paper stocks the editors used and the careless printing jobs were statements of their disdain for established journals.

Douglas Blazek, one of the more dynamic of the younger poets, who also became an important editor in what was known as the mimeo revolution, began publishing *Ole* in 1964 from his home in Bensenville, Illinois. He called his publishing company the Mimeo Press. On the title page of the magazine he declared that *Ole* was "dedicated to the cause of making poetry dangerous."

Blazek was born in Chicago in 1941, the same year Bukowski left Los Angeles to begin his years of wandering. In his junior year in high school, Blazek read Jack Kerouac's *On the Road*, a book that affected him profoundly, as it did many of his generation. J. D. Salinger's *The Catcher in the Rye* also influenced his development. Indeed, like Bukowski, he even developed a bad case of acne and found himself rejected by many of his classmates. This rejection, based purely on his physical appearance, heightened his growing rebelliousness. He identified himself increasingly as a poet, and his mistrust of the world grew. Only in poetry did he find the means of reconciling himself with the world.

When Blazek started his magazine he solicited poems from Bukowski, whose address he obtained through Ron Offen, editor of the *Chicago Literary Times*. The poet promptly responded and Blazek speeded up plans for his literary venture. Bukowski's words gave him a direction, one that led away from the path taken by the Beats. "I could identify with Bukowski from working in the foundries. That real grittiness. I saw that I needed to make myself, and my writing, more authentic. Bukowski opened up an aperture to explore another point of view," Blazek states.

In searching for a name for his magazine, Blazek chose *Ole*, pronouncing it "ol," thinking of a word he had used in an early poem. Others kept calling it "olé," using the Spanish pronunciation, which he conceded to, realizing it expressed the spirit that he wanted his publication to stand for. Furthermore, "olé" stood for the slaying of the beast in a bullfight.

"Poetry is dying on the vine like a whore on the end stool on a Monday night," Blazek quoted Bukowski in this opening essay to the first issue of *Ole*. From there, the young editor expressed his own belief that poetry stood a chance to be recharged by a new generation, one that knows that "there is no special procedure in writing poetry or in living life." Blazek wrote that "OLE is hoping to prove Mr. Buk wrong. We want to build poetry up . . ." He did that in his own rip-roaring manner over the next few years with such poets as Bukowski and Harold Norse, with whom Hank maintained a voluminous correspondence, helping to lead the charge.

Blazek stood on his own, reaching out through the network of small poetry presses. Besides Bukowski and Norse, he encountered the works of other older poets. It was through the mails that most of the editors, poets, and magazine backers came together, a far cry from the idea of the literary café society of Paris and San Francisco. This literary movement via the post office box suited Bukowski's temperament.

For Blazek, just at the beginning of his career, finding a voice like Bukowski's two thousand miles away in Los Angeles, unattached to any literary movement or academic institution, was a revelation. Here was a man who lived and wrote without preconceptions, who tossed fuel onto the flames of literary anarchism. Blazek trusted the L.A. poet. Bukowski's involvement with *Ole* helped propel him back to prose, an event of no small significance in his life. In fact, it led him to eventually be able to support himself as an artist and to gain a truly international audience.

Blazek wrote to Bukowski in the winter of 1964 to announce that the first issue of *Ole* had been mailed to him. He informed him that "you have taken the art away from the college profs, the creeleys, the william carlos williams, the pounds & eliots." Then, in a romantic gesture, he stressed that Bukowski had brought poetry back to the financially unstable, ordinary people of the country, saying that "YOU are the prime example that the poetry of tomorrow will be the poetry of the fighting, struggling, unprofessional poet."

The editor of *Ole* shied away from direct political statement, another reason for Bukowski and him to feel like literary soul mates. His anger at American society was not unlike what is found in the writings of Henry Miller. Blazek believed that poetry, on its own, without any connection to an organized political movement, could affect people's lives for the better.

Blazek's belief that life and ideas must come together in the poem found justification in Bukowski's work. It is interesting to note that he saw the enemy not just in the colleges and universities, but among modernists like W. C. Williams and younger poets such as Robert Creeley. He viewed them as one step removed from the freedom that was necessary to art and poetry beyond literary convention. Essentially, he went right back to Walt Whitman's earthiness. For Blazek, everything centered on risk taking and a lack of polished mannerisms.

Douglas Blazek's letters are filled with the same kind of rich imagery and personal accounts of the foibles of daily life as Bukowski's. He found a sympathetic ear in the older poet, who had lived through much of what Blazek suffered. This is not to say that the relationship was one-sided. Bukowski poured his deepest feelings onto the page and fed them into envelopes addressed to the small town of Bensenville.

In December 1964, Blazek wrote a long letter to Bukowski in which he talks of having to go back to the factory in three hours' time. He goes on to say:

> If only i possessed a few lousy bucks i'd stay home & count the snowflakes listing them in a journal like past memories to ghost me at some future playing of Bach's Tocatta or sleepdreaming eyes open back lying bed soft & gushy fingers in terror of what i have to go through.

In the same letter, Blazek writes:

> how could you ever survive 44 years having to prostitute yourself doing things you hated? look, i'm not even 30 & i'm ready to plunge the knife to the merrygoround to initiate the void. how could you last so long? & what keeps you going now having to work for common laborers wages? is it drink or drugs or are you finally insane?

He then says not to take him too seriously, that he is really asking these things of all artists and writers everywhere who, like himself, have to face the grim prospects of trying to survive.

Bukowski welcomed Blazek's openness and vulnerability. He knew that the younger poet had no trouble taking stock of his own condition. His polemical style also attracted Hank, who liked his statement that "the poetry of this generation is a poor man's offering. a struggling, fighting man's offering. Great poets will no longer appear from an upper-middle class family that is financially comfortable in some way." Blazek, as a worker in a local factory, was the kind of young poet Hank could feel some identity with, and *Ole*, badly printed on a cheap mimeo machine, impressed him with its raw power when it arrived at his mailbox. Bukowski was represented with three poems, "watchdog," "freedom," and "age." The first one led off the poetry section and the latter two brought it to an end. Two of Bukowski's editors contributed as well—Carl Larsen, who had published *Longshot Pomes for Broke Players* a few years earlier, and Marvin Malone of *Wormwood Review*. In the magazine notes, Blazek wrote that Bukowski "resides in Los Angeles where he writes mad, beautiful letters & is trying to stay sober. Presently, he is preparing to accept the Nobel Prize for poetry which he deserves as much as Martin Luther King." Bukowski believed that *Ole* represented an exciting new development in poetry. He liked the rough edges around Blazek's production. "I had this feeling that Blazek and the rest of us were doing something important. There were others, William Wantling, who was in prison at the time, or had been, and Steve Richmond. We were a fairly tough crew. American poetry needed a good going over. This seemed like the right way to go at the time." One of the toughest in tone was the poet Harold Norse, an expatriate living in Europe. Norse, like Bukowski, was a literary maverick and an underground legend. He had also published in *The Outsider*. Now, through *Ole*, he served along with Hank as a father-confessor to the younger poets.

William Wantling, born in 1933, shared the spotlight with Bukowski as one of the major poets of the mimeo revolution. Blazek published a collection of his work, *Down, Out, and Away*. A voluminous correspondence between Wantling and Hank lasted over a period of several years. Hank admired his poetry in the same way he did Richmond's or Blazek's. Raw and earthy, his voice was that of a young man who lived entirely outside of the academic literary scene. Wantling had been in and out of prison and spent five years in San Quentin. When Hank and I published our own magazine in 1969, *Laugh Literary and Man the Humping Guns*, we included Wantling's work. He and Wantling traded long, oftentimes rambling discourses back and forth. In response to Wantling's interest in capital punishment—he had known longtime death-row inmate writer Caryl Chessman—Hank wrote to him on the subject in December 1965 and then went on to comment on the entire justice system:

> I guess what I figure mainly is that almost the whole structure of everything is wrong, so why pick at the parts? I mean, let's sink the whole ship, the ship of state, the ship of the world. A bomb? anyhow, what I mean is, take even jail. we don't need jails. we don't need morals. all we need is a common working sense and easiness and instinct. religions senseless. morals senseless. so-called decency senseless. laws senseless. a fucking cop pulls me over because I am driving 80 mile an hour while drunk. the theory is that I don't know what I am doing and that I am endangering other members of society. bullshit. he doesn't know what he is doing. he is a wooden pigeon with a badge. WE CREATE AN ACTUAL MONSTER ON THE THEORY THAT WE MIGHT PREVENT A POSSIBLE MORAL AND SOCIAL WRONG. get it? you were jailed for getting caught using drugs. they were worried that you were getting something they didn't have. it's a hell of a society when you are told it's wrong to use drugs but it's all right to kill yourself in a factory for a pitiful and demeaning wage.

The second issue of *Ole* appeared in March 1965 with a cover of yellow paper stock printed in red and black. A notice on the first page proclaimed that the magazine was "for all those unacknowledged legislators of the world, especially those who are *really* unacknowledged . . . " The playoff on Percy B. Shelley's well-known dictum from his "Defense of Poetry" set the tone for what lay inside awaiting the reader. Blazek included an essay in which he proclaimed that "literature is like the incredible shrinking man, emaciating into a sweet nothingness of whip-cream . . . " At the end of his "talk" he printed a letter of outrage from the editor of a poetry review, who wrote in response to the first issue of *Ole*. She said she could hardly believe that there were enough vulgar and inhuman people in the world to keep *Ole* supplied with poems. Hank liked the way Blazek kept up a running attack on the literary establishment without appearing too political.

Calkins must have been even more horrified by *Ole*'s second offering, for it was more of the same, and included a red-hot Charles Bukowski special prose piece entitled "A Rambling Essay on Poetics and the Bleeding Life Written while Drinking a Six-Pack (Tall)." The title accurately describes the state of Bukowski's mind when he wrote it. Explaining the essay later he said, "It was a drunken manifesto. I felt like the Ezra Pound of the mimeo scene. You know, it really seemed like things were happening then and so this essay was supposed to say the way things were or should be." He created a literary hand grenade to lob at the academy and at complacent types who sat in positions of cultural power. Highly personal, the essay provided Bukowski with an opportunity to let out onto the page much that had been welling up inside. He went right to the beginning of his days as a writer, giving a highly personal sketch of himself, a notebook of poetic sensibility that presented him as a solitary figure ranging across the landscape:

> In the days when I thought I was a genius and starved and nobody published me I used to waste much more time in the libraries than I do now. It was best to get an empty table where the sun came through a window and get the sun on my neck and the back of my head . . . I did not feel so bad that all the

books were dull in their red and orange and green and blue covers sitting there like mockeries . . .

The "Rambling Essay" goes on in the same conversational tone. "Whether I was a genius or not did not so much concern me as much as the fact that I simply did not want a part of anything," Bukowski wrote. He wrote about how amazed he had always been at watching other men work at regular jobs, and he underscored his desire to constantly escape the system, to drown himself deliberately in wine. He then mentioned his father as "that brutalized monster who bastardized me upon this sad earth." Then he landed back at the library table feeling "the dullness, the death."

From Bukowski's letters Blazek learned of the years when he had written prose. Judging by the passion, wildness, and natural wisdom of his letters, Blazek urged him to write the essay. "Those letters he wrote to me were marvelous prose examples of freedom of oneself. They showed me that one could take anything happening between man and the world, using language that is alive, and the things themselves would be read. It was language through the blood."

Blazek recalls that his subscribers identified with Bukowski's prose. It brought them the voice of an older man who wrote on the edge of madness with an Artaud-like sensibility:

> Then I was lost and young; now I am lost and old. There I sat in the library, the knowledge of generations there and not worth a damn to me, and not a living voice in the world that had spoken anything of what I was thinking.

That was not quite true. Bukowski might as easily have talked about the young Saroyan or about John Fante's *Dago Red* and *Ask the Dust*. He wasn't being totally untrue to himself. He still felt attached to the likes of Henry Miller, who wrote of burning all the books and moving on with one's own self as the master of destiny, who underscored the importance of relying on one's own voice, one's own personal vision. Hank did not know at the time that many prose books lay ahead. He had already begun sharply defining the shadings of the character that later emerged as the world-wise Henry Chinaski.

As the essay progressed, Bukowski led the reader back into the library once more, through the philosophy and religion room, to Chatterton and Dostoyevski. The reader learns of his early attempts at prose and is told how he wrote many of his stories by hand because he had no typewriter. Then he invokes images taken from his early years, such as riding on track gangs, hitting the Filipino over the head with his portable typewriter in the flophouse corridor, and taking a creative-writing class at L.A. City College.

He defined himself outside of the tradition handed down through Keats and Shelley, as well as that which came from W H. Auden, Stephen Spender, T. S. Eliot, and Ezra Pound. "Call me a hardhead if you wish, uncultured, drunken, whatever," he proclaims:

> I've never said this before but I am now high enough as I write this to perhaps say that Ginsberg has been the most awakening force in American poetry since Walt W. It's a god damn shame he's a homo. It's a god damn shame Genet is a homo. Not that it is a shame to be a homo but that we have to wait around and let the homos teach us how to write.

He exhorts the reader to cancel subscriptions to the academic poetry journals and "come here to *Ole* where you have to squint at what you read and laugh because we can't spell or punctuate."

How ironic that Bukowski, who had devoured books in the public library as a young man, could now call himself uncultured, a hardhead. Yet, like Henry Miller, who, after all, wrote *The Books in My Life*, a paean to the art of reading, Bukowski felt it was better to experience life firsthand, not to rely on the past, on other people's impressions of life. The point he hoped to make, was that a writer must create his art from the world around him, not from others' voices.

The essay received such a positive response from readers of *Ole* that Hank eagerly set to work on new prose pieces. Blazek encouraged him, although the poet really didn't need much urging. He liked returning to prose for a while, discovering a fluid style that read with the same clarity found in his poetry.

Mimeo Press soon offered two short prose books by Bukowski, *Confessions of a Man Insane Enough to Live with Beasts* in 1965, described in the fourth issue of *Ole* as "prose accounts from one man's hellish dealings with life," and *All the Assholes in the World and Mine* a year later, "a humorous account of one man's hemorrhoid operation." For Hank, these two forays into prose brought him back into a form of expression he had left years before. At the time, he told his friends of his desire to be able to quit work and simply to write for a living.

In *Confessions*, the character of Henry Chinaski is brought to life. As with "Rambling Essay," Bukowski wrote this work of autobiographical fiction quickly, literally as fast as his fingers could move across the typewriter keys. He fought against manufacturing a literary piece. He let the visceral elements rule, listening to the blood roar through his veins as he poured out fragments of his life. His prose ranged over his love affair with Jane, his acne operations, and his life in cheap dives and dead-end jobs.

Listening to his own "ear," which meant that he wrote as he spoke, Bukowski produced a document that reads like a practice run for his later prose. *Confessions* consists of random episodes laid out one after another without thought of chronology. Form and content, shaped by the moment of creation, were not belabored. Nor had he done an outline before he sat down to write.

Bukowski portrays Chinaski as wild-eyed and weakened by nonstop bouts of guzzling cheap wine, having been unsuccessful at finding his usual life-saving job as shipping clerk or stock boy. Chinaski applies for a job at a meat-packing plant. When the boss asks if he is strong enough to handle the job, he replies: "I'm nothing but guts. I used to be in the ring. I've fought the best." His description of a bar has the feel of Céline: "it was just another bar—dull, imperfect, desperate, cruel, shitty, poor, and the small men's room reeked to make you heave . . ."

The style of *Confessions* had little to do with avant-garde writing of the time. If anything, much of it was a throwback to his prose of the thirties. Some of the stories from *Confessions* resurface in Bukowski's novels of the seventies, *Post Office* and *Factotum*.

Echoes of the past rose up in Bukowski's mind as he composed *Confessions*, including dialogue between him and Jane, whom he calls "K." They are sitting in their apartment, practically penniless:

> K: "Shit, I c'd stand a drink."
>   I'd still be in bed smoking the last cigarette.
> ME: "Well, hell, go down to Tony's and get a couple of ports."
> K: "Fifths?"
> ME: "Sure, fifths. And no Gallo. And none of that other, that stuff gave me a headache for two weeks. And get two packs of smokes. Any kind."
> K: "But there's only 50 cents here!"
> ME: "I know that! Cuff him for the rest; whatamata, ya *stupid?*"

In an episode that follows, Hank is at the hospital being treated for his acne:

> It was like a wood drill, it might have been a wood drill, I could smell the oil burning, and they'd stick that thing into my head into my flesh and it would drill and bring up blood and pus, and I'd sit there the monkey of my soul-string dangling over the edge of a cliff. I was covered with boils the size of small apples. It was ridiculous and unbelievable . . .

The writing seemed very believable to Steve Richmond, then in his early twenties and a regular contributor to *Ole*. He first became interested in poetry in his last year of law school at UCLA when he attended a class given by poet Jack Hirschman in 1964. Hirschman introduced him to the work of Antonin Artaud. Richmond began writing poems and sending manuscripts to little magazines. In *Ole* he found Bukowski's address listed in the magazine along with those of other contributors, and wrote him, asking for poems for a magazine he wanted to put out. He had just graduated from law school but had become a full-time poet. He opened a small bookstore in Ocean Park, Earth Books and Gallery, mainly handling little magazines and other small-press publications—all were placed there on consignment.

Richmond published his magazine out of his store. He wanted to visit Bukowski, whom he saw as the best poet in America. But at the same time he didn't want to bother him. In almost every letter, Richmond wrote that he wanted to visit but recognized Bukowski's need to be left alone. Bukowski could read between the lines. He wrote back to Richmond and told him to come over on a Friday evening. Blazek found out about the upcoming meeting and told Richmond to make sure and bring over a six-pack of beer. He went over to De Longpre: "Bukowski's face was incredible. He was forty-four, but his face looked old, not like he was going to die, but just old."

They drank through the evening, making a few liquor store runs every now and then. For Richmond, the evening was magical. Bukowski gave him a stack of books, including *The Outsider*. Mostly, Richmond listened as Hank talked. "Are we going to just sit here and look at each other?" Hank asked. He was intrigued by the young poet who sat before him. While driving home, Richmond felt he had met one of the sages of the planet. He thought of the poem "Freedom" which he had read in *Ole* number one, a work he later included in a publication of his own.

In 1966, Richmond put out a broadsheet of poetry by himself, Bukowski, and a friend from UCLA, Jim Buckner. On the front page, in large letters, were the words FUCK HATE. Underneath, also, in bold letters, were the words WHEREBY WE THE ABLE MINDED CREATORS TELL THE ESTABLISHMENT, FUCK YOU IN THE MOUTH, WE'VE HEARD ENOUGH OF YOUR BULLSHIT. Beneath it Richmond wrote BEINGS OF BEAUTY. The broadside then opened to a drawing by Richmond, surrounded with poems by the three contributors. Both of Bukowski's poems dealt with the subject of emasculation.

Richmond printed ten thousand copies and found people to distribute them. *Fuck Hate* was stacked up in a corner of Earth Books. Some people who came in became distributors of the broadside: they walked in empty-handed and left with at least one hundred copies each. Over a two-week period ten people were arrested by the Santa Monica Police for distributing what the authorities considered an obscene publication. Richmond knew that the police would soon be coming to Earth Books to pay him a visit. He took all remaining copies from the store, but had neglected a few crumpled copies, which the police found in a wastebasket when they finally arrived and began their search.

Richmond was taken to the Santa Monica police station. To his amazement, a bail bondsman was there to bail him out. How he got there has remained a mystery to him, but he suspected a family member. After he was bailed out, the case dragged on for four years until it was finally dropped in 1970.

Douglas Blazek regretted that, in spite of their long friendship, he had never had a chance to meet Bukowski in person. The time finally came in 1967 when he moved his family from Bensenville to the West Coast. On his way to San Francisco, he came to L.A., calling ahead of time to let Hank know of his imminent arrival. When Blazek pulled onto De Longpre, along with some fellow poets, Hank stood on the driveway waiting. As the group approached, Hank asked, "Who is Blazek?" After a few minutes of confusion, the young editor identified himself. Hank led them all into his place. Blazek felt as if he were entering a hallowed ground, thinking to himself that he was in the room where *Confessions*, *All the Assholes*, and great poetry had been written. One of the first things that caught his eye was Hank's typewriter.

Blazek and the others stayed well into the evening, getting drunk, talking. As the hours passed, he had that feeling one often gets when meeting a mentor or hero: "scaling somebody down to just flesh" is how Blazek describes it. Thinking back on that meeting, Hank recalls that Blazek seemed on edge and defensive. Preconceptions that had been formed earlier in correspondence now had to be readjusted in this face-to-face meeting. Just as the younger man had thought of the older one as being larger than life, so Hank had tended to build up Blazek in his mind as a heroic laborer from the Plains.

Perhaps in an effort to lighten things up, and to end the small talk, Hank would say a particular word and then tell a story based on that word. He might say "Love" and then begin a tale of love. Though Blazek enjoyed this, when the evening ended, there was no lasting warmth between the two men.

Carl Weissner, a young editor, a man destined to make Bukowski famous throughout Germany, began corresponding with him. The West German, a tall, broad-shouldered man with a keen sense of humor and a quick mind, speaks English peppered with Americanese. While talking to him, one is struck by street lingo that is reminiscent of Nelson Algren, Raymond Chandler, and Bukowski himself. Weissner was born in Karlsruhe during World War II and has enough memories of the American bombing raids then, and of the subsequent American occupation, to give a colorful replay of bombs dropping and soldiers handing out chocolate candy.

Bukowski's future translator learned his English in the classroom and on the streets. After the war, his neighborhood was occupied by GIs and their families. Directly next door to him lived a black master sergeant with his wife and children. He became versed in American lingo and developed an interest in jazz, especially Duke Ellington and Woody Herman. In high school, he played in a band, often performing in American NCO clubs.

Weissner's university years were spent in Heidelberg and Bonn during the early sixties. The former is a picturesque city whose older section, where the university is located, sits under the shadow of the immense castle of the Palatinate Electors. Skirting the edge of the old city is the Neckar River. As far as Weissner was concerned, the university curriculum was as old as the stones of the ponderous castle. There was hardly any interest shown in American literature. The one professor who did talk about it focused mainly on Ezra Pound's *Cantos*, ignoring anything newer that might disturb his theses. The other professors zeroed in on English literature, cramming Thomas Hardy and William Blake into the curriculum. When Weissner read Jack Kerouac's *On the Road*, which was popular in Europe at the time, he realized that an important aspect of contemporary literature was being completely ignored in the German universities. He began reading the Beat Generation writers and following their exploits in Tangiers, Paris, London, and in the United States. Along with Kerouac's work, Weissner began reading Henry Miller, William Burroughs, Gregory Corso, and other American writers. The stultifying and bourgeois intellectual climate of the university could not compete with the power of Burroughs's *Naked Lunch* and Miller's *Tropic of Cancer*.

In the *Times Literary Supplement* he came across an article offering a directory to many of the little magazines and shoestring literary presses. This prompted him to begin his own magazine, *Klactoveededsteen* named after a tune by Charlie Parker. He printed it in mimeo and published a lot of American writers, and also reached out for work from Mexico City, London, and the avant-garde poets of Calcutta, the most prominent being Malay Roy Choudhuri. He wrote to Douglas Blazek and other editors and soon found himself engulfed in a massive correspondence. Broad in his appreciation, he published straightforward narratives and experimental work, including examples of the cut-up technique developed by William Burroughs, Harold Norse, and Brion Gysin.

Harold Norse met Weissner in Heidelberg back in the early days of *Klacto*. Norse describes him as dynamic and intellectually honest, with a relentless enthusiasm for the new writing. "At that time, Weissner had a strong interest in the cut-up technique," Norse says. (This method of writing involves splicing together random words or texts into a unified whole). "He was interested in experiments being done by Burroughs, myself, Brion Gysin and others. I originally heard from him while I lived in Athens back in 1964 or so. I sent him a piece called 'Alarm' that later appeared in my book, *Beat Hotel*."

In the spring of 1966, Weissner received·*Iconoature*, a magazine from a small town in England. He gave it a perfunctory reading, and found most of the poetry to be the usual mundane stuff he always came across. But then his eyes stopped on a page of poetry that demanded his full attention. He read the six poems and kept glancing at the name of the author: CHARLES BUKOWSKI. The work impressed him as having a direct, earthy appeal unlike any modern poetry he had ever come across. Bukowski's anger, humor, and lack of poetic adornment caused Weissner to not merely read the poems but to study them. After several readings he knew that he had to get in touch with Bukowski. Anyone who could write a line like "I am going to rob a bank or beat hell out of a blind man any day now, and they'll never know why" needed to be heard in as many places as possible. He wrote to Alex Hand, the editor of the magazine, and got Bukowski's address. Unbeknownst to Weissner, John Bennett, an American living in Munich, had published a poem of Bukowski's in 1965. Weissner only became aware of Bennett after he and Bukowski began corresponding.

Once in touch with Bukowski, Weissner began to receive the first few of a series of four- and five-page letters. Along with the first letter came a couple of poems hot out of Bukowski's "machine-gun." Weissner, who had very little money, somehow managed to get his magazine out and keep up with his growing correspondence.

Carl Weissner maintained an appreciation for the international avant-garde. He refused to focus on only one nationality. The new writing popped up everywhere: India, London, Paris, New York. Few people in Europe, however, looked as far as Los Angeles. At any rate, *Klacto* was a magazine without barriers. Homeported in Heidelberg, it nonetheless ranged everywhere. As to the forms contemporary literature took, Weissner was equally at home with the prose cut-ups of William Burroughs as with the direct, linear sensibility of Bukowski: in both he saw a true rebellion against the established order.

In his letter to Weissner, Bukowski did not disappoint. The editor of *Klacto* found an amazingly openhearted voice emerging in Bukowski's correspondence. The letters were long and ranged over a wide variety of subjects, the major theme being Bukowski himself and how he suffered from an excess of alcohol and from a slim bank account. Weissner found that Bukowski was as supple and brilliant in his letter writing as in his poetry. Bukowski wrote: "we are all drunk around here, all unhappy. we can't sleep. we are tired of talking. When we shit we sit on our ivory stools dumbfounded that something actually seems to be happening at last . . ." The tone was dramatically different than the one that came out of the stifled, carefully controlled mouths of Weissner's teachers and colleagues. As for poetry, Bukowski wrote that "you can talk about poetry and talk about poetry and all you end up with is an old rubber tire full of shit."

Weissner knew that Bukowski could succeed as well in Germany as he had in the American underground scene. Writers in his own country had a built-in censor, as though the spirits of the great classical writers were looking over their shoulders. Weissner yearned to see a book such as *Naked Lunch* done by a German. None was forthcoming. Nor did any of the German writers have the uninhibited quality that permeated Bukowski's poetry. Weissner envisioned Bukowski as a best-seller, as one who could hammer away at the stolid facade of German cultural materialism and even spark a revival of German literary innovation.

Driven by the excitement that seemed to be happening everywhere but in Germany, which Weissner found oppressive to his spirit, he applied for a Fulbright scholarship, choosing as his thesis an essay on the poet Charles Olson, author of the epic "Maximus Poems" and *The Archeologist of Morning*. In the summer of 1967 he got the Fulbright and headed for New York. He went to Buffalo, where he found that several other people were working on studies of Olson. Not wanting to cover ground already gone over, he dropped the project. Instead, he wrote *The Braille Film*, published three years later in San Francisco, and guest-edited an issue of *Intrepid*, an avant-garde poetry magazine edited by Allen DeLoach. He also put together a documentary on New York poetry for the German Avant Garde Archives. While doing the latter project, he lived in a poor neighborhood on the Lower East Side. All through this time, he was hoping to eventually make it to L.A. and meet Bukowski. He came to the West Coast in the summer of 1968 and stayed with poet-editor Jan Herman in San Francisco, where he explored the North Beach poetry scene. Weissner helped Herman edit his literary magazine, *The San Francisco Earthquake*.

During this time he went to Los Angeles to visit Hank, who was supposed to meet him at the airport but got lost on his way there. The editor from Germany thought that Bukowski was drunk and maybe he forgot to come, or he crashed on the freeway, or maybe he had finally committed suicide as he often threatened to do in his letters. Weissner waited more than an hour, then took a bus into town. De Longpre Street looked like a decayed highway (he would write about it in the introduction to a book of Hank's poems a few years later). He kept thinking that the scenery fit his image of Charles Bukowski. There were gigantic slabs of concrete strewn around, flat wooden houses with paint peeling off, burnt grass, dusty old hedges, junk littered everywhere. He walked by the tall palms lining the street and came to 5134 De Longpre, an address he knew well. It was from the battered little court that lay in front of him that so many miraculous letters had arrived at his apartment in Heidelberg. Just to round out the mildewed and raunchy cityscape, a '57 Plymouth with a new oil stain under the motor sat on Hank's front lawn. Weissner walked onto the porch and saw a note on the door which read:

> Carl. Don't bother to knock. I'm probably in transit. Just step through the door. It's broken anyway. Welcome to the United States.

Weissner tried the door. Just as Hank had said, it was unlocked. The environment seemed perfectly suited to his image of Bukowski. Window shades shut the world out. The room reeked of dirty socks and prolonged bouts of beer guzzling and cigar smoking. On the side of the room farthest from the street there was a couch with stuffing pouring out of a gaping wound. To Weissner's amazement, a set of tires sat propped up in a corner. He looked at the bookcases crammed with journals Bukowski had appeared in and his books of poetry. There were old newspapers and magazines littered around. In front of the window facing the street was a small table on which an old black Remington sat with a ream of typing paper next to it. Weissner took it all in. He had entered Hank's lair and found the poet's world laid out before him, with only the poet absent—but not for long. As Weissner smiled at the photographs, newspaper clippings and drawings tacked onto the walls, he heard a voice, one he knew from a tape recording that had been sent to him by Hank: "Amigo. I think you've got shit in your ears." Weissner turned around and found himself face to face with a grinning Bukowski.

"You sure are on your toes for a man your age," Weissner said.

"Man, sometimes I've gone down for the count," Hank rejoined as he handed Weissner one of the cold beers he had just brought in with him. "If I hadn't figured out it was you, I'd have had something else in my hand right now," Hank said, grinning. "Sorry I couldn't meet you at the airport," he added.

He told Weissner that the night before he had been in a studio at a local alternative radio station, KPFK, with a microphone in front of him and a bottle of rotgut Mexican liquor in his hand. "I bullshitted until I fell off of the stool. Then everything is blank." He explained that he had been given a handful of red pills. "Reds! Alcohol. Horrible combination! I can warn you. No asshole can handle it."

He went on to say, "When you've lost a whole month's wages at the racetrack and come back to your shitty little place at ten in the evening, and you sit at your typewriter, it would be damn difficult to write any sort of pretty rosy bullshit." Hank talked as usual about the bars, the track, the years of wandering, of Jane, and of his daughter, Marina, whom he had continued to visit often after he and Frances made separate living arrangements. Then he said something very insightful about himself: that in all those years of wandering and working dead-end jobs, he had made a deliberate choice to use a limited vocabulary in his writing. "With this little bit, I tried to hammer out what was inside it. Beside that, I'm just another suicide case in a bug-ridden hole or burned-out Plymouth down Laurel Canyon, or in the sea or on the railroad tracks . . ."

Everything Hank said made the trip down from San Francisco well worth it for Carl Weissner. "I was struck by how Hank spoke as clearly as the way he wrote. He didn't add any literary adornments. It came right out of him, straight talk." Weissner listened intently as Hank complained about the image that others were foisting onto him. "What I don't like," he said, "is this shitty image, this Humphrey

Bogart image of me, or those who worship me as some totally wild Hemingway, or some slum-god from the sewers of L.A. or what have you . . . Many people who read my stuff don't seem to be clear about this."

Hank told his visitor something of his long years living in poor neighborhoods, adding, "I still live in Hollywood's skid row just like before, but I know it thoroughly. There I learned how to work, and that's why I ain't so fast on changing anything . . . A few bars where I have credit, a few magazines, and a little kitchen . . ."

Weissner later put his visit to practical use. When he edited a book of Bukowski's poems some years later, one destined to become a poetry best-seller throughout Germany, he included an introduction telling of his visit. He recounted their conversation and offered invaluable biographical information along with keen insight into the qualities that make the poetry important. In his description of Hank, he wrote: "There he stood. Approximately 110 kilos. Thick hanging shoulders, bowlegged, baby worn pants, sweaty plaid shirt opened in the front." Next, he examined Hank's "battered" face, saying that "against that even Eddie Constantine would probably have difficulties." But Weissner had other work to do aside from translating Bukowski. When he returned to Germany, he edited an anthology of cut-up writings, which included Claude Pelieu, Jan Herman, and William Burroughs, among others. He also put out a final issue of *Klacto*. A publisher located in Darmsatdt, J. Melzer, financed the magazine, helping to get out three thousand copies. Shortly afterward, Weissner translated G. Ballard's *The Atrocity Exhibition*, a work he points to as a watershed of twentieth-century thought. Always at the forefront of his mind loomed the image of Bukowski.

NINE

HANK and I were in his apartment on De Longpre Street late one night in 1965 discussing everything from John Steinbeck's early novels to Ernest Hemingway's suicide.

He commented on the striking difference between the smoothness and smallness of his hands in comparison to the rest of his body.

"Look at my hands," he said. "See how precious they are? These are the hands of a true artist."

"Hands of a lover. Right?" I rejoined.

"Hands that can belt you one right across your cheeks," he fired back.

This particular night Hank had stocked enough beer in the kitchen to take us through a weekend siege. Keeping up with Hank meant lifting a great many bottles. Two trips a night to the liquor store up on Sunset and Normandie were not uncommon. I had already gone on the porch twice to vomit from too much beer. When my head began to swirl from the alcohol, I told Hank that I had to go home.

"Be a man," Hank fired back. "The evening has just begun. Have another beer."

I protested that it was 2 A.M. and time to get some sleep.

"For Christ's sake, kid. Let's go a few more rounds."

"Don't you have to make the track tomorrow?"

"Sure. I'll get there. The track is waiting. The post office waits. I'm on the cross at all hours. Even in front of the typewriter."

His typewriter sat on a table near to the front door—a racing form lay on top of it and there were several empty beer bottles next to the big black machine. Wet East Hollywood air entered through a partially opened window, and the fecund aroma of tall hedges clinging to the side of the old building caused a tingling sensation in my head. Those hands of Hank's seemed to leap from his body as he handed me a new bottle of Miller beer.

"Aren't we running low on beer?" I said, knowing that we weren't.

"No!" he insisted. "I've still got four six-packs in there. By the way, this guy is coming over in a few days—John Martin—a collector of literature. You can be here if you want. I believe he wants to make me famous."

"Listen, Hank . . . I'm going."

He blocked my exit. "You can spend the night again, kid. You know, you've done that before."

"You sleep so late," I protested. "I don't know what to do when I get up."

"Split. That's okay. I just want to talk a while. My landlord, Peter Crotty, was here earlier—he and his wife. They want to know if I'm famous now. I said, 'Sure I am,' and joked about letting them raise the rent. The truth is, I'm getting fucked at the post office. Ever since *Open City* they've been tightening the screws. I want to quit, but you know, it isn't that easy."

"Why not? You can write your way out of the post office if you try."

"Not with poetry. It has to be prose. You know, the only way a poet makes real money is by teaching in a university, and that is the final murder of the soul."

He brought out his tape recorder. Back in the sixties he made a considerable number of tape recordings, usually pointedly aimed at literary matters but other times simply drunken talks between himself and his guest. This night he began, "The major poet Charles Bukowski and one other person are about to begin a recording. We are here together, two men, and there are no women present. Take note: The great Bukowski has no woman at this time . . ."

A Rachmaninoff symphony blared out of the radio. Hank announced that we were going to engage in a literary conversation. With his introduction completed, he handed me the microphone. I talked about Steinbeck's *In Dubious Battle*. I said that it gave a solid, lean portrayal of labor violence in California during the thirties. Hank agreed, making a point of how difficult it was to work as a fruit picker in the hot sun of Central Valley, and then went on to criticize some of Steinbeck's later books, which he believed were marred by sentimentality. As he talked, I remembered that Hank disliked the use of such words as "star," "moon," or "infinity" in poetry—they were, in his opinion, sure tip-offs.

"Blood on the line . . ." he always said. "Writing has to be blood on the line. Steinbeck faltered when he forgot that."

From Steinbeck, Hank focused his sights on Hemingway, speaking of his early admiration, but ending by criticizing the great novelist for giving in to notions of fame, so much so that it marred his writing. This was a common theme of Bukowski's. He always said that fame laid a trap for the mind. "You see, kid," he said, "the parties became endless, and the interviews. Hemingway had no time to think. He wrote himself out. Then, one day he finally realized that it wasn't fun anymore."

"We can knock the big writers," I said, "but they still sound exciting."

"I know," Hank said. "You mention Hemingway or Dos Passos and I kind of get chills. It's like they stand sixty feet tall."

After rampaging through the American literary scene, Hank brought up the name Pablo Neruda. "When he writes down the word 'blue' he makes you feel it."

"What do you mean by that?"

"I mean he gets it down without literary preconception. You know, like the professors who come by with their little fucking six-packs of beer and they want to know the secret, but there isn't any damned secret. It's just day by day, day by day living."

[181]

When I told Hank that I had gone to a big antiwar rally up in San Francisco he sneered at me for following the crowd. Some of his readers would have been shocked by this. Those who knew his work well, however, couldn't have been surprised. His mindset was about as far from the political mainstream as possible, but he held the anti-war movement in contempt as well. "Lot of these people are blind. They got into the antiwar movement because they're lonely hearts. They have no ideas of their own. These same people, if they were in control, would be just as bad as Johnson or Westmoreland." No matter how strongly Hank dismissed current events, he often seemed to have a fair knowledge of what was going on in the world.

Just before the sun rose he went into his bedroom, and came back with a blanket that he threw onto the couch, saying, "Okay. I guess we'd better turn in. Maybe this John Martin guy will bring me luck."

One of Hank's main themes was the notion that a writer must exist on his own, not supported by anyone. This is evident not only in his conversation, but in his poetry as well. "As a poet I have no responsibility except to myself," he said. "Not to any politic or religion. When we start adding too much ideology to a man's writing we get bullshit. In other words, to be unattached to a fixed position is what I call for. I am not concerned about saving the world."

"What about the news from Vietnam?" I asked. "Don't you feel responsible for what we're doing over there?"

Hank lunged up from his chair and shouted. "Hell, I didn't send them over there. I didn't tell them to start that fucking war."

"All the killing, doesn't that affect you? The things we read in the newspaper?"

"You want to know what I feel? Nothing. Not a damn thing. If I see a dog killed in the street, before my eyes, I feel it. If I see a man killed before my eyes, yeah, I'm going to feel something, but if I hear on the radio forty orphans died in a fire up in Vermont, well, shit man, it's not going to be the same thing. How can I feel it? It's just information coming over a dead wire."

"And the protests against the war?"

"Remember what I said in 'The Genius of the Crowd'? I warned about people who scream for peace. They are the ones who will murder you in the end. I really meant what I said."

The poem Hank referred to had been distributed as a mimeographed chapbook by D. A. Levy's Seven Flowers Press. It served as a rallying point for younger poets much as did the prose works Blazek published. Levy, whose own poetry appeared in *Ole* and other magazines of the mimeo revolution, admired Bukowski as a leader in the cause of a poetic anarchy. Along with many of his friends, Levy was under nearly constant harassment by the authorities in Cleveland for his advocacy of marijuana legalization and for publishing "obscene poetry." For him and his colleagues, Bukowski's poem became a manifesto of the artist in perpetual war with "straight" society. The poem is a polemic aimed at the average man, who comes under attack for being treacherous, hateful, and violent. The poem warns:

> *Beware*
> *The Average Man*
> *the Average Woman*
> *BEWARE. Their Love*
>
> *Their Love Is Average. Seeks*
> *Average*
> *But There Is Genius In Their Hatred*
> *There Is Enough Genius In Their*
> *Hatred To Kill You, To Kill*
> *Anybody.*

Crucial to the intent of the poem is Bukowski's view of how the average person views the creative artist:

> *Not Wanting Solitude*
> *Not Understanding Solitude*
> *They Will Attempt To Destroy*
> *Anything*

That Differs
From Their Own

Not Being Able
To Create Art
They Will Not
Understand Art

The poem goes on to say that they will turn their failures as creators against the artist,

And Their Hatred Will be Perfect
Like A Shining Diamond
Like A Knife
Like A Mountain
LIKE A TIGER
Like Hemlock

Their Finest
ART

When John Martin appeared at Bukowski's door, he knew something significant would happen. The soft-spoken Martin managed an office and furniture supply company in Los Angeles, but he would soon direct his energies to building an independent publishing company devoted to fine printing of contemporary poetry. Although he did not mix around in the local literary scene, Martin kept abreast of contemporary literature with an all-consuming passion. He collected rare books, and owned an impressive library.

Martin had not received a formal university education. He taught himself about modern writers, beginning with the classics in a library left by his father, an attorney who died in an automobile accident in 1939, and moving on to such moderns as Kenneth Patchen and Henry Miller. He particularly admired the openness of form and meaning of Whitman's *Leaves of Grass*, and he believed Miller's *Tropic of*

Cancer and *Tropic of Capricorn* to be true American classics, equal to Herman Melville's *Moby-Dick*.

Martin first read Bukowski in *The Outsider*, and recognized his genius right away. He thought a poet like him deserved a much wider audience. When he found out that Bukowski lived in Los Angeles, he requested a meeting. Intrigued by Martin's request, Bukowski wrote back, saying that they could get together after the Christmas season.

By the time he visited Bukowski, Martin knew he wanted to begin a press, even though he hardly understood the difference between a publisher and a printer. The door was open when he arrived, and he peered through the screen door into the dimly lit room where Hank was typing. When Martin knocked, Hank came to the door and said, "All right, come on in." As Martin stepped inside, he took note of the beer cans, the papers scattered about, a rickety book shelf, a desk in a far corner loaded with envelopes, magazines, and more beer cans. Off to one side was Hank's typewriter. As they talked, Martin was impressed with his host's soft, gentle voice and his courtesy. Eventually Martin brought up the idea of publishing. He explained that he wanted to do some broadsides for which he would pay thirty dollars per poem. Hank agreed. Since the post office didn't pay well in those days, this represented a substantial amount of money to Hank.

"You could say when Hank and I met it was not unlike Mr. Rolls meeting Mr. Royce before they made the cars," Martin recalls. He discovered an untapped literary treasure when he asked Hank if he had more material that could be published, and the poet walked over to the closet, kicking a few empty beer bottles out of his way, and opened the door. There sat a stack of carbon copies of his poems done on onion skin. The stack reached at least two and a half feet tall. Looking at it, Martin thought, "My God, you don't have to wait around for this guy to produce. You can pick what you want out of this tremendous backlog."

Martin had already picked a name for his publishing company, Black Sparrow Press. He didn't have a lot of resources, although for Hank, Martin seemed like a wealthy man. In reality, he had very little money in the bank and was taking home less than six hundred dollars per month. He sold his entire library of first editions to the University of California at Santa Barbara, earning seed money for his press, which enabled him to make long-range plans. At the start, he made use of the print shop at the company he worked for, paying costs to the printer, Phil Klein.

Hank's impression of John Martin on the day they first met was of a meticulous and kind man, with a very faint, perpetual grin. He liked the future editor's clear, businesslike attitude. Instinctively, he knew that this man was just the kind of person he needed to help guide his burgeoning literary career. Knee-deep as Hank was in the shadow of the postal service, he saw Martin as a possible key to making it on his own.

John Martin's emotional stability, and the fact that he stood by his word, never failing Bukowski, helped create a lasting friendship. A serious, soft-spoken man, he never played into the Bukowski myth. They did not spar around verbally like so many people did in order to encourage a performance of the poet as disorderly drunk. Martin, in fact, was a straitlaced, church-going man, neither a drinker nor a smoker, who lived a sedate, comfortable family life. The contrast with Bukowski is obvious, and in later years, Martin often pointed out that the two of them made quite an odd couple.

The Bukowski broadsides, the first publication of Black Sparrow Press, appeared in the spring and summer of 1966. These included the poem "True Story" in April, "On Going out to Get the Mail" in May, "To Kiss the Worms Goodnight" in June, and "The Girls" in July. Thirty copies of each broadside were printed. Twenty-seven copies of each were numbered and placed on sale. Three were lettered not for sale. In the fall, Martin printed a broadside by poet Michael Forrest, followed by Hank's "The Flower Lover," again in an edition of thirty copies. When Martin handed Bukowski his first payment of thirty dollars for "True Story" the poet was ecstatic. He barely took home one hundred dollars a week from the post office at that time and had never expected to be paid that much for a poem.

Martin's admiration for Bukowski grew as the months passed. He began adding other poets to his Black Sparrow Press list, including San Franciscans Robert Duncan and Ron Loewinsohn, and avoided becoming the house organ to any particular literary trend. He didn't go out and seek poets who wrote like Bukowski. Unlike Jon Webb or Douglas Blazek, he did not publicly expound his reasons for publishing—he had no axe to grind. His publishing house had no mandate except to print the highest quality books. By the end of 1968, there were fifty-one Black Sparrow broadsides and books. Few writers could be as far apart in terms of sensibility as Bukowski and Robert Duncan, or Bukowski and Jerome Rothenberg, yet they all appeared on the same list. While Martin had no aspirations to be a major house in the traditional New York sense, he still thought in terms that were monumental when compared to most small presses that concentrate primarily on poetry. In 1969 alone, twenty-six new titles were printed under the Black Sparrow imprint. Martin had already secured himself a permanent place in the history of American letters. Black Sparrow Press brought a new element of care and refinement to the small-press scene. Collectors began buying up each of his publications as they appeared, and, when the press began doing full-length books in larger runs, Black Sparrow took its place as one of the most innovative small presses in the country.

In the meantime, beginning in May 1967, Hank became a local hero due to his weekly column, *"Notes of a Dirty Old Man"* written for *Open City*, an alternative paper founded by John Bryan.

Bryan had edited several small-press magazines, *Renaissance* and *Notes from Underground*. He had been part of the San Francisco scene in the early sixties. While there he edited an alternative paper, *Open City Press*, which published a few prose pieces by Bukowski. In L.A., a few years later, he asked Hank to write a weekly prose column, to which he readily agreed. In terms of readership, there was no comparison between distribution of the poetry journals and Bryan's paper. Whereas *The Outsider* and *Ole* might find their way to several hundred hands, *Open City* reached thousands of readers. Although not the widest circulated underground paper in Los Angeles, it nonetheless made a significant impact on the counterculture. In his column, Hank covered whatever came to mind. He delved into the heart of the sixties rebellion, and his appeal quickly spread far and wide. "There was no money in it, really, but it kept me in good form and I feel that the writing kept getting better." It was a practice run for the novels that he would write later on for Black Sparrow Press.

The first assignment Hank took on for *Open City* was a review of A. E. Hotchner's biography of Hemingway, *Papa Hemingway*, which appeared on May 5, 1967. It was titled "An Old Drunk Who Ran out of Luck." The piece showed that Hank still held on to some of his youthful admiration for Hemingway. Although he had long since stopped reading him, there remained a lingering interest in the novelist's career. In the last few sentences of his review, Bukowski expressed how he felt about this great master of the American novel, writing that Hemingway

> lived on war and combat and when he forgot how to fight he quit, but he left us some early work that is perhaps immortal? but something with the cape movement there. some flaw. oh, who the hell cares? let's have a drink for him!

A week later, the first installment of *"Notes of a Dirty Old Man"* appeared. The one-page column concerned Hank's run-in with two policemen who tested him to see if he was driving while drunk. He begins:

> Well, you see what happens when a couple of cops stop me when I go out for cigars? I want to change the whole social penal structure. don't misunderstand me—I am not saying that the drunk driver is a superior citizen . . . but I am saying that there are too many cases where a man can make it home without harming a fly's butt and he is interrupted and thrown into jail, because when jails are there, jails will be used . . .

In "Notes" Hank treated his readers to slices of autobiography, a portrait of himself as the eternal outsider, or as he puts it "the frozen man." He wrote freewheeling essays, like the one quoted above, in which he presents his viewpoint on society and politics. Young people in the late sixties could empathize with the seventeen-year-old Bukowski battling it out with his father after coming home drunk one night, or participating in an ROTC competition that he won without really wanting to. Readers of the alternative press could hardly resist reading Hank's portrayal of himself as the ultimate rebel against authority of any kind:

> I guess my father finally recognized the Frozen Man in me, but he took full advantage of the situation for himself. "Children should be seen and not heard," he would exclaim. this was fine with me. I had nothing to say. I was not interested. I was frozen. early, late, and forever.
>
> I began drinking about 17 with older boys who roamed the streets and robbed gas stations and liquor stores. they thought my disgust with everything was a lack of fear, that my non-complaining was a soulful bravado. I was popular and I didn't care whether I was popular or not. I was frozen. they set great quantities of whiskeys and beer and wine in front of me. I drank them down. nothing could get me drunk, really and finally drunk . . .

In the columns one did not find the parlance of the times. Whether talking about himself or society, or his half-crazed friends, or how the writing of poetry can put a person on the cliff's edge, Hank wrote in the no-nonsense style he had begun with back in the early forties. In the heart of the sixties, he remained untouched by hippie terminology, employing it only sarcastically to prove a point. From time to time he made it very clear where he stood politically, which was neither on the right nor the left, nor in the center, but on the outside. Thus, he remained clear of anti-Vietnam War rhetoric. In one column, commenting on presidential elections, he said choosing between the Republican or Democratic parties was similar to trying to make a choice between warm shit and cold shit.

When he did venture into the political arena, Hank lunged right ahead:

THE LITTLE MAN HAS SIMPLY GOTTEN TIRED OF TAKING TOO MUCH SHIT. it's happening everywhere. Prague, Watts. Hungary. Vietnam. it ain't government. it's man against govt. it's Man who can no longer quite be fooled by a white Christmas with a Bing Crosby voice and dyed Easter eggs that must be hidden from kids who must WORK TO FIND THEM. of future presidents of America whose faces on TV screens must make you run to the bathroom and puke.

Many people equated Bukowski with the youth-oriented counter-culture, not knowing his relatively long history—including his wild and lonely apprenticeship as a prose writer going back to the thirties. His attitudes and opinions, formulated decades before the youth re-bellions of 1967 and 1968, cast a veil of anarchy over the prevalent, ideologically inclined philosophies of the left. Young people who followed *"Notes of a Dirty Old Man,"* often understood implicitly that an older voice spoke to them, one as defiant as they themselves strove to be.

Bukowski's prose had the same kind of lean imagery as Henry Miller's. The sense of the Whitmanic man prevailed, unattached to ideology, yet acutely aware of his own needs and desires and exactly where he stood in relationship to the life around him. The columns were never planned—he did not know where he might be led to next. When he did focus on a social issue, it was usually subordinated to narrative deriving from his own experiences.

In 1967, John Bryan asked John Thomas to edit an issue of *Open City*. He loaned Thomas a stack of Bukowski's poems and Hank came over to Thomas's to read them aloud for a recording. Bryan reclaimed the poems after the recording session and in the confusion that ensued lost the only copies. It then fell to John Thomas to transcribe the lost poems from the master tape and it was this copy that convinced John Martin that the collection would make a wonderful first book of poetry for the Black Sparrow Press. The book, *At Terror Street and Agony Way*, was published in May of 1968. The first printing of eight hundred paperbound and seventy-five hardbound copies sold out almost immediately.

While *Terror Street* was being put into shape by Martin, Hank decided to write a long prose work. As of early summer 1967 he had completed seven chapters of his novel—tentatively titled *The Way the Dead Love*. But due to overwhelming personal problems, mainly the increasing difficulties of working long stretches at the post office and the pressure of meeting deadlines for his column, he abandoned the project. He wrote to William Wantling:

> I haven't written a poem in 3 or 4 months and don't care. but have been doing a weekly column for the new L.A. paper *Open City*, editor, John Bryan. don't know how long I'll continue. have written, I guess, about a dozen columns.

Perhaps sensing that he wasn't the only one aware of his difficulties, and knowing that he wanted to finish the novel, he applied for a sixty-five-hundred-dollar Guggenheim grant, but was turned down. Because of the notoriety of his *Open City* columns, the postal authorities decided to give old Mister Cool, mail sorter Charles Bukowski, a little push in making a decision about whether or not to stay on for the long haul with the postal department. It came in the form of a summons to the personnel department. Word got around the building. Was old man Cool going to crack? If they made Bukowski knuckle under, then they could get to anybody.

He went for the interview. In a standard bureaucratic trick, he was left in the waiting room for forty-five minutes. When he received his call to enter a Kafka-like maze and find his way to a small conference room, he saw shock on the faces of his interrogators. They had expected a younger man, possibly a hippie type with beads and long hair. Instead, it was Mister Los Angeles. A man about the same age as they were. Scars on his face. Hair combed neatly back. As polite as anyone could possibly be.

At first, he was asked if it was true that he was not married to the mother of his child. "That's true," he said. "We are not married." When they inquired as to how much child support he paid, he said nothing, reasoning that it was none of their business. Then, an old gentleman, neatly dressed, with a very serious expression on his face, reached into a cabinet and brought out several copies of *Open City*. Apparently, one of Hank's co-workers had brought them to the attention of the authorities.

"They were waiting for me. I said things that weren't pleasant to the average ear," Bukowski comments. "I was real cool. When they asked if I wrote the columns called '*Notes of a Dirty Old Man*,' I said 'Yeah. Sure.'" Then, with the intention of intimidating the authorities, he brought up the First Amendment, followed with an eager expression and the question, "You mean, I can't write any longer?" He mentioned the American Civil Liberties Union, to further intimidate them, knowing that he had put some fear into them already. "*I don't know what we're gonna do with you!*" one of the men said. There was much handshaking and Bukowski was free to return to his duties.

A short time later, they called him in for a second interview. During this meeting, one of the interrogators told him that he had two sons who were attending journalism school and that they would never write things like in the *Open City* columns. Bukowski said, "Don't worry. Even if they wanted to, your sons will never write this way." Again, the authorities made no headway. Once again, there were handshakes, smiles, salutations. "Jesus. It was as if we were all old friends who had come together to bullshit for a while," Bukowski recalled.

He became a hero. Word got out that he had stood defiantly against the authorities. He would come to work each morning and workers would whisper, "Hey, there goes Bukowski," or, "Man . . . look, it's the guy who writes for *Open City*." He acted wise and all-knowing. They would come up to him and tell stories. Now, though, the supervisors were afraid of him. They would say to the employees, "Hey you can't talk to him." As Bukowski puts it, "The printed word strikes fear in everybody. It was pointed out to me that one of the guys who interviewed me was from Washington. He said, 'Did you write this column?' I said, 'Yeah.'"

Bukowski began to make a practice of sending poems to John Martin on a regular basis. *The Days Run Away Like Wild Horses Over the Hills* came out in 1969, a collection of poems from Bukowski's first four books, including *Poems and Drawings* from *Epos* and numerous works brought together from a myriad of poetry journals. Martin chose the order in which the poems appeared and divided the book into three sections. For all future poetry collections of Bukowski's, Martin followed the same practice of placing the poems in an order that he then sent to Bukowski for approval.

John Martin describes his relationship with Bukowski as being "like two gentlemen meeting over coffee." The poet would often say to friends, "Martin is one hundred percent. He has never disappointed me." For a man who distrusted others' motives, that represented quite a vote of confidence. Their relationship was deeply professional. Martin seemed to bring out a sense of propriety in Bukowski. Never, in all those early years, or later, did Bukowski talk to Martin about his childhood or his affairs with women. When he did talk about personal matters with Martin it usually took the form of blowing off steam over an argument with a friend.

Hank looked at John Martin as an anchor in his life, a safe harbor. Thinking of Martin firmly at the helm of Black Sparrow Press gave Hank a sense of security—and he especially liked the idea that, early on, Martin himself had packed and shipped his books. Having worked as a shipping clerk many times in his youth, he appreciated this hands-on involvement.

Encouraged by his success as a columnist, Hank thought more seriously about being a full-time writer. He drank as much as ever, still mostly Miller beer, which he bought by the six-pack at a liquor store a few blocks from his apartment. The owner and he engaged in track talk as beer, cigars, and cigarettes crossed the counter—all three of which Hank shared with an increasing stream of visitors. He constantly battled to find the time for writing, to balance his vital solitude with his obligations to friends, acquaintances, and strangers. He didn't want to seem like an ungracious host, and usually found himself taking vast chunks of time out of his day to meet his growing social obligations. Not a few arrived who genuinely wanted to spend time with a writer they admired, while others came to test and probe the Bukowski legend. Some eventually ended up staying long enough to watch him become drunk, occasionally challenging him to a fight. Among the writers who knew him, the subject of his drunkenness came up often in the conversation. Drunk, sober, or hung over, Hank also enjoyed talking about literature, even as he protested. He had never completely shaken off the early excitement over the sheer bigness of his early heroes.

"Fame is the biggest whore of all," he often told his friends, joking about the increased attention he received, not only from the small presses, but from the popular underground media. Much earlier than the late sixties, he wrote a poem entitled "love & fame & death," which begins: "it sits outside my window now / like an old woman / going to market . . ." But despite his misgivings, Hank felt excited by the ever-increasing attention focused on him. The notoriety and fanfare that the *Open City, Nola Express*, and *Free Press* columns brought were one thing, but coupled with the editions brought out by Black Sparrow Press, he knew that his dream of financial independence might not be far off.

He stated categorically that he did not feel a part of the underground, even as he became one of its heroes. But like Henry Miller, he took the position that war signified total madness and that he would not be a part of it. He went even further, saying, "I am neither for war or against war. It's too easy to take sides. I just deal with what is directly before me."

A visit to Disneyland would not entice Hank. When I suggested we go there together he told me I was insane. "I'd rather sit in an emergency room." When I mentioned Busch Gardens, however, just over the Hollywood Hills from L.A. proper, he was ready. You paid your admission which gave free access to several beer pavilions spread out over the complex, and enjoyed a stroll through gardens, sprawling lawns, animal acts, a variety show, amusement rides, picturesque ponds, and the like. There was also a brewery tour to see how the Anhauser-Busch Company brewed their magic elixir.

We drove out there one Sunday afternoon, paid for our tickets and headed straight for the first pavilion. To our delight, you were allowed two beers each. We drank our limit and went to find the next pavilion. Somehow we ended up at a bird show. Four cockatoos were performing with two trainers. We stayed for part of the show, vaguely amused, but in need of more beer. Leaving the amphitheater we found another pavilion, had two more beers and then headed back to the first one. "You go first," I said. "Take off your jacket. Go up to a new server." I figured that they wouldn't be able to tell we had our turn already and we'd be able to get another round and drink on into the night.

Hank went inside and stood in line for his beer. He held his jacket on his arm and managed to find a different server. I followed behind. Soon enough we were sitting on a verandah looking down at orderly rows of roses with beers in our hands. The roses were red, yellow, and pink. People strolled among them, enjoying themselves. We heard a parrot screech in the distance. "I love this," Hank said. "If you'd just get rid of the gardens and the people, it would be a wonderful place."

We went up for our second beer. Everything was working like magic. We moved on to another pavilion, for variety's sake, wandering past a bamboo grove, a children's zoo and some amusement rides. Soon we came to a new beer pavilion, satisfying our thirst, and bought an order of pretzels. The gardens were becoming increasingly crowded, but we managed to find the fourth, and final pavilion, which featured Michelob beer, my favorite at the time. Here we dropped all pretense and just kept coming back for more beer. No one seemed to mind. By five P.M. we were thoroughly soused.

Although the park was not going to be open much longer, we decided to rush back to the second pavilion. We were able to drink four more cups of beer each, so cold, so foamy.

Halfway through the last round a smooth-faced security guard in full military regalia approached us. He inquired as to how much drinking we'd been doing. "Just the normal amount," I said. "Nothing more."

"I had a report about two guys fitting your description."

"Wrong guys," I told him.

"Well, this is a family park. I don't think I got the description of this guy wrong," he responded, pointing to Hank.

"Listen, my son and I were just out for a good time," Hank interrupted. "My face may look like the roadmap of hell . . ."

The guard withered. "I'm sorry, sir. There must have been a mistake." And with that the guard walked away.

We left this pavilion for another across the park, where we continued drinking. By this time we were both smashed. We walked outside and wandered. When we reached the small peninsula of bamboo that jutted out into a pond, Hank lay down and stretched himself out amidst the ornamental leaves. I followed suit. We must have lain there for a good hour when suddenly the same guard who had questioned us earlier showed up accompanied by two more guards.

He gently nudged me. I opened my eyes. "Yeah?"

"You guys have to go."

"What the hell . . ." Hank said, getting up, brushing his pants.

"You two lied to me back there . . .We want you out of the park, now."

As if to encourage us, a monstrous guard, probably the granddaddy of them all, grabbed Hank's arm. "Don't touch me, mother fucker," Hank barked. The man let go.

I explained that we'd be happy to oblige, but that we hadn't broken any rules.

"We haven't even taken the brewery tour," Hank added, coyly. "Besides, I could use more beer."

Not amused, the guards walked us to the front gate. People were staring, wondering what crime we had committed. We wondered too as we left Busch Gardens under escort. Hank swore that he'd return, which he and I did a month later. We were more restrained the second time, and afterwards stopped off at a beer bar in North Hollywood to get our fill. It was Happy Hour and beer was only 25 cents a glass.

By 1969, Hank and Lawrence Ferlinghetti were exchanging letters. Ferlinghetti, famous as Beat poet and a major voice of the San Francisco poetry renaissance of the late fifties, earned equal fame as the publisher of Allen Ginsberg's *Howl and Other Poems* under the City Lights imprint. Ferlinghetti began taking notice of Bukowski in the mid-sixties, mostly from poems and short fiction he saw in the little magazines. In a letter to Ferlinghetti in the fall of 1969 Hank begins with a graphic description of his ever-growing myth:

> Well, here it is one a.m. and I am sitting here in my shorts with the usual cheap cigar and beer—something very bad on the radio—and my head hurts, let me finish off this bottle—THERE!—christ, yes, that's better. Now let me get another one.
> . .

He goes on to discuss the differences he sees between the little literary magazines and the more established ones with typical Bukowskian cynical aplomb. What he tells Ferlinghetti is a part of his standard repertoire in condensed form, wherein he attacks the entire literary scene, leaving carnage behind him as his rhetoric fells all the fortresses of entrenched literary success. He wrote:

> Frankly, the littles are more disgusting than the bigs, because even tho they both publish SHIT, at least the bigs conduct themselves in a business manner. And by a business-manner, I mean something about MOTION, about the calendar, about getting it DONE, for christ's sake. Too many children playing with littles while having big Romantic ideas and fading like cocksuckers at a lesbian's ball. All right.

What prompted him to mention the magazine scene was his own preoccupation with *Laugh Literary and Man the Humping Guns*, the poetry journal he and I began in February 1969. It had been planned as a major new literary journal. Financial considerations, however, trimmed us down to a thirty-two-page stapled magazine done on twenty-pound paper in a photo-offset edition. Bukowski originally thought he had a backer on the line, someone he had known in high school. He wanted to call the journal "The Contemporary Review: A Non-Snob Journal of Active Creativity Now." When I protested, telling him that the title fit neither his wildness nor my own sensibility, he told me to go home and wait until he came up with something better—and I did, hoping I might beat him to it. Three days went by. Late one evening, the phone rang. "This is Hank," he said imperiously "Now, I've got it. You ready?" I said, "Yeah, man. Go on." He answered, "*Laugh Literary and Man the Humping Guns*,' published by the Hatchetman Press." I agreed.

He explained that the title was his way of laughing at the staid literary world and of bringing humor into the scene. "We've got to laugh at ourselves," he said, "and we have to not take ourselves too damn seriously. Maybe the title will reach people that way."

We collected poems for the first issue. Even before we had enough poems, however, we argued over the cover, though we both agreed that we wanted something dramatic. "To shake 'em all up a little," I said. "No, to make them angry and bring the enemy crawling out of their comfortable little closets," Hank retorted. I wanted a photograph of us, along with a few nasty comments about our enemies, real or imaginary. Hank wanted words, his words, and so he sat down and wrote by hand on a piece of typing paper: IN DISGUST WITH POETRY CHICAGO, WITH THE DULL DUMPLING PATTY CAKE SAFE CREELEYS, OL-SONS, DICKEYS, MERWINS, NEMEROVS AND MEREDITHS—THIS IS ISSUE ONE OF VOLUME ONE OF LAUGH LITERARY AND MAN THE HUMPING GUNS. He signed his name at the bottom, figuring that to be quite a brave gesture.

Hank had thrown a rather diverse group of poets together in his handwritten condemnation. Robert Creeley and Charles Olson—

both associated with the Black Mountain School, and later, with the new American poetry that emerged in the post-World War II era—had broken from tradition, each in his own way, and both were considered major innovators by the Beats. In the Bukowski pantheon, however, they were all too conscious of their trailblazing and therefore contrived. He stated that Creeley's poems were nothing more than a rehash of the English love poem, and that he played it safe. Olson he looked upon as a bombastic figure, too often caught up in rhetoric that didn't go anywhere. As for the remaining poets on his list, he categorized them as dull and tedious crowd–pleasers, hemmed in by academic concerns, creating artifice at the expense of art. He wrote of Robert Creeley in a letter to Harold Norse back in 1966 complaining that "Creeley doesn't fuck, he makes love." He told Norse that the poet had tried to become one of the boys by writing a poem about watching a woman pee in a sink.

There is hardly a poet who isn't tinged with parochialism. Obviously, Bukowski himself didn't remain immune. He had written enough poems on the subject of poetry to fill at least two fat volumes, most of which blast academic poets and what he calls the "quick and modern poem-makers." In a poem with that phrase in the title, he wrote:

> it is quite easy to appear modern
> while in reality being the biggest damn fool
> > ever born;
> I know: I have gotten away with some awful stuff
> but not nearly such awfulpot as I read in the journals;
> I have an honesty self-born of whores and hospitals
> that will not allow me to pretend to be
> something which I am not—...

As an editor he knew what he wanted in a poem. His faith in spontaneous poetics and his own sense of what seemed contrived or real remained steadfast. He had developed an instinctive sense of line and breath in the midfifties, and it remained intact—the well from which he drew for guidance. I thought that his choices were too close to home, too imitative of his own style. Recognizing this, he did make a not-too-successful attempt to stay clear of his imitators.

"You know, I'm wondering what kind of heat we'll get for my cover?" he confided. "Maybe they'll write back to us—some of the people we attacked—and we could print responses." I nodded in agreement. None responded, though—instead, we were flooded with submissions from all over the country and from Europe.

In addition to Bukowski, poets in *Laugh Literary* included John Thomas, T. L. Kryss, Douglas Blazek, Jerome Rothenberg, Jack Micheline (a Beat poet from the Bronx, New York, who had written "Streetcall New Orleans"), Don Cauble, Harold Norse, and S. S. Veri, the pen name of Frances Smith. The contributors list represented a mixture of people in Bukowski's orbit and some who had sent poems to us randomly, as well as a few I had come across independently. Norse, who acted as our contributing editor, brought us poems from Sinclair Beiles, a poet living in Greece at the time. In a letter to me discussing the editorial business of the magazine, Bukowski wrote, "I am busting my ass reading this garbage that's coming in and sending it back. It takes hours and there are more submissions each day."

One night, while editing the first issue, Hank called to tell me that he had found a young genius, a poet who lived in the San Fernando Valley and came to some of the local literary gatherings. I remembered him as a bad poet, prone to misplaced surrealist imagery, a poetry without focus, wandering nowhere. It was two A.M., and I pleaded Bukowski, "Can't this wait until tomorrow?" He protested, saying I had to come over to his place right away. I gave in, and drove down Santa Monica Boulevard, taking a right on Normandie until I came to De Longpre. I parked in front of Hank's court, knocked, and went inside. "Grab a beer, kid," Hank said as he gestured toward the anxious young poet, who sat in an overstuffed chair underneath his "Outsider of the Year" plaque from Loujon Press. I got a beer from the refrigerator in the small, messy kitchen and came back into the living room. Hank sat next to his radio with a smug and self-satisfied air. He handed me a sheaf of the poems by the new literary genius, who, like so many visitors, ended up drinking through the night. I took them and tried to avoid the young poet's eyes. Slowly I read. After twenty or so poems, I handed the stack back to Hank. He sat on the edge of his chair, wondering what my response would be. The young poet barely breathed. His eyes were wide open. I said, "Hank, take another look at these."

He obliged and read through the entire manuscript, finally looking up at the young poet, then at me. "Jesus Christ. Neeli is right. These poems are terrible." Just then a ray of sunlight streamed into the room and formed a near perfect halo around Hank's head. The young poet rose violently from his chair and screamed: *"Neeli ruined it! Bukowski loved my poems . . . He ruined it for me . . ."* He grabbed his manuscript, a life's work, and ran out the door, all the while threatening to write an article exposing how Neeli Cherry, as I was known then, secretly controlled the great Charles Bukowski.

Another time, Hank and I were reading a stack of poems from various writers when a demon seemed to take possession of the room. The result was that we began crumpling up manuscripts and writing mean-spirited rejection notes, such as, "Sorry, baby, but these won't do," or "We couldn't publish this crap if our lives depended on it." In the midst of this madness, Hank went into the kitchen, broke an egg into a dish, and dipped manuscripts into it, letting the egg dry. We then spilled beer on a few submissions. We took the entire batch to the post office—living up to our press's name: Hatchetman Press.

For the second issue of our poetry journal, which we brought out in December 1969, I did the cover, writing with a large black marking pen: "LAUGH LITERARY AND MAN THE HUMPING GUNS, this is issue #2, volume 1 DIRTY POEMS FOR YOUR SUICIDE LIVES." At the bottom, we each signed our names. Our contributing editors were now Norse and Steve Richmond. We included poems by Norse from his European sojourns, several local poets, and a poem Bukowski and I wrote together under the name Simpson Freyer. He wrote a few lines, then I added some, and then Bukowski again. The Freyer poem began:

call the police
call the mice
call the f b i
call hours of the sleeping whores
call mercy
call mama . . .

. . .

tell me about black men
tell me about mongolian idiots
tell me about the gas company—. . .

Our final issue appeared in February 1971, by which time, we had both gone on to other things. Bukowski's preoccupation with earning a living as a writer didn't afford him the luxury of keeping the magazine afloat, and we had argued mercilessly over the magazine's production. Yet, this last issue had some interesting entries, including a story by Bukowski about the day he knocked out Ernest Hemingway. The cover for this issue was of Bukowski and I with an eighty-five-year-old window-washer who happened to be walking by as we posed for our picture in front of Hank's apartment.

The summer of 1968 Hank and I were going to a party at the home of Norman Taylor, known as Crazy Jack in Bukowski's stories. He was a painter who made pen and ink drawings on biblical subjects, urban American life, and from his own surreal mindscape. The house was perched on a hillside in Silverlake. For the previous two days we had been on a continuous drunk, buying six-pack after six-pack and making runs for greasy chicken-to-go on Hollywood Boulevard. Mary, Norman's girl friend, had called to invite us over. "It's a celebration for Jack's drawings," she said. "Everyone will be there." For Mary, everyone meant an assortment of hippies, addicts, and small-time hustlers. But I loved her and I loved Norman's drawings.

Hank continued drinking on the way over, but somehow seemed perfectly sober. "Kid, I hope these people don't bore me," he said.

"You like Mary."

"I know, and Crazy Jack is wild enough. It's the others that worry me. I'm not much with crowds."

"Unless you're the center of attention."

"You have a point there."

We started up the steps on the narrow sidewalk leading to the house, when we were called over by a man working in his garden, separated from us by a white picket fence. He turned the earth with a tiny spade and had done a neat planting, a flotilla of petunias.

"I'm all alone," the gardener suddenly blurted out. "That's right. There's nobody left."

He was balding, with a large indentation running across his forehead. His eyes were pale brown, his lips thin. Something about his face did not inspire confidence.

"What the hell," Hank said. "Why are you alone?"

"My parents died. Now there's just me. All alone in this house. All alone in the world. Where are you guys going?"

"A friend is having a party up the street," I said.

"Can I come, too?"

Immediately, Hank chimed, "Yes."

"Hold on a minute." The man dropped his spade and ran in the front door of his house. A moment later he reappeared with a tattered coat and his hair haphazardly slicked back.

"Thanks for letting me come along. I don't get to talk to many people. I get so lonely."

A few minutes later we were at Norman and Mary's door. Mary, an exuberant, dark-haired woman with large brown eyes, greeted me with a hug, then turned to Hank. "Mary, baby," he roared, handing her the six-pack we had brought along.

Our lonesome guest shook her hand and walked inside. He sat on the sofa between two beaded hippies. Bukowski and Crazy Jack were huddled in a corner with the poet Marv Conners, and Mary. I went into the kitchen to forage through the refrigerator.

Somehow the conversation got around to the Vietnam War. Mary thought it was all madness and that nobody should take sides. Norman, high on pot, began chanting, "Ho, Ho, Ho Chi Minh, the

Vietcong are gonna win . . ." As the talk went on, the tempo began to shift. Mary believed that the United States had no business in Vietnam. Others agreed. Hank cut in with "who gives a sacred fuck," and I said we would earn the hatred of the Vietnamese people. It was about then that our lonely sap from down the block sprang up from the sofa and announced that he had killed ten men back in the days of the Korean War.

"So what?" Hank said.

"So I could kill more if I had to," he said.

"That's sick," somebody shouted.

"Yeah!" Norman agreed as he threw some of his drawings onto the coffee table.

The lonely man suddenly ran toward the door, turned, and pulled out a gun that he waved back and forth. "Okay, now, listen up. I am a killer. It really doesn't matter to me who I kill or where."

I tried moving slowly toward the kitchen, hoping to escape out the back door and go for help. But he caught me in his eye and motioned me back to where I had been standing. "Don't nobody try anything," he warned.

"Yeah? Who the hell do you think you are?" Hank retorted.

He ignored Hank and addressed us all, "You people never been on a battlefield. You don't know what killing is all about."

Hank prodded, "I don't think you're man enough to pull the trigger."

"Oh yeah?"

"Yeah," said Bukowski as he walked up to the madman, stuck his belly into the gun barrel and challenged him to shoot.

"Go on, baby. I'm ready to die. Shoot," Hank taunted.

The man suddenly began to cry as Hank reached out and took the gun away. After emptying the bullets, he handed the revolver back and told him to leave. But the man pleaded to be allowed to stay at the party. "I was just kidding. I promise I'll be good. I didn't mean nothing bad."

"You could have killed someone," Mary shouted. "Get out of my house."

I opened the front door and watched as he walked dejected down the hillside to his place. Hank rejoined the party.

Later, back at his apartment, I asked Hank why he had confronted the man, wanting to know if he had been frightened.

"Hell yes," he answered. "I was scared . . . but I had the guy psyched out. He wasn't going to shoot anybody. It was all bluff. I saw it from the beginning. He was just a lonely heart trying to put some excitement into his life."

In 1969 Bukowski was included in the Penguin Modern Poets series. The series had gained a wide readership, not only because of Penguin's worldwide distribution network, but because it published three poets together in a single volume, most of whom already had their own loyal followings. Ginsberg, Ferlinghetti, and Corso were in the series, as were other American poets, and many from England. Bukowski appeared with Harold Norse and the San Francisco surrealist poet Philip Lamantia, a writer closely identified both with the Beats and the San Francisco poetry renaissance. Bukowski's selections came from his Loujon Press books, along with a short biographical note.

The project began when the new Penguin poetry editor, Nikos Stangos, approached Norse with the idea of doing a single volume of Norse's poetry. Norse was shocked, telling Stangos, "I thought only T. S. Eliot, W H. Auden, and Ezra Pound got single volumes from publishing houses like Penguin." Stangos responded that he wanted to bring newer poets into print, to modernize the Penguin outlook. Norse asked how many copies such a book would sell. The editor said about three thousand to four thousand copies. Then Norse inquired about the Penguin Modern Poets series. Stangos said that those volumes sold ten thousand or more. Figuring it would be much better to be in the series, Norse told Stangos he had two other poets in mind: Charles Bukowski and Philip Lamantia. Stangos didn't know Bukowski's poems, so Norse lent him copies of *It Catches My Heart in Its Hands* and *Crucifix in a Deathhand*. Stangos read the books and told Norse that he was right, Bukowski had a rare gift.

Meanwhile, Hank tried to keep in close touch with Frances, who wrote often but never stayed in one place for very long. In 1968 Frances and Marina lived for a few months in San Francisco with Frances's oldest daughter, Patty, on Potrero Hill, a neighborhood of old Victorian houses overlooking the warehouse district of the city. Marina attended kindergarten there with her mother's grandson. At first this seemed like an ideal situation. But Frances grew restless and decided to move back to Los Angeles. Bukowski welcomed the news that Marina would soon be close to him again.

Frances stayed in Mar Vista for a few months, but soon left for a commune in New Mexico, called New Buffalo, near the town of Rio Hondo. Hank expressed strong disapproval: he wanted his daughter to settle in one place, and *not* one where the inhabitants espoused some ideology. He spoke to his friends disdainfully about Frances and her hippie commune in the Southwest.

As life at New Buffalo became next to impossible to bear in the harsh winter months, Frances moved to Placitas, New Mexico. She cooked beans every day in a big pot for the people living with her in a large house. Her small monthly check fed a whole group of people until her money was stolen, presumably by one of the residents. She went back East to visit her family, where a birthday party was held for Marina. Frances kept in close touch with Bukowski no matter where she lived, assuring him of his daughter's good health and general well-being.

Early in 1969 mother and daughter moved to the Silverlake area of Los Angeles and then back to Mar Vista. Marina, at age six, didn't attend school during the 1969–70 year, a decision Frances made largely on her own. Bukowski's spoken preference was that his daughter should not attend school, but he didn't know of any practical alternative. A few years earlier he had written a cartoon for *Open City* in which he advised Marina never to go to the university. In his discussions with Frances, however, he did say he wanted her to eventually go back to school to receive at least a primary education.

The following year Frances and Marina lived in Garden Grove with Frances's mother, a move made out of financial necessity. Once there, she sent Marina back to school.

Once settled in the Los Angeles area, Marina would go over to her father's apartment once a week. He picked her up after school, never failing to be on time no matter how bad his hangovers were. Marina recalls, "He respected the way other people were unpredictable, but he was always on time . . . And he was really there. He would come and talk to me and we would go to eat somewhere, maybe down by the beach. He talked to me about life, even though I was just a little kid. He didn't hide things from me."

Hank was relieved when Marina began to stay put in Santa Monica. As she grew older and participated in school plays and other productions, he came and sat in the audience. Marina had no idea then that he felt anything less than comfortable milling around with stalwart PTA types and the local Santa Monica gentry.

She had a sense that her father was different than the other fathers she knew: "Being a child brought up completely as an outsider, I felt that we had something special that everyone else was missing out on . . ." Not so many kids came from divorced families back then, and this, in and of itself, made her feel different. At one point she consciously asked herself whether or not she would have been better off with a father who went off to work every morning in a business suit, with a briefcase in his hand. "I really thought about it. I just didn't say I wanted a father like Hank out of loyalty. But I saw my father as a person, a friend, not just my father, not merely someone in a father's role."

TEN

I N the closing days of the sixties, Hank continued to work at the post office and to battle against its arcane system of rules and regulations. He found it increasingly difficult to be stoical about the daily foibles at the Terminal Annex—among them, his co-workers' animosity toward him, and the write-ups he got for minor infractions of postal rules. His bosses put the pressure on hard, wanting to run him out of there. Once, for instance, a particularly spiteful supervisor saw him standing near an open window. He approached Hank and said very sternly, "You're not allowed to open that window!"

"I was just standing here. I didn't open it."

"You must have opened it because you're here."

He didn't even answer the bespectacled, tight-lipped supervisor, who suddenly began screaming. Instead of fighting back or lobbing one of his well-hewn rejoinders, Hank remained silent. The supervisor finally turned around and went back to his post.

Aside from pressure brought on him by his superiors, there were the grueling hours and squabbling with his fellow clerks. One night he decided he could not take the sniping any longer. Everyone kept verbally knifing one another unrelentingly. So Hank asked the entire mail-sorting room to stop what they were doing. He had something to say to them. He began, "Look, we have a hell of a job, we've got to work very hard, with supervisors on our ass all the time. We attack each other. We tear the shit out of each other. We're always thinking of nasty things to say to each other. The job is hell. We're making it a worse hell." Then one of the guys said, "Hank, can I say something?" Hank said, "Sure." He said that among all the people in the mail room who attacked one another, Hank had the sharpest and most vicious tongue of all. When the man finished speaking, Hank returned to his position and said no more, realizing that his detractor had spoken the truth.

He had an ongoing battle between himself and one of his black co-workers. "This one individual always attacked me. Always jumped on me. It's habitual. You learn how to do it and you can't let go. It wears you to pieces. I had to survive, being one of the few whites . . . So, this guy said to me, 'Your grandparents made slaves of my grandparents.' I said, 'My grandparents didn't have any slaves. They were in Germany. They didn't have slaves there. What are you talking about, motherfucker?' He said, 'Hey, listen. I guess you wouldn't invite me to your house? Right, Hank?' I said, 'Sure. You can come over anytime, Leroy.' 'Well, I'd come in the back door so the neighbors won't see me. I'll have a white chick with me.' I answered, 'Good. When you arrive I'll be sitting on the couch with a fifth of whiskey and I'll have a black chick on my lap. Okay, baby?' This would go on all night. Sticking mail and fighting. Just trying to kill one another off—white, black, young, old."

One incident impressed Hank with just how far people allow themselves to be turned into obedient, uncomplaining cogs in the machinery of their jobs. He turned to a fellow postal clerk while sorting mail at the Terminal Annex and asked, "Don't you sometimes feel like dumping all the mail on the floor and just running down the halls screaming?" The guy looked at him with dulled eyes and said, "No. I've never felt that way." Having answered he turned back dutifully to his job. For Bukowski, the writing made the suffering of twelve and a half years on the job bearable. He believed that without the writing during those years, he might have robbed a bank or killed somebody.

Partially because they saw it as a way for Hank to earn enough money that might hasten his liberation from the post office, friends convinced him to give his first poetry reading in the spring of 1969. Having no appreciation for the oral tradition, his reluctance to enter that arena was understandable. Once he took the plunge he recited his poems as if he had always been doing it. He didn't look forward to the event with much enthusiasm. The reading was held at the Bridge, a gallery performance space on Sunset Boulevard run by a German named Peter, with help from his girlfriend, Bonnie White, a black folksinger-poet. There were books for sale, candles, paintings, and pottery. The Bridge reading series featured Harold Norse, John Thomas, and other local poets. It usually attracted thirty or forty people. For several days before the event, word spread that Hank was scheduled to read his poems, and more than three hundred people showed up.

As Hank walked from the parking lot of the market, across from the Bridge, he railed on and on against "those half-assed idiots who attend poetry readings . . . lonely hearts . . . people with nothing else to do." Inside, many of the recognizable L.A. poets were talking to one another, anticipating a wild evening. Hank stood at the precipice. He swaggered in front of the crowd in the hall, ready for anything. Before reading, he made a few comments designed to provoke the crowd. A long-haired biker shouted, "Cut the bullshit!" John Thomas, massive and bearded, sat menacingly, as if ready to jump into action if the need presented itself.

When the crowd quieted down, Hank cleared his throat and took a long swig of beer. "Okay. Let's begin this thing," he said. His cool, methodical, resonant voice filled the room. He had command, and remained in control throughout the long reading, never missing a beat. In the audience were a few hardened writers, many hippies, starry-eyed before the booze-inundated guru, and a few professors from the local colleges. He read many of the poems that evening right off the galleys for *The Days Run Away Like Wild Horses Over the Hills*.

Every once in a while, Hank paused for a drink. He called out to John Thomas for moral support, and then kept on reading. Many of the poems were familiar to his fans, while others were just off the typewriter, machine-gunned onto paper. "Okay, here goes . . .Watch it ..." Hank said as he began one of the poems from the Loujon Press days. After the reading, he didn't hide his elation. "Well, what the fuck. The gods have been good to me. I can do no wrong." He spoke this way on the drive back to his apartment, but then began complaining about not having a woman. A few hours later, he thought back on the reading, reviewing how difficult it had been to stand before people who meant nothing to him. He reasoned that doing public readings could turn into a profitable enterprise, however, one that would help him stay afloat financially. The crowd was such that many people were turned away. The following night Hank gave a second reading at the Bridge before an equally large crowd.

Hank and I visited Harold Norse at the Venice Beach apartment he shared with his mother. We were received in a large room filled with evidence of the expatriate poet's years of travels. There were stacks of books, wall hangings, and art work. I sensed that Hank liked having a contemporary to talk with, someone who represented a tradition much different from his, a man who had known W H. Auden and been a part of the academic New York poetry scene of the 40s and 50s, but who had ultimately thrown his lot in with the poets of the common language. Hank whispered, when Norse stepped out of the room, "Christ . . . think of it . . . He knew William Carlos Williams and Tennessee Williams."

The time with Norse had gone particularly well, although I had this underlying feeling that something was bothering Hank. Essex House, a North Hollywood press specializing in pornographic books, had just released a collection of Bukowski's *Open City* stories, *Notes of a Dirty Old Man*. It didn't take long for the twenty thousand copies printed to completely disappear from bookstore racks. This success resulted from Hank's exposure in the L.A. underground newspapers and helped enhance his status as a cult figure.

Taken as a whole, the stories underscore how Bukowski shadowboxes on the edge of despair, among ludicrous people and even more ludicrous situations, yet emerges in full control of himself, even when he portrays himself as a loser. Bukowski makes formidable icons out of the most ordinary situations, flooding them with passion and humor. It is L.A. street news delivered with hard and fast punches, delving into the superficiality of our culture, the flat and boxed-in mentality of the people he sees around him, and his own sense of apartness. He doesn't look for a connection point to some vast world-soul. With a leanness like that of Hemingway's in *The Sun Also Rises*, and the gutsiness and instinctual sense of unadorned human speech of Nelson Algren's writings, Bukowski tells his stories.

Still, this night Hank seemed out of sorts. His voice had a dark edge to it, and he had made a few openly sarcastic comments on the L. A. literary scene—not so strange for him—but more acerbic than usual. As we left Norse's, Hank mentioned the dismal atmosphere of Venice Beach. Norse's building surrounded a huge, squalid courtyard. You had to cross over from an elevator in the middle of the court on a narrow ramp leading to a balcony. Harold's place was on the third floor. "This is like a prison," Hank said. When we were on the street and heading toward my car, parked two blocks away, he was unusually somber. "I'm so tired of literary talk . . . give me a bookie at the track or a half drunk bum on the Row," he groaned. We walked along in silence after that. I felt awkward; Hank radiated nothing but bad vibes. Unable to restrain myself, I asked what was wrong. "Did Harold or I say something that bothered you?"

"Leave it alone."

Generally, when we left Norse's, Hank would be amused by the conversation, invariably finding something funny to talk about. Now, he grew more and more withdrawn.

As we approached my car, he said that he was tired of people, tired of the writer's life. "In fact, I'm tired of you."

I started off along the speedway, turning toward Lincoln Boulevard and the entrance to the Santa Monica Freeway. It had rained earlier, kicking up a cool breeze. I had the window halfway down. Hank reached for a half pint of whiskey that had been hidden in his coat pocket. He hauled it out and uncapped the bottle. I knew then that trouble lay ahead. The last time I had been with him when he drank hard liquor he had vomited on the sidewalk and smashed his hand into the door of his car before running off into the night. When he called the following evening, he wondered if he had been rolled because he couldn't find his wallet.

I asked him why he had kept the whiskey hidden. His response was to take a nip and tell me I couldn't have any.

"Why are you drinking whiskey?" I asked. "You know it's safer with beer."

"I'm drinking because I'm Bukowski . . . because I've been feeling bad lately . . . because you mothers depress me . . . Norse, John Thomas, Neeli Cherry, this one, that one . . . Boyer May, Frederick Franklyn, Cardona-Hine, Jory Sherman, Peter, Bonnie . . . Jesus, what a ball-breaking mess."

"Is that all?"

"It's enough."

Maybe so, but he said it with bitterness, not in his usual high-spirited manner tempered with that slow Bogart drag of a voice. When we reached the junction where the Santa Monica intersects the San Diego Freeway, he instructed me to head north. I obliged, knowing it was only nine P.M. or so, and our evenings usually went into the early hours.

"Where are we heading?"

He thought for a moment. "Maybe downtown. . . not home, not yet anyway." Then his eyes widened as he turned to face me. He said, "To the rich people and the co-eds . . . the comfortable people with their murderous eyes and well-pressed clothing . . .Westwood Village." The area is a business district adjacent to the campus of the University of California, a haven for the students, faculty of the university, and the well-to-do of West Los Angeles. There were trendy movie theaters, bookstores, fashionable shops of every kind, and plenty of restaurants and cafes. The sidewalks were kept clean and the people had an optimism and sense of good health rarely seen in other parts of Los Angeles. The Dirty Old Man of East Hollywood wanted to sing his song of darkness to the bright-eyed college kids, the professors and their families, and anyone else roaming the Westside night of Los Angeles. We were driving from poverty and degradation, from the slow murder of us all, to an enclave of the upper crust, the ones who had already 'made it.' I felt unsure of myself. Perhaps there were demons that could only be expunged by hard liquor and the lights of Westwood. Whatever it was, I remember vividly how his face took on an ever more tortured expression. The tough mask that he wore. As though to prove it, he guzzled from the bottle, letting much of the liquor pour onto his shirt.

"Go easy," I warned.

"It's all shit, don't you realize that? The whole edifice is made out of shit. I see night everywhere . . . a dropping off into the void . . . ruins . . . people in towers deciding who shall live and who shall die . . . presidents who lie and kill . . . soldiers who drop off into nothingness . . . my heroes are madmen pacing back and forth in their cells . . . I'm nothing . . . less then nothing."

What I took note of was the change in tone. I had rarely heard Hank like that before. His voice had grown deeper, sadder, firmly set in despair. Maybe I'd glimpsed it before, but never with such intensity. I didn't know what to say and so I said nothing.

I continued on, trying to come up with a comic routine, or even a literary anecdote. Nothing. Even as I fought for control, I knew I didn't have it. The Old Man was in the driver's seat.

"You're all sniveling bastards. I didn't get into this writing thing to know other writers . . . everyone's jealous . . . Bukowski knifed me . . . Bukowski sucked Martin's ass . . . Bukowski talked behind my back . . . he can't write anymore." I began to feel defensive. Still, I knew it would not help matters. He'd sneered at us all before, but when he was lonely or had the blues he didn't hesitate to call one of us.

"Darkness reigns . . . the exits are blocked."

There was an ever more menacing timbre to his words. "Some times I feel like taking a razor to my throat . . ." That gave me the chills. It hardly seemed play-acting the way he said it.

I swung off the freeway exit and made my way to Westwood Village, where he wanted to play out his tragedy. Why he wanted to be there, I didn't know, but I was willing to help him play out his wishes.

"Park the car and get the hell out of my sight. I don't want to see any of you. I'm worthless, more worthless than you or any of them. The game is over. It's all over. The writing. The poems. The stories. Open City. Hippyland. Timothy Leary." My God, I thought, he's composing a poem.

We parked behind an ice cream parlor filled with happy looking faces, mostly young, mostly well-to-do judging by their clothing. Hank walked inside, but not before finishing his bottle of whiskey, which he threw against the wall of an adjacent building. As he entered, I followed. "Listen, man, I told you to get the hell out of my sight," he barked. I hesitated a moment, thinking of fighting back. Not wanting a scene, I turned around, walked out of the door onto the back lot, then found a window where I could look inside. Hank made his way slowly to the front of the parlor, stopping every now and then to wave at people and talking to them as they sat at fancy little tables with their cones, sundaes, and glass goblets of ice cream. I couldn't hear what he said, but judging from the reactions, it wasn't very nice. In fact, two football jocks were heading toward him. Hank hastily fled toward the front door. Instinctively, I ran into the parlor, shouting, "My friend is drunk! He's not himself!" The two jocks backed down. I passed them and followed Hank outside. There were people milling about everywhere. Hank, however, had disappeared from sight. I scanned the avenue, then passed a woman's clothing shop, a record store. I thought I saw Hank, so I called out. I was mistaken and continued my search, growing increasingly frantic. It was one thing to soliloquize in the car, and quite another matter to rant on Westwood Boulevard. This was not friendly territory, though I felt sure that plenty of Bukowski fans were wandering these very streets.

Then I caught sight of him, unmistakable this time. Charles Bukowski. Hank. The Dirty Old Man. Author of "The Genius of the Crowd." The title referring not to himself, but to the actual genius for hatred that a crowd can possess. He stood at the center of a group of movie-goers, mouths ajar. He shouted obscenities. Then he unzipped his trousers and glancing my way, he smirked and exposed himself to the evening's passers by. He danced, singing an old-time ditty, a sort of delicate ritual, almost elegant in its contempt, then he cursed everyone in sight with a volley of vulgarities. "Hank, please, stop . . .You'll get arrested." He wouldn't listen. I was part of the crowd, nothing more. It was of the crowd I began to think . . .wondering if they would react in some collective way, some violent way. Remembering Hank's poem, I thought of his line, "they will kill you in the end." What I did see were horrified and outraged faces, but not the face of a mob. These people simply wanted him to go away.

I fought my way through the milling mass of strollers, clearing a path for myself, and watched as Hank darted into the traffic. I crossed over as well, hoping to waylay him on the other side of the street.

As he stepped onto the sidewalk, nearly swiped by a taxi cab, I ran up beside him. He dodged. I panicked. This was my friend and he seemed determined to either get arrested or beaten up on the streets of Westwood Village. Hank had metamorphosed into one of his outrageous characters. I blamed the alcohol, and cursed myself for not having taken it from him.

Embarrassed, I turned away. A man with a bulldog face glowered, pointing to Hank. "Get the hell out of here or I'll call the cops on you!"

"You are the scum of creation," Hank shouted to everyone within earshot, and there were plenty of people, lured onto the streets by the balmy summer air.

"I'm the immortal writer Charles Bukowski," Hank yelled. "Greater than Hemingway . . ."

The crowd grew threatening. Mothers covered the eyes of their children. Coeds held onto their boyfriend's arms. I looked around to see if any police were in evidence. Just as I did people began to call for them. Hank, sensing danger, zipped up, but continued yelling wildly. I worked my way through the crowd, which had now surrounded him and grabbed hold of his arm. At last, he let me lead him away. People parted so that we could pass. They didn't necessarily want the law; they just wanted this crazy man out of their sight.

Hank said nothing. We got into the car and I drove away. For a good ten minutes he remained silent, but as we progressed well down the Santa Monica Freeway, he became talkative once more, only this time his voice was stranger then earlier. He touched on many subjects and people, as if his mind were unspooling and thoughts and images were tumbling out. It was much the same as before, the same expletives. He said Norse and I appeared so ridiculous in Venice . . . we were so convinced of our opinions . . . so literary . . . and so phony . . . and the same was true of the whole L.A. poetry community. "I like the track because people are more honest there . . .you feel their greed . . . the ones who want to lose and the ones who want to win . . ." Then he went silent again, all the way to De Longpre Street. When we arrived at his place, I parked and stepped out of the car along with Hank. A warm, gentle breeze had kicked in. I looked up at the dark outline of a palm tree, wondering if Hank wanted me to come into his place. I hoped so. After so much excitement, I didn't want to be alone.

He said, "Go home, man. There's no use coming in. I want to be by myself."

"Do you realize what happened in Westwood?"

"I don't remember a thing . . . but I want you to go. Please. I'll see you another time." He disappeared onto his porch, behind the banana leaves and I drove to my own place on Alta Vista.

Worn out, I fell asleep quickly. I must have been asleep for two or three hours when the phone rang. Groggily, I fumbled for the receiver, knowing full well who'd be on the other end of the line.

"It's me . . . let's admit it, kid, I can't drink hard liquor without going nuts. What the hell happened out there?"

"Listen, Hank," I said. "You exposed yourself before a crowd of Westsiders. I mean it was . . ."

"I did what?" he said incredulously.

"You heard me. It was wild. I parked and we went into an ice cream parlor. It was a fancy place, wire legged tables with glass on top. Pink walls, I think. There were nice people sitting there."

"Jesus Christ . . . I hate nice people. No wonder I went insane."

Hank wondered why I had driven over to Westwood Village. I explained that he wanted me to go there. He said, "Hey, you know, if they'd arrested me, it might've been good for book sales . . . the dirty old man goes down for the count. What the hell."

"You sound fairly sane, now."

"You know me, Neeli. I can be wild one moment and the next moment I'm good time Charley. I took a bath when I got inside. The whiskey must have drained out of me. But, listen, let's keep this quiet. Or maybe we can work it into a story."

"Someday," I said.

Nearly twenty-eight years later I asked myself what did this episode mean. On the surface, it seems to me, Hank simply became drunker than usual and acted out some dark corner of himself that had long lain dormant. Or perhaps he deliberately wanted to play out one of those mad characters from his short stories who seemed closer to him that night. Spurred on by the hard liquor, that might well have been the case. Whatever the motivation, Hank never repeated the performance. It remains a discordant note in the casebook of a hard-drinking man who usually held his liquor well.

Hank and I went to the Norm's on Sunset. Norm's was part of a chain of low-priced restaurants, catering to working-class Angelinos. In the windows they put up big posters advertising various specials. They had big parking lots, inexpensive food, and heavy-duty waitresses. Norm's was the chosen hangout of the moment where we went for the steak and eggs special at the end of our drinking sessions. The food made us feel good about ourselves and eased the oncoming hangovers that were the inevitable result of our habits. We pulled onto Sunset Boulevard flanked by a somber hodgepodge of warring architectural styles and drove east. Each of us took turns soliloquizing on the Los Angeles night as we zoomed through it. We saw two drunks battling it out on one street corner and a crazy guy dancing in the middle lane a few blocks further on, all was normal in the city of wounded angels. At four A.M. we pulled into Norm's parking lot, both of us feeling the effects of our drinking. We stumbled inside, waved to the manager who was used to us, and took our usual booth across from the main waitress station. The harsh lighting annoyed me, especially after our long car ride, but gradually my eyes adjusted. Our favorite waitress, a large, red-headed woman with huge, meaty arms and a torso to match, brought us coffee.

"You boys look like hell," she said.

Hank answered, "That's what we are. . . We are hell. This is my son," he added, pointing to me.

"I've heard that before," she said. "You look like you could be his grandfather."

We all had a good laugh and then we ordered two specials that arrived with steak sauce and a copy of the *Los Angeles Times*. There would be no time to read it, however, as Hank was about to launch into another one of his stories, one that might find its way into a notebook and eventually into print.

"Okay, fat boy," he began. "Take our waitress . . . she had a husband who died of a heart attack twenty years ago. She's about sixty, right? So she was forty, give or take a few years. Her old man was a big, stocky mother with a balding scalp, like my landlord Crotty. He had massive shoulders, a bulldog neck, fat thighs, and he ate hearty meals. He worked as either a shipping clerk or a yard man for a lumber company. Let's say it was in the lumber yard for the sake of argument. The boss was a mean fucker . . . he rode our man from morning until quitting time, always trying to squeeze a little more out of him, wanting that extra yard. So in the end, the job turned out to be a river of shit, like most jobs. The years went by and our man, who must have had a spark or two in him when he was younger, became dulled, stupefied. He'd come home and argue with his wife. No matter what she did. No matter that she was also part of the drone class. Hell, she was there and she was a mark for his anger, his sense of failure."

About this time our steaks arrived, along with two eggs swimming in a pool of butter. Hank thanked the waitress, Alma, then dove into his steak before continuing with the tale. "So, we've got him turning into a wife beater. Then, you know, she'd run into the bedroom, slam the door and sob on the bed. There's a picture of Jesus in a Woolworth frame on the far wall. He's got blue eyes, golden blond hair

[220]

and a chickenshit expression. Alma looks at Jesus, but Jesus doesn't have anything to offer. He's just dead meat in the wilderness."

He stopped for a moment when Alma brought more coffee.

"They had a kid and the kid would be in his own room, frightened by all the anger, all the yelling, hating his father for hitting his mother. And, to trim it all down, she had to get ready for the night shift. She always pulled the night shift."

He stopped there and asked me to continue. I thought about it for a moment. "Well, the old man starts getting these pains at work but he doesn't tell anyone. Eventually he's no longer able to pull his weight. The boss calls him in for a talk. Still, he doesn't confess that he has these pains. He's afraid of being fired. So he tells the boss not to worry. He goes back to work and with tremendous effort is able to lift the lumber like he used to . . . he's back to being king of the yard, but only for a few days. Every step is pain. A wrenching feeling hits his chest every time he bends to pick up even a small piece of lumber. The brave act he puts on begins to wear around the edges. Finally, he calls in sick. He's out three days with no pay. Then he goes . . ."

"Hold it," Bukowski said. "Let me finish this." I was glad to stop, as my food was getting cold.

"Now, he goes back to the lumber yard. He's operating the forklift, picking up a load of boards. Suddenly, he bolts upright in the chair and lets go of the controls. The forklift runs into a stack of lumber. Our man slumps over, dead of a massive heart attack, maybe a stroke. What's the difference."

"Then what?"

"Then there's our night shift waitress, alone. Well, she's got the kid, sure, but he goes bad real quick. She doesn't have time for him. Works all night. Sleeps most of the day. It's an impossible situation. And, of course, they have to move to a smaller apartment. So it's the old song. A real dead-end."

He cut his steak in half, ate, dug into his baked potato, watching the sour cream ooze down the side, and gulped some coffee. We both felt a twinge of sadness. But Hank had not yet finished. "The kid joins some kind of Hollywood gang. He gets in and out of trouble.

Alma thinks it's just growing pains, right? But the kid wants to graduate. . . not from school, but from the gang. He hears about bigger
action. He meets these guys who are robbing stores. They've been
going over to Bell Gardens and towns like that, pulling smalltime
robberies. So the kid joins them. He drops out of high school, right.
He wants to make money. Even gonna help his mom. Yeah, like hell."

We had nearly finished with our food by then. Hank had more to
tell. I suppose I could have embroidered more myself, but this was
Hank's show.

"So, now we've got the kid pulling bigtime heists. They've got guns,
right? The cops come by looking for him. Alma is out of her mind,
yet she holds on. She goes in to work day after day, the sun is down,
the moon is a white disk of cancer in the sky, I mean, it's a slide, baby.
Well, the kid is picked up. There's a trial. He's pulling down time.
That brings us to Norm's on Sunset . . . end of story . . . eating the
steak and eggs special, Charles Bukowski immortal genius of poetry,
the gutsy man himself . . . and one other person."

Back at Hank's place we celebrated the emerging day with a new
six pack. It was going to be a forty-eight-hour marathon of drinking.
There would be no sleep, though I yearned for it.

"Listen, Hank" I said at last. "Maybe we ought to call it a night. After all, the dark is over."

"Be a man," he said. "And by the way . . . did we ever finish the story? You can fill it in, right now."

"Hank, you've piqued my interest. I feel like a new man."

I started to speak, pulling the waitress's hapless son out of jail and
on toward a new life. "He's going to enroll in college," I said. "Somehow, during his stay in prison, he developed an interest in film. He
wants to be a lighting technician."

"Hey, that's no good," Hank wined, pounding a foot on the floor.
"You're going to ruin the story with a bit of sunlight and we just don't
want the sunlight."

But as I saw the sun streaming in between the shuttered blinds
of Bukowski's front room I continued over his protest . . . making
things right.

In the fall of 1969, Bukowski mailed a copy of *Notes of a Dirty Old Man* to Carl Weissner in Mannheim, Germany, who had already read many of the individual pieces in *Open City*. Seeing them together in one volume made quite an impact on him. He showed the collection to J. Melzer, heir to a publishing company with a long tradition of books on Jewish mysticism. The owner of the firm had brought his son home from the Israeli army to help reestablish the press. He developed an interest in new American writing and was ready for anything, including the scatology and stark sexual imagery of *Notes*.

Melzer picked up the book, opened it to the preface, and read two pages. He turned to Weissner and said, "I want to do this book. Can you get me a contract for the German rights? And will you translate it for me?" Carl said yes, hoping Melzer would bring out a good, inexpensive edition easily available to university students, the group most likely to be interested. He tried to convince Melzer to do a low-priced paperback edition, something for twelve marks or so. But the publisher believed in an old myth that an important author, such as Bukowski, deserved a good hardcover edition. And so it turned out the book cost too much for students to afford.

Notes appeared in the spring of 1970 under the Melzer imprint. Probably due to the high price, it only sold twelve hundred copies. The edition looked somber and highbrow, in no way appropriate to the wild writing that lay inside. Ironically, there were many favorable reviews, including one in *Der Spiegel*. A tenuous inroad to the German reading public had been made. Weissner knew that he had come close. It hadn't yet occurred to him to translate a book of Bukowski's poetry and see how that would do.

On January 2, 1970, Hank quit his job at the post office. Before the end of his last day, he overheard a fellow worker remark, "That old guy has a lot of guts to quit a job at his age." On his way home he stopped off at Ned's liquor store, buying a few more six-packs than usual. He celebrated his new life behind drawn shades. A few friends dropped in during the first few days of his freedom, having heard the news as it traveled through the local poetry community. The Crottys, his landlords and longtime drinking companions, who lived down the court from Hank, came over and celebrated. "You sure you did the right thing?" Crotty asked. "Seems crazy to me."

Hank complained to visitors that he needed writing time. He feared that he might not really make enough money as a writer if he did not concentrate on a long prose work, and for that he needed hours of isolation each day. He had the rent to worry about, even though it only amounted to $37.50 per month. Combined with child support, money for the track, and beer money, his expenses didn't look so small. John Martin paid him a modest monthly stipend to help him along, and promised to raise the amount as time went on. Hank had retirement money coming and some savings, which helped to keep him solvent. So, gathering his courage he decided to write a novel.

Hank plunged into writing *Post Office* the day after he quit his job, letting the words roll out of him: he completed the manuscript in less than three weeks. He rang up John Martin every so often and assured him that he wouldn't let him down. In the end, he had 120,000 words, which he trimmed down to about 90,000. The project allowed him to look back through the years of suffering as a postal clerk. He relived each incident with a distance, free as he now was from rules, regulations, supervisors, and his fellow employees. As for writing about his job, he says, "It wasn't possible to write about it like I did in *Post Office* until I left. Only then, when I could look back on that time, did things break loose." In *Post Office*, he compares quitting the job to breaking out of jail; writing the novel came as a cathartic release, a means to finally purge himself of a bad situation.

Hank fell into a kind of trance the day he began the novel, and did not take any days off until he finished. Typing began at 2:30 in the afternoon and went on until midnight, when he would stop a bit, maybe go out and eat something. He'd revise as he wrote. "Here's where it took all day long, it was very nice there because you could see people pass on the sidewalk . . . you knew the world was there: I'd type up these pages and lay on the couch and pass out. Then, in the morning, I'd walk out and look at ten or twelve pages . . . and get rid of the gibberish. Usually, in the last few pages there would be more of that than in the first ones. Well, you think you are magic and a genius . . ." On the day that he completed the manuscript, January 21, 1970, he called Martin: "It's done."

"What's done?" Martin asked, genuinely in the dark.

"My novel. Come and get it."

"What's the title?"

"*Post Office.*"

In *Post Office*, Chinaski is portrayed as a fearless man who will not buckle under to unfair orders, nor let himself be defeated by the system or its agents. He calls the boss, Johnstone, "Stone" right to his face, unlike the others who only use the name behind the feared man's back. In retaliation for Chinaski's rebelliousness, Stone sends him home day after day without an assignment. Next, he hands him the toughest mail route of all. Chinaski is always disappointed by the failure of other men to be decent. He comes to expect their indecency, and is surprised whenever they turn out to be men of their word, men of dignity. Chinaski's own sense of decency is underscored by his sense of humor, which is never far from the action. At one point, when lost in a storm on a mail run he calls out, "Johnstone in the Sky, have Mercy!" and asks himself (and the reader), "Was I some kind of idiot, actually! did I make things happen to myself?" He reaches out to the reader in such a direct, disarming fashion that one cannot help but empathize. Bukowski gives us a hero who is just like most people, victimized at one time or another and feeling hopeless in the face of situations seemingly beyond their control.

Hank's job at the post office served as an anchor in reality—a cruel one for a man who needed to write, who felt compelled to put his life down on paper, but an anchor nonetheless. The daily responsibility of his job and, above all, his writing kept Bukowski from going the way of many of his contemporaries who had succumbed to drugs and alcohol. To understand how he merges pain and humor, failure and humor, loss and humor, in the fabric of his writing is to find a kind of road map to the meaning of his writing. The public image of the hard-drinking, wild Bukowski is partially true, but only up to a point. When everything is said and done, he is a survivor.

Post Office set the tone for the later novels. Antihero Henry Chinaski, victimized by society, emerges as a government unto himself. He starts with the sentence, "It began as a mistake," and then ranges over his life as postal clerk, lover, and racetrack habitué. As with John Fante, Henry Miller, and Jack Kerouac, Chinaski's actions closely follow the writer's own life. "Why look further than one's own life?" had always been Hank's motto. The entire post office episode of his life stood fresh in his mind. Rather than write a dark book, he utilized the human comedy, as he had in Notes, plowing through the drudgery of a dull and difficult job so as to make it all seem like a monstrous series of comic clips. Despite unfeeling supervisors and failed love relationships, he comes through victorious, taking his own life in hand and quitting his job.

Editing decisions regarding *Post Office* were not monumental. There are none of the slash-and-cut stories that one associates with Thomas Wolfe or Jack Kerouac. The manuscript Bukowski gave Martin had been worked over at least three times by the author. A number of the editorial changes were about a few pages that were repetitious, but most of the others were simply typesetting details—Martin thrived on being a good detail man. He found Bukowski to be one, too: nothing could get past him. Regarding this first novel and all subsequent ones, Martin says, "I'd show him what I did on editing and he would agree or not. If I do something he doesn't like and know he might object, I sort of hold my breath and wait, and he always finds it . . . Many times I'd want to do some little thing to improve it and every time he'd find it and take it out. Because it's not him. It's not the way he thinks. He doesn't want any embroidery." Martin makes the point that Bukowski is always right on these editorial issues, emphasizing that "Bukowski hits really well, a left to the jaw is his best punch."

Publication ninety-nine from Black Sparrow, *Post Office*, quickly became a best-selling book. Martin's impressive list, which had begun with Bukowski's broadsides, easily rivaled that of any small press in the country. The novel became a high-water mark not only for the author but for his publisher as well. Martin printed it in January 1971, one year after Bukowski walked out of the post office for the last time. The edition of two thousand paperback copies quickly sold out, prompting a new printing and eventually the sale of more than forty thousand copies.

While *Post Office* was being readied for release, Linda King, a cherubic brunette destined to become Hank's long-term girlfriend, went to the Bridge one night late in 1970 to hear a poetry reading by a writer whose name she forgets. She met Peter, the owner, and the two of them began talking about writers in L.A. Linda asked Peter who he thought wrote the best poetry in Los Angeles. He told her Charles Bukowski was the best poet in L.A. Linda picked up a copy of the first issue of *Laugh Literary and Man the Humping Guns* from Peter. This included a Bukowski poem called "The Grand Pricks of the Hobnail Sun." Linda liked what she read. When she came to the line "God tongues out your asshole," she began to wonder about the poet's sexual preference. Standing in front of the Bridge, she asked Peter if Bukowski was a homosexual. Peter said he didn't know. Quite unexpectedly, Hank and I showed up right then. Peter saw us in the parking lot at the market across from the Bridge. We had just gotten out of Hank's car and were playfully wrestling in the lot and making a considerable amount of noise, secretly hoping to attract attention to ourselves. "That's Bukowski coming right now," Peter informed Linda. I came up to the door first and Peter told me that this woman wanted to know if Hank was a homosexual. Not to be outdone by the generally wild Peter, I tossed off, "Well, he doesn't play around with me."

Linda watched as Hank swaggered up to the door and walked inside. He and I sat with Peter on a mattress at the center of the room as the reading began. Hank and I both began making snide remarks, first under our breaths and then loud enough for everyone in the room to hear. Linda, who had come with her sister Geraldine, sat in a far corner. We were entertaining ourselves with beer, wine, and conversation.

A few weeks went by before Linda returned to the Bridge to find a bad poet reading to flute accompaniment. She turned to Peter and asked, "God, doesn't anything exciting ever happen in this town?" Peter excused himself, saying he wanted to make a phone call. He returned to Linda a few moments later and said, "I'm taking you over to Bukowski's place on De Longpre. It isn't far from here." She knew that Peter wanted to bring her and Hank together. Hank intrigued her, but she had no idea that she would eventually fall in love with him. She had arrived at her own conclusions about the relationship between men and women, having learned in her previous marriage that a woman had not only the right but the obligation to live on equal terms with her male partner. Her former husband was old Italian stock, she says, believing that a woman should stay home, clean house, make meals, and take care of the children. Linda had just freed herself from their ten-year marriage and wasn't about to rush into anything serious, especially with a man twenty years older who had a reputation for hard living. In truth, she looked on the visit as a lark. Besides that, she had responsibilities taking care of her two young children and did not feel she would even have time for an involved relationship.

She had introduced herself to Peter as Morona. "I used Morona at the time," Linda says, "because my sisters had been telling me that I should admit that I was stupid, and this was my humorous way of admitting it." In a letter to me dated July 12, 1970, Bukowski wrote,

> the typer sounds good today . . . I may be able to con some immortal shit out of this afternoon. the girls come by—Bonnie, Liza Williams, Morona, but we just talk and I look at those bodies and think, no, no, no, the price is too high, the price is always too high, and the bullshit act beforehand, degrading and stupid, like a beggar, god damn them, I let them go, goodbye, goodbye, yes, come again, oh yes it was nice, come again, and then I walk over to the typer and write a story about rape . . .

Peter introduced Linda as Morona. Hank said, "Come on, what's your name?"

Linda insisted that it was truly Morona. "It's it," she said. "I just want people to know right away I'm Morona . . . kind of dumb . . . so they will know what to expect. They can never say I didn't warn them."

"Okay, Morona, sit down," Hank said.

Linda noticed right away that Hank looked at her as if he were appraising her body. Hank and Peter fought one another for center stage. Peter whispered, "See. Look who I've brought you," while directing his own sexual innuendoes at Linda.

Linda began her own performance. She jumped up on Hank's wobbly, cluttered coffee table, which sat in the middle of his small living room, partially obscuring a portion of the filthy rug. She wiggled her hips, flung her hair from side to side, and shouted lines from her own poetry. It was the kind of show that Bukowski liked, and he admired her that evening. The crazier she became, dancing around his room like a hyped-up flamenco dancer, the more he desired her. He saw her as this beautiful, semidivine woman. Peter did not appreciate Linda's performance, especially because he knew Bukowski hated the poetry she recited. What Peter failed to comprehend was that Bukowski paid more attention to Linda's body gyrations than her poetry. He may have had enough of her poetry, but the mysteries of her body were something that he wanted to explore. After a while, Peter left. Nothing sexual transpired between Bukowski and Linda that evening.

As Linda danced, Hank thought of the sexual drought that had afflicted him for the previous four years. Since Frances, he had not had any relationships that amounted to anything—so he hoped that something might develop between him and Linda. Perhaps it would now be over, he thought to himself as he continued to admire the performance of the voluptuous woman who had come screaming into his life. She seemed just the right age, being under thirty-five years old.

A short while later, Linda sent a poem to Hank, in which she called him "an old troll" and exhorted him to come out and dance in the open meadows with what she termed female fawn creatures. To do so would give Bukowski great wisdom, she thought. The next morning after he received the poem, Linda drove over to De Long-pre Avenue, parked down the street from this place, walked up to his apartment, and knocked on the window. No response came from inside. "Open up. It's me, Linda." she called. She caught him in the midst of a hangover and offered to come back later. Quickly, he told her to stay. They talked for a while, and eventually she told him that she was a sculptor and wanted to make a bust of him—which caught him off guard, since no one had ever asked to do a sculpture of him before. He agreed to come over to her house and sit. Linda wrote down the address. She lived in Burbank.

Linda began to look on Hank as a challenge, though not necessarily as a sexual one. In her playful way she wanted to tame "the wild beast," and show him that a woman could be as powerful, if not more so, than a man. (She did not realize that Hank already knew this.) In a piece she wrote that was largely tongue-in-cheek, called *To Think I Fell in Love with a Male Chauvinist*, Linda confided that Hank told her that he had not had sex for nearly four years. "Oh, I was sly, and over the clay I gave him hot looks, then turned to put more clay on the head like I was just studying his eyes or his mouth for the shape," she wrote. She claims that she didn't have any intention of making love to him when she began the sculpture. As far as she was concerned, he was a very good writer, and an interesting, humorous, and insightful man—but not really her type.

He definitely presented a challenge. Her instincts told her that he would be hard to catch. Having read his poems, she knew he was no ordinary man. She admired him, but did not stand in awe of him, or of his work. Gradually, she realized that they might actually become lovers. For Linda it would be a seduction played out with a peer, nothing more, nothing less.

The breakfast nook of Linda's apartment in Burbank served as a studio. There she began shaping the clay into an image of the poet. She not only observed her subject, but listened to his stories as she worked and probed him concerning his past, his feelings about his writing, and his attitude toward women. For Linda, he was much more entertaining than any comedian she had ever heard. "He made me laugh," she said. "Some days I couldn't stop laughing, even after he had gone away. But there was another side, too. That dark side. The tough side. And it was just as strong." Not being a shrinking violet, however, Linda was fast on the retort and could always hold her own in conversation, whether one-on-one with Bukowski or in a group. She wasn't knowledgeable in literary matters, but her wit held her in good stead when they bantered back and forth.

They worked out theories on the battle of the sexes. In Hank's mind, and the same held true for Linda, there really was an ongoing battle. It did not have only to do with sexual matters, but also with manipulation and possessiveness. Hank felt Linda was playing games with him, that she was deliberately being coy. He confessed that his having gone without sex for some time made him feel deprived. Linda understood his vulnerability. Hank could play the tough guy, but he did not fear exposing his intense desire for sexual gratification.

Over the course of making the bust, Linda learned a great deal about Bukowski. He did not hold himself back. Eventually, Linda began to feel enormous pressure. She had been bothered at first by his reputation as a male chauvinist and by his age. The "dirty old man" had turned her off, but what put her off the most was his alcoholism. Her father, who had recently died, had also been an alcoholic. Linda knew firsthand what liquor could do to a person, and what a drunk person could do to others—even one with a mind and heart like Bukowski's. But now she witnessed the sensitive side of the poet, that lyrical part of him that so often surfaced in his poetry and prose.

One day, after many weeks of sculptural courtship, Hank got up and followed her to the refrigerator as she went for beer. He grabbed her, but Linda resisted his advances, explaining that they had to finish the work. A few minutes later Linda's older sister Geraldine came over and her presence defused the tense atmosphere. The King sisters, Linda, Geraldine, and three others, had written a book of poetry together, which Linda had given to Hank. "Their poems had a lot of humor, and plenty of sexual imagery," he recalls.

Linda and Hank continued their sessions in the breakfast nook and the bust took form. He hinted about what he termed as "the man-woman thing," and talked of his past affairs with Jane, Frances, and Barbara Frye. Hank wrote her that he was beginning to feel desperate about "your denial of any total act between us." He said that older men have to settle for little tidbits, "and be damned glad of that." This kind of honesty set the tone for a barrage of letters that began to flow from De Longpre Street to Linda's apartment in Burbank.

Hank played on the theme of "the old troll," referring to Linda's poem about him. They both knew that sooner or later they would make love. The letters came with such frequency, and in them Hank laid himself bare with such honesty, that Linda was overwhelmed. He wrote about his years of being a loner, his self-described ugliness, his caution in dealing with matters of sex, his distrust of other people, his dedication to writing. Taking down his mask was almost like his wearing one; that is, by being so open and honest he was almost saying, "Hey, look at me, I have to be great. See how open and honest I am?"

As Linda came to know Hank better, through both correspondence and their encounters in her kitchen, she began to find him as irresistible as he found her. She viewed Hank as a mass of ego balanced by sensitivity, humor, a lack of confidence, and touches of alcoholic gloom. She began to see through all of that down to the core of the man, the strong sense of self that had been defined as a child on Longwood Avenue and honed down to a fine point as a young man traveling from city to city, surviving on the margins of society in rooming houses.

Meanwhile, the bust was nearing completion—scars, large nose, small eyes, full lips, and all. Hank surveyed it, told Linda it looked beautiful, and then began to talk about sex. Within moments, they had both undressed and gotten down on the linoleum floor of the kitchen. Just as they were about to consummate the long-awaited act, a loud, insistent knock on the front door stopped them. The knock was followed by a plea from her daughter, who had just cut her finger. They quickly dressed and the child's finger was attended to by Linda, the doting mother, as her soon-to-be lover looked on, half amused.

While the courtship continued between Hank and Linda, *Laugh Literary*, issue number three, was edited. We held a party for the magazine at Hank's apartment early in March 1971. Linda arrived dressed flamboyantly. She seemed to be everywhere at once, especially where men were standing around. Because most of the people there were men, she didn't have to go very far in the crowded front room. Hank drank more than he usually did, and became increasingly bothered by Linda's flirtations, though they still hadn't become lovers and he had no real claim on her. He warned her to stop fooling around. By the time they were alone he had forgiven her and they went into his bedroom, lay down, and spent their first night together. After they made love, Linda said he had better decide upon a name for the child that was sure to come from this encounter. "Call him Clyde King Bukowski," Hank said. Later on Linda told him, "The only thing that saved me was that your sperm were pickled with alcohol." This early argument, even with its humor, foreshadowed the tone of their entire relationship, which would almost wholly be a tempestuous one, with few calm interludes. As John Thomas observes, "They were both into the jealousy game." Yet their relationship flowered.

Being nearly twenty years younger and an unpublished poet, Linda learned from Hank. He taught her a lot about writing, both by commenting on her work and by example. As she learned of the long, hard road he had taken to his recent success, she paid even closer attention to what he said. Hank had endured. He believed in himself. When he talked about his lack of confidence in high school, after the acne had permanently scarred him, she was able to better understand his insecurities and the *noche oscura* that sometimes overtook his otherwise humorous spirit. She began to see that his work took precedence over everything. No matter how much he needed the love of a woman, his writing dominated. Without it he would have been lost.

A poem that Linda wrote soon after they became lovers reflects her state of mind.

> *This man was*
> *as new as creation*
> *as old as fifty*
> *as giving as the sun*
> *after night and cold*
> *as crazy as a trapped animal*
> *as jealous as a horney dog*
> *who'd found a bitch in heat*
> *. . .*
> *he gave me his soul*
> *he also gave me his hangovers*
> *his rages his insecurities*
> *and he gave me love*
> *it came from the center*
> *of him to the center of me*
> *and I gave him love*
> *love he wanted to be*
> *finished with*
> *once a week . . .*

ELEVEN

IN 1971, during the editing of *Erections, Ejaculations, Exhibitions and General Tales of Ordinary Madness*, Bukowski's short-story collection published by City Lights Books, Linda King went to Escalante, a small town near Boulder, Utah, to visit with her sisters, explaining to Hank that this family tradition of returning to the Boulder area for the fourth of July could not be broken. Hank protested, even though she planned on returning soon. Linda told him that she was eager to return to L.A. and pick things up where they had left off.

This was not the first time Hank and Linda had been apart. In fact, they had been splitting up on a regular basis since they became serious with one another. They squabbled over other people: usually Hank was jealous of Linda, with little or no basis but his fear of losing her. Once Linda was going for dental work and Hank accused her of sleeping with the dentist.

"I need to go," Linda said. "My teeth are hurting."

"Don't lie to me!" he told her. "I know what you're doing at his office. Your teeth aren't really bad."

On an outing at MacArthur Lake, Linda asked a fisherman what he used for bait. Hank became furious. Linda protested that she had simply asked a question. Hank ran off, convinced that she had been coming on to the guy.

Hank and I, along with Paul Vangelisti, at the time were editing an anthology of L.A. poets (a book that, incidentally, included work by Linda King). Whenever I went over to Hank's he barraged me with his many ideas on "that man-woman thing." Mostly, this concerned the issue of how a man should treat a woman who constantly flirted with other men. He had convinced himself that this was the problem with Linda, though he admitted that his distrust of her was like his basic distrust of everyone.

"People are difficult," he said, "and as for sex, it is even more difficult. Everybody has a theory about it. And nobody really has any answers."

"Maybe you have to open up more," I suggested.

"No, I can't do that," he replied. "Linda only has youth and beauty. I have Bukowski."

"But you have to be more open . . ."

"Uh-uh. You just don't give pieces of your soul away. *Women* are relentless."

"What will you do, then?"

"One day at a time, I guess. We're fighting, always. Hell, you've seen us—jealousy, blind rage."

"Can't you learn to relax about it?"

"Not really, kid. It's a war, really, with moments of tenderness and peace. So I have to be on guard at all times."

Linda told Hank of a dream she had in which he became very rich and famous. Amidst all the adulation, he was hanging from a cliff and needed someone to keep him from falling. In the dream, Linda was the one who came to rescue him. She later said, "Bukowski really knew that he had it made as a writer. Things were really happening for him about the time we became seriously involved. Fame and money were on their way. The checks began rolling in for readings, short stories, and the like." The activity that centered around Hank excited Linda, and she herself began publishing, even producing a mimeographed collection of poems by herself and Bukowski.

Linda's youthfulness attracted Hank and appealed to his vanity. Even as the fights wore him down, they also brought an element of tension and vigor that he liked. Linda, like Hank, was very exuberant and playful; and just as she had found his wit charming when they met, so he liked her ability to be playful and humorous. They were at their best in public when they bantered back and forth, talking about sex, the battle of the sexes, literature, or politics.

Linda could describe for hours Hank's best points, and a day later she might be cursing him, announcing the end of their affair with bitter finality. To write of his outrages and accept them became the game plan for much of her poetry. "It has to be love Bukowski / It just has to be," she writes after describing a series of outrages. She tried to come to terms with their continual fighting through her poetry. Perhaps one of her keenest insights was her belief that love was not something that he could trust, and that he drove it away from him before it had the chance to fail.

She tried to balance the difficulties of living with a man she looked upon as a creative genius with her own desire to define herself as a poet and sculptor. She made no secret of how much she admired him, both in conversation with her friends and in her writings. He stood as a field of boundless energy she could play off against. His wit and irony were all weapons she enjoyed sparring with, and testing herself against.

By the fall of 1971, Hank was saying, "I wanted to break up with Linda from the beginning. She knocked on my door and threw herself upon me. I'd been trying to get away from her. I used every available excuse. When I decided on this writing game it meant blood on the dotted line. This means that there are no traps in the world that would stop me writing as I felt. So this beautiful woman came and laid a trap on me. She kissed me and loved me. After that, and before that, I knew there would be traps." He went on to say, "She wanted my soul, with all her beauty and body and everything. She wanted my soul on the line. She knew I was Bukowski, the tough guy. She deliberately walked in. Look at me, my face, my heart, you know me. I'm not really tough."

One afternoon in 1972, while I was living in San Bernadino, an hour east of Los Angeles, I received a postcard inviting me to a book party Hank and Linda King were giving for their joint publication, *Me and You Sometimes Love Poems*. Hank telephoned me the afternoon of the party. "Linda and I wrote these damn poems, but all you guys are gonna make money from the collectors with the copies we sign for you. Martin's got a bunch of them already. You can do the same thing." He went on to tell me that while the book was a good collaboration, he and Linda were fighting more than ever. "You know, it's a chore, finally. I'm the old troll. I'm the man who has to perform for all of you. I'm always performing. I was just supposed to be this guy sitting before a typewriter."

"Consider the alternative."

"I know. Remember…I was alone for a good many years. After Jane…"

"You had Frances, right?"

"She was just some clawing phantom in the night. But she did give me Marina."

As usual, even as he expressed his hatred of parties, he wanted to make sure I'd be there. "We'll have fun. The whole gang will be there. Big John Thomas. Your pal Vangelisti. Some of Linda's friends."

"For a guy who doesn't like parties, you sure know how to throw them."

"This is for Linda, my man."

I got off the phone and prepared to leave. Just as I was stepping out of the door the phone rang again. "Kid, it's Hank. I want your help tonight. I'm about ready to belt this woman. We just had another argument. It's too much to bear. She's twenty years younger, a wild woman…You know Linda. Help keep things cool, alright?" I agreed, suggesting that he lay back and not worry about entertaining the rest of us. "Yeah, I'd like to take your advice, but you know me." I also knew he was a jealous man, capable of seeing any attention to Linda from his poet-colleagues as a come-on or threat to his sense of dominion.

The party went well at first. Linda's ramshackle rented house, surrounded by shrubbery and trees halfway up a hillside overlooking the Silverlake Reservoir, north of Sunset Boulevard, had a country feel to it. The air was atypically cool and refreshing. Fronting the entranceway was a patio of cracked concrete with decrepit patio chairs and a wobbly table. We were crowded into the small living room with plenty of beer, dancing, and loud conversation. There were a lot of old faces mixed in with people unfamiliar to me, ones Hank had met in his new role as a local celebrity. Midway through the evening, Linda, as vivacious as ever, seemed to be everywhere at once and always with a different man. Was every male in the room dancing with Linda? Bukowski drank with increasing frequency, often nudging me and pointing to Linda. "Listen, man, like I told you over the phone, there's going to be trouble. Maybe you can think of something?" But I couldn't.

There was an inevitable confrontation brewing, one that would surely ruin the festivities. I did make an attempt to help matters, however. I took a copy of the mimeographed book to Linda and asked that she read from it. She flung it aside and continued dancing from man to man. I noticed that Hank was in a corner now, isolating himself from his guests. He had a bottle in his hand, an empty one, and looked as if he might throw it at any moment.

There was still time for a little fun and games before the storm. Hank had put down the empty and was now guzzling another bottle of beer. I walked over to him. "She's pissing me off now more than ever. This is deliberate. I may be the old troll, but I've got a powerful punch left in me and I can clear out this whole damned room if I put my mind to it." I mentioned that he had expressed a desire for a calmer evening than that. "Yeah, but Linda's on the warpath. She wants trouble."

Late at night, the party had boiled down to me, John Thomas, Paul Vangelisti, a poet named Tony Quagliano whose writing had appeared in *Laugh Literary*, and Linda. Hank came forward from the corner which had served as his observation post. I reasoned that he had chosen to save his big scene for the stalwarts, those of us who had witnessed them before. "Okay, I've had enough," he exclaimed.

"Linda has been asking for trouble all evening. She can't seem to keep her hands off anyone, including you guys."

Linda yelled, "Can't I have any goddamned fun without you getting jealous?" Her cheeks turned crimson and she fell back against a table stacked with copies of their joint publishing effort, a few copies of *Me and You Sometimes Love Poems*, fell to the floor, unceremoniously.

Hank grabbed an empty beer bottle, just as before, but now he was holding it like a weapon. "Okay, which of you guys is first?" he provoked, backing slowly against a far wall and looking each of us directly in the eyes.

Tony stepped forward, a massive man with a thick neck and gigantic hands.

"You want her, right?" Hank asked.

"No, I don't," Quagliano answered flatly, holding his ground as Hank took one step in his direction.

"Bullshit," Hank roared.

"You calling me a liar?" Quagliano shifted his weight from right to left and readied himself for an attack.

Just then John Thomas moved in on Hank from one side and Vangelisti from another. Hank suddenly threw the bottle to the opposite wall, where it shattered. He turned and stormed out of the house, across the patio and down the stone path to the driveway where he had parked. Moments later we heard his engine rev up and he was backing into the street.

Linda decided to run after him. She managed to get close enough to his car to bang on the hood and scream, "*I hate you. Oh I do. I hate you, you son of a bitch!*"

When she returned, we settled down for more beer as Quagliano made his goodnights, clutching a copy of *Me and You Sometimes Love Poems* under his arm.

Half an hour later the phone rang. I was sitting near the phone and Linda asked me to answer it. I think we both knew who would be on the other end. "Hello," I said.

"This is Bukowski. Put Linda on."

"Linda, it's Hank."

"I don't want to talk with him!" she snapped, loud enough for him to hear.

"Tell me, who's with you there?" Bukowski asked.

"John and Paul. Tony just left."

"Which one of you is going to end up with Linda tonight?"

"None of us."

With that he hung up.

We finished drinking and Paul went on his way, leaving me, John and Linda.

Hank called again.

"Yeah?" I asked.

"Who's left?"

"Me and Big John. Why don't you come back? We're only talking."

"I want you guys out of there," he barked, hanging up before I could say anything in response. I glanced at the clock and noticed it was 1 A.M.

Five minutes later, the phone rang. *"You sons of bitches better clear out. I'm real mad!"*

"Hank, I . . ." But he had already slammed the receiver down. Linda laughed and handed me a beer.

It wasn't long before Hank pulled up the driveway. When he entered the room, Linda bolted from her chair, ran to him and began scratching his face. "You ruined my party!" she bellowed.

"Yeah? Well, I can ruin more than that if you want."

Big John had slipped out unnoticed. I managed to get their attention, a failed peacemaker. "Goodnight," I said.

As I drove down the San Bernardino Freeway I realized I had left my copy of the Bukowski-King collaboration back in Silverlake.

Two weeks passed before Hank called me. I had wanted to phone him, but was cautious, fearful of his reaction.

"Hey, I've got your copy of the book," he said.

"That's good."

"Meet me at De Longpre. Come over tomorrow night."

The next evening, I drove to Los Angeles and Hank's apartment, first stopping off at Ned's Liquor for two six-packs. I knew I was headed for a long evening.

Hank turned the conversation to the subject of women. He declared Jane the only reliable woman he had ever known, adding that he had failed her. At the same time, he went on about Linda, saying that maybe he did love her. "She's like a black widow spider," he moaned. "She said she has to spin her web. She wants me totally under her control and I can't allow that."

Eventually, Hank brought up the subject of the book party. "You know, I was truly mad at you guys. But madness aside, I find it hard to trust anyone around her. Linda has this power, a life force that can seduce any man."

"Maybe so," I said, "But you had nothing to fear from any of us. At least not from me or Paul or John."

With that, we continued drinking. Near to the break of day, with nothing resolved, Hank turned in and I curled up on his couch, as I had done so many times before back in the 60s.

During a particularly difficult time with Linda, Hank began seeing Liza Williams, who had become a popular figure in the underground newspaper scene. When they began seeing one another, in fact, they both wrote for the *Los Angeles Free Press*, the largest alternative newspaper in the city. Her column, named for herself, often seemed to parody Bukowski's, but was not without its own brand of wit. One of her stories, appearing in the June 30, 1972, issue of the paper, talks about the difficulties of living with a genius and gives us a character called "Hunk" who seems suspiciously like Bukowski. In response to the unnamed female character's cryptic theories about poets, Hunk says, "You're making me sick, your sentimental hardness . . ."

Hank met Liza Williams during the sixties when she and her boyfriend visited him on several occasions. From the beginning, he saw her as a freewheeling hippie entrepreneur, a woman who had her hand everywhere. She seemed to know all the *right* people in the underground, the poets, cartoonists, political activists, and musicians.

She worked at one time for Capitol Records and then for a major British record company.

Sometime in the winter of 1972, Hank ran into her while delivering an article he had written for an entertainment magazine in Hollywood. Linda accompanied him. When he left the office he saw Liza sitting in her car, a brand-new Mercedes. He walked over to ask how she was doing. They talked for a few minutes. During their conversation Liza told him that she was living alone and needed a new boyfriend. He wrote down his telephone number for her and told her to call sometime. Linda could hardly contain herself. She knew that if she had handed out her phone number to a man, Hank would have gone berserk. She told him that it was obvious he would be calling Liza at some point.

Hank went to the harness races that evening and won a large sum of money—and managed to forget Linda for a while. Yet he couldn't resist calling her from the track to provoke her with his victory, and to let her know that he could do without her. When somebody answered he yelled into the receiver that he was a winner, that he wanted to end things between them. He stopped to catch his breath, and a calm, bemused voice informed him that it was the babysitter. Linda had gone out for the evening. This enraged him. He had thought he would be able to irritate her, to get under her skin in some final way; instead, she had turned the tables on him. On his way home from the track he began to imagine Linda out for an evening of hot, unbridled sex.

He was lying in his bed when the phone rang the following morning. Linda announced that she had gone dancing. After long diatribes back and forth, Hank slammed the receiver down and drove over to Linda's with the bust she had made of him—a ritual that become legendary among their friends.

They reconciled, but their troubles soon grew again. One day Hank pulled up at her house to find that she had vacated it. He unlocked the door, went inside, and found that she had left the air conditioner he had loaned her. Along with it he discovered a note telling him that she was gone for good. He remembered Liza Williams and decided to give her a call. She immediately invited him to come visit her at her place in the Hollywood Hills.

Liza was about eight years older than Linda King, who was in her mid-thirties. Unlike Linda, she lived almost totally in a rarefied world of music-industry parties and talk of big record contracts. Hank was excited by her, although completely turned off by most of her friends—he viewed them as phonies hustling after whatever small fame and fortune could be made on the hip music scene.

Once Hank was inside Liza's house, which she shared with another woman, she encouraged him to talk openly about himself and Linda. He freely admitted that he missed her, even with the craziness of their troubles. He talked about the wild accusations on both sides, and of the frantic, insane phone calls, and of running over to her place with the bust whenever they had a particularly vicious fight. He told Liza that he doubted if he could ever get over the loss.

Linda was in Utah at the time. She preoccupied herself with writing and sculpting, and also prepared her poetry book for publication by John Bennett's Vagabond Press. Hank sent a letter to the address she had sent him, to inform her that he and Liza Williams were together. Linda did not take the news well, and fired back an angry letter.

Hank had already decided that Liza had a good figure and a pretty face. She was less antagonistic than Linda King. "Liza is less grating," he once told me. "With Linda I've got to be on guard. She's always flaunting herself all over the place," he said. "Maybe because Liza is older or something, maybe that's it."

Much of what Hank saw as flirtatiousness on Linda's part was merely her natural exuberance, the very thing that had attracted him in the first place. Also, as Linda became increasingly conscious of herself as a poet, spending a lot of time with other poets, mainly male, she naturally began to assert herself more, and this often caused trouble between her and Hank.

Soon after his first visit to Liza, Hank described himself as a much more cautious man. "After Linda, I've found out how to guard myself. My theory is that you don't fall in love. You guard against it," he said. "That way you're protected from both ends." When I asked if he planned on a long-term commitment, he was emphatic: no. Yet I could see that the great loner preferred being with someone to moping around the house alone. I reminded him of a few years earlier, when he used to constantly complain about not having a woman. "You were miserable," I said.

"I'm miserable with them or without them," he responded, unembarrassed by the cliché.

Hank and Liza Williams went on numerous trips outside of L.A., mostly financed by Liza. It soon became a constant round of excursions, and many of them included encounters with the slick-talking music-industry people Hank abhorred. Soon he couldn't even remember where they had been. One week it was off to the mountains, and another week they were speeding up Pacific Coast Highway. There were parties where Bukowski usually stood off to one side playing the quiet observer, amused and yet bored by the pretensions of the fashionable young people Liza knew.

While involved with Liza, and writing long letters to Linda, Hank met a young aspiring director in L.A. named Taylor Hackford. Like so many others in the L.A. area, he first came into contact with Hank's work through *Open City*; only later did he read Hank's poem "dirty old man" while sitting in a barbershop, leafing through a magazine distributed in barbershops.

A few years earlier, Hackford had done a concert with the group Traffic at the Santa Monica Civic Auditorium, financed by Island Records. The president of the company at the time was Liza Williams. One day Hackford and Liza were talking. Hackford asked her what she was doing in her life. She mentioned that she had fallen madly in love with this local poet, Charles Bukowski. Hackford remembered Bukowski's poem and said he loved his work. Liza told him she would be happy to arrange a meeting with him.

Hackford's first meeting with Hank included a ride on the train to the Del Mar horse racing track. "When Bukowski wants to go to the track, he doesn't want to talk about anything else," Taylor emphasizes. "It was an introduction to Bukowski through horse racing." Hank, Liza, and Hackford got on the train. "We had this whole day at the track. I lost. Bukowski had a pretty bad day. I think he had two winners . . . seven losers, and I was really pissed. I was so angry. Hank doesn't like people who are good losers." They left the track and went back to Liza's. The three of them sat around commiserating over their bad luck, an excuse to get drunk. Hackford perceived a riveting clarity in the way Hank talked about the track, and realized that the daily pilgrimage to the race track served as an important ritual in the poet's life, if not the most important one.

Hackford worked at the time in the Cultural Affairs Department of KCET, the public television station in L.A. The department decided to do an ongoing feature on Los Angeles area artists. He said he wanted to do a program on Bukowski. None of his superiors knew who Hank was, so Hackford tried to explain his importance, calling him the quintessential L.A. poet in his effort to explain that he was a major underground literary figure. He told Hank of his idea for a film designed for KCET. Hackford was convinced that a well-done documentary could be as involving and dramatic as a feature film especially if it dealt with a larger-than-life personality such as Bukowski.

Hank agreed to the project and Hackford began hanging out with him, spending two or three nights a week getting drunk with him, going to his haunts, walking up to Ned's liquor store up on Normandie and Sunset, a few blocks north of De Longpre. They did the rounds of the tracks, from Del Mar to Santa Anita. They followed the entire southern California racing scene. Occasionally Liza came along, but usually they went on their own.

Meanwhile, Liza planned a trip to Catalina Island, twenty-seven miles off the coast of L.A., a middle-class tourist spot Hank would never have thought of going to on his own. But his newfound lover could hardly wait to hit the shops in the small town of Avalon and lounge around on the beach.

For Liza, the island offered endless delights. No so with Hank. He was bored by the glass-bottomed boat, bored by the old dance hall perched on a slip of land in the Avalon harbor, and bored by the people. Although he enjoyed much of his time with her when they were alone, he could not share Liza's appreciation for the shops filled mostly with cheap tourist souvenirs. Nor could he join her in the small talk she made with shop owners and fellow tourists. Eventually, he told her that he wanted to stay holed up in their hotel room and drink. He had brought a portable typewriter along, so he sat down and wrote a few poems.

Hank was sure that Liza had really fallen in love with him, and he certainly liked her. On their way home from Catalina, she had a look of longing in her eyes. They talked of taking other trips together. Hank realized that she belonged in a different world than he did, and he had known it from the beginning. As crazy as things were with Linda, there had been an unspoken contract between them: they were playing an emotionally dangerous game, and they knew it and liked it.

Hackford witnessed Hank's wavering between the two women. Hank confessed to Hackford, "You know, Liza is a nice woman, but there's another one I've been seeing, Linda King." Hackford could see that Liza lavished gifts on Hank and introduced him to a comfortable lifestyle. On the other hand, as Hackford saw it, there was the "wild and young Linda," who Hank longed for. Inevitably, this triangle became a major subject for the film—as did the drinking, the racetrack, and his poetry.

Hank became a kind of graduate school for Hackford, who admired the fact that the older man didn't try to hide his quirks and failures, even after agreeing to the film. He remained his old self, pouring forth to Hackford his emotional turmoil over the women in his life. The younger man saw that Hank's womanizing was a kind of orchestrated Divine Comedy, written and directed by Charles Bukowski. "He was constantly stirring the pot. He would always try to provoke either Liza or Linda into some sort of crisis," Hackford observes. "He would say, 'Oh these women are crazy. They're going to destroy me.'" Yet it seemed to Hackford that Hank himself enjoyed creating emotionally pitched situations, all of it feeding into his art—it provided him with things to write about. What seemed clear to Hackford was that Hank kept setting up one situation after another, what he describes as "this wonderful opera" that went on continually. Both women knew that Hank manipulated their emotions, but they acquiesced regardless.

As Hackford observed Hank closely, he became convinced that the writer's reputation in some quarters as a man who hates women was unjustified. He saw him rather as an individual fascinated with the battle of the sexes, even obsessed with it, much as one of Hank's heroes, James Thurber, had been. He knew that the women in Hank's life would have to be a major subject for his projected documentary. What he wanted to do was to examine Hank from the perspective of the turmoil he created in his life, and, at the same time, to have the women Hank lived with provide commentary of their own. In the film, Hank tried to come off as the aloof, superior one who sits back pontificating on the women in his life, and their stealth, while the women looked on him with a bemused attitude, describing how he manipulated them into various situations. Hackford thought they were brilliant in their analyses, easily as honest as Hank was about his strengths and weaknesses.

Hank revealed to Hackford his abiding obsession with the fact that he has small, almost dainty hands that stand in dramatic juxtaposition with the rest of his body. He said that his face represented his character, but his hands were his heart and soul: the hands of an artist. This revelation was the kind of personal detail Hackford wanted in the film. He wanted to avoid the usual interview situation, which only skimmed the surface. He saw Hank as the perfect subject because he didn't fear exposing his foibles either in writing or on the screen.

Another quality Hackford saw in Hank, and one that he would bring into the film, revolved around the poet as philosopher of L.A. He came to see firsthand that what had been written down in *Post Office*, the columns for *Open City*, and in his poetry, was not mere literature, but truly a reflection of how Hank lived and how his writing emerged directly from his own day-to-day experiences battling with life in L.A.

Hank's reunion with Linda came soon after Catalina. Hank and Liza were together at De Longpre one evening when the phone rang—he knew right away that it was Linda. She was calling from Utah to tell him how much she missed him. Liza left the house as Hank and Linda continued talking. They spoke for a long time, repeating how much they missed one another and how good it would be to get back together. The combat was forgotten. Hank could almost see Linda's flushed, chubby cheeks and playful eyes. That same evening he broke the news to Liza that he was going back to Linda.

Linda arrived back in town with her two children and her dog. One of the first things Hank told her was that he had to go and see Liza one last time, not wanting to just callously drop her without explaining things. Linda protested, but he told her that it was only a matter of a one-time meeting.

He saw Liza and then returned to Linda, who gave him the third degree; when he passed it, convincing her that he was not really serious about Liza, their life returned to normal—meaning that the fighting began again. Once more, Hank reveled in it, amused yet partly annoyed by his inability to live a calm, stable life with a woman. Perhaps he couldn't live without the turmoil, although he often said to me, "It has to end, the fighting. I can't take it. These things keep me from my work." But still he advanced on all fronts. He remained dedicated to his work no matter what difficulties he had in his personal life. Poetry and prose continued to flow off his typewriter.

On June 1, 1972, John Martin published *Mockingbird Wish Me Luck*, a book containing "The Mockingbird," one of the publisher's favorites. "Bukowski is so direct. To be able to uncover a truth so quickly . . . I'd never encountered that in poetry before. It was like digging into the side of a hill, and all of a sudden at the end of your pick is this solid gold nugget."

Bukowski's use of ordinary speech heightens the dramatic insight that "The Mockingbird" provides; the realistic vision plays off against a detached acceptance of life. Bukowski is the calm observer who doesn't romanticize himself, a poetic journalist simply giving the facts. He evokes the same set of images as in some of Robinson Jeffers's shorter poems, the animal at war with its own kind or with another species, or with the forces of nature. Unlike Jeffers, Bukowski finds the brutal facts of nature right in his own driveway:

> the mockingbird had been following the cat
> all summer
> mocking mocking mocking
> teasing and cocksure;
> the cat crawled under rockers on porches
> tail flashing
> and said something angry to the mockingbird
> which I didn't understand.
>
> yesterday the cat walked calmly up the driveway
> with the mockingbird alive in its mouth,
> wings fanned, beautiful wings fanned and flopping,
> feathers parted like a woman's legs,
> and the bird was no longer mocking,
> it was asking, it was praying
> but the cat
> striding down through centuries
> would not listen
>
> I saw it crawl under a yellow car
> with the bird
> to bargain it to another place.
>
> summer was over.

It has always intrigued me that Hank found his greatest poetic inspiration in Robinson Jeffers. There are similarities Jeffers was a loner like Hank, a man who had no truck with the infighting of the literary world. He believed that poetry had become slight and surface oriented, too precious. It needed bigness, more room in which to flex its muscles. Jeffers embraced Nieztsche's phrase from *Thus Spake Zarathustra*, "The poets lie too much." Because of that sentiment he strove not to go with the fashion of his time, either in form or content, but to be true only to himself, to rely on his own emotions. He didn't want to, "say anything because it was popular, or generally accepted, or fashionable in intellectual circles . . ." unless he believed it himself. The young Bukowski, reading Jeffers, whose narratives of tragic splendor played out against the isolated land in and around Big Sur or along the vast coastal stretches between California's urban centers, admired the harsh territory that Jeffers chose to celebrate. For a poet who laid claim to the urban environment, and often mocked nature, Hank remained true to Jeffers right up to the end of his own life.

Hank had read "Roan Stallion," learning from it the power of narrative poetry. The violent passion in that story poem held their appeal to his nature. He was writing prose at the time and it fascinated him that a poet could compose a story so haunting, so visceral and filled with such dark foreboding, and not be writing of the city. Hank liked phrases such as "the phantom rulers of humanity," "a woman covered by a huge beast in whose mane the stars were netted," and "A smear on the moon-lake earth." There were no primrose paths in Jeffers. Man stood as something of an aberration on the land. Organized humanity was not to be embraced, but recoiled from. Man was called on to find his own truth and insist upon it and ascend to his own idea of beauty. Hank did not probe deeply into the philosophical framework behind Jeffers. That was not his way with any poet. The jagged edges of Christian thought and of Greco-Roman mythology found in Jeffers only added to the boiling cauldron of words. He responded to Jeffers writer to writer, admiring the older poet's ability to stake his ground, the untamed land of coastal California, and the tragic lives of the people on it. There was no easy living in Jeffers. Hawks rose higher than the aspirations of humankind, and rocks along the coast held more majesty than all the man-made wonders of the world.

[251]

Hank felt drawn to his renegade soul: "his voice was dark/ a rock-slab pronouncement/ a voice not distracted by/ the ordinary forces of/ greed, cunning and/need. . ." It was from Jeffers that he would learn to carve out his own territory, attend to a strong, but focused vocabulary and work with a few well-chosen motifs.

In his Jeffers reading, Hank came across "Haunted Country" in which he found, "Children for all their innocent minds/Hide dry and bitter lights in the eye, they dream without/knowing it." He was in his early twenties when he discovered these lines. Jeffers also wrote of, "The inhuman powers, the servile cunning under pressure,/In a land grown old, heavy and crowded." Hank, about to break loose from the geography of his youth, and head out on the open road, felt this poem resonate within him. It was a haunted country. Jeffers said it well, and it was best to live in the shadows, best not to be a part of the servility. Hank remembered his own childhood, how he had been forced to hide so much of himself, how he couldn't trumpet his early writings before his parents. "I think what held me in that poem was the 'dry and bitter lights' part of it. I had teachers send me to the principal's office just for what they saw in my eyes. I didn't have to say anything. They read defiance and rebellion."

Jeffers saw terrifying beauty in the waves that hit the California shore. But these brooding, rhapsodic odes to pounding surf, to enduring rock, to the coast bending inland or jutting out in a long thin earthen arc, did not find their way into Hank's writings. Jeffers could live and die near the sound of the ocean, the smell of sea air, under the shadows of seabirds. In Hank's world, "the sea stinks/ and makes flushing sounds/like a toilet/it is a bad place to die. . ." In another poem he writes of a boy looking out a train window and saying of the passing ocean view that it isn't beautiful.

Hank learned many lessons from his old master, but he had his own turf, his own set of images and his own battles to wage. The ravine of water rushing down to the sea in a Jeffers poem became, in Hank's opus, a flow of cars on the Harbor Freeway, the rolling hillsides of "The Woman At Point Sur" became empty lots or "avenues of the dead" in Hank's realm.

In Jeffers there is a steady movement away from any central authority other than the haunting myth growing out of a single individual. This is what Bukowski, the aspiring novelist, the young man who dreamed of duking it out with Papa Hemingway, admired. "You know what I say about schools and all that stuff?" he asked one night on De Longpre Street. "I'm going to answer that . . . because I remember the dullness of the classroom. I can still hear the lies, the dead sentences. I say that a man should grow up like a single seed dropped out of a window and be allowed to grow upward into the sky and upward into God if there is a God, and if there isn't, upward into God anyway . . . a man has to take his own path." He was responding to a poem I had written about education which we published in *Laugh Literary and Man the Humping Guns*. Man is threatened in Jeffers because he subscribes to old, outmoded codes of conduct. Bukowski leveled his sights at poets who subscribed to old patterns, especially those who thought that the common life around them wasn't the stuff of poetry. He may not have known it back in 1955 when he began writing poetry in earnest, but he was reiterating Whitman's call for a poetry of the streets and the common man, not from a shelf. "There comes a time when you have to put the books aside," he said.

Hank's poem "Destroying Beauty" was written with Jeffers in mind. It is the kind of writing that stopped editors in their tracks. They were used to poems about finding beauty, celebrating it, not an assault like this: "a rose/red sunlight/I take it apart/in the garage/like a puzzle. . ." He compares the petals to "old bacon" and tells us that they fall to the floor "like the maidens of the world." What does he do at this point? This man who dares to dismantle a rose with the hope of discovering something profound about the world glances at a calendar hung on the garage wall, then touches his wrinkled face and smiles in the realization that "the secret is beyond me."

Regarding "Destroying Beauty," Hank confessed that it came from an image of long ago. "I must have written it in the mid-fifties, at the time when I had just begun to publish in the little magazines, but the title had been floating in my mind for decades. You're living in rooming houses all over the country, drinking cheap wine, wanting to get laid, waiting for an editor to take your short stories . . . other guys are in Europe fighting in a war that meant nothing to you. There's a bed, a table, a chair, a landlady in the hallway and you don't even have a typewriter. So, you might think about destroying beauty." Once, in St. Louis, he paused before a crack in the pavement—it was after a long drunk—and saw some weeds growing. "It was a beautiful sight," he said. "I loved those weeds. They grew right out of the grime."

"Destroying Beauty" is a steady drift toward the realization that there is a secret the poet cannot touch. He sensed that secret during his years of wandering. It is no wonder that he later saw himself as an outsider, with other men going off to fight in the war while he remained home, interested only in writing. To aid him on his quest for a writer's life he drank and deliberately chose to live by his wits. He had this romantic notion stuck in his head: toss yourself into the life of the streets and simply see how it turns out. It was enough to write. Sometimes he could rely on a typewriter, but mostly he had to settle for notebooks in which he scribbled over three hundred short stories in a decade's time, publishing only a handful, losing the rest.

Hank still looked to Jeffers in later years for inspiration. What he continued to admire was Jeffers's sense of endurance: the mind is resilient enough to fashion art out of the unending tragedy of existence. In "Jeffers," one of Hank's finest later poems, he spells out his admiration for the older poet's "blood-smeared horizons," and describes Jeffers's hawks, a recurring motif, as casting "shadows of doom," that seem to stretch over Hank's wholly urban universe. From "Roan Stallion," he re-echoes Jeffers's "stallions greater than men." The poem is a rare tribute by a poet who measured out praise sparingly. Hank wanted his readers to know that he had a debt to pay to an older master.

TWELVE

Early in 1972 Hank received an invitation to read in San Francisco for the City Lights Poet's Theater. All around the country English professors were lining up to bring Bukowski to their schools. By this time, he had already given readings at Bellingham, Washington, and at the University of New Mexico. The event in Frisco would be the first of several readings in the city of poets. At all of these readings Hank did his best to promote his image as a boozing, sex-crazed character.

Linda accompanied him to San Francisco and was as shocked as Hank to find that he had achieved celebrity status, at least in the literary community. Much of this had to do with the fact that *Erections, Ejaculations, Exhibition and General Tales of Ordinary Madness* did particularly well in the Bay Area.

Taylor Hackford saw the San Francisco reading as an excellent chance for making his film project a reality. For months he had listened to Hank philosophize on women, the racetrack, beer drinking, and life in general, but he had no film footage to show for it. Hackford decided to fly north with the poet, to document the trip and the reading. He hoped that this would provide enough material for the whole movie (especially since he only had a budget of twenty-five hundred dollars). As it turned out, this journey to the north became only one of many episodes in the film.

Nothing was posed. Hackford worked in cinema verité style, keeping the camera trained on the action, capturing Hank in his airplane seat by Linda, as he bought mixed drinks and leafed through poems. During the flight Hank ingenuously asked Hackford which work he should read. Because Hackford had a profound knowledge of Hank's work, he was able to help shape the reading as the plane flew north.

Hank and Linda stayed at Ferlinghetti's cramped, three-room apartment above the City Lights publishing office in the heart of North Beach, the city's old Italian neighborhood, dominated by Telegraph Hill to the north and Russian Hill on its south flank. To be holed up in the city's bohemian quarter did not appeal to the bard of East Hollywood. Only when he met Ferlinghetti, an easygoing man with soft blue eyes and a kindly disposition, was he able to relax. He enjoyed the treatment he received as the peer of a world-famous poet, a man widely read and translated since the mid-fifties. After a visit with their host, Hank and Linda went into the Trieste Café, a local coffeehouse and literary hangout. They ordered coffee, sat for a while, and then met with Ferlinghetti at the U.S. Café, an Italian restaurant on North Beach's main thoroughfare, Columbus Avenue. A writer for the *San Francisco Chronicle* who joined them for lunch later compared Bukowski to Hemingway. As they conversed, the appetizers appeared, but rather than wait around, Hank said that he needed to be alone before the reading. He and Linda walked out, and after going a few blocks, he leaned against the side of a building and vomited—a typical prereading occurrence for him, which would be repeated through the following years when he went on the road from college to college reading his poems.

Doug Blazek, who then lived in Sacramento, heard about Hank's reading and drove to San Francisco. He waited at the City Lights editorial offices, hoping to surprise him. When Hank arrived he didn't recognize Blazek, whom he had not seen for five years. Blazek waited a few moments, then said, "Hello, Hank," and Bukowski responded, genuinely pleased to see the younger poet. Blazek asked Hank teasingly,

"Why don't you grow more . . . change more as a person?" Blazek had undergone tremendous changes of his own, even repudiating his efforts as editor of *Ole*. His question was as much a reflection of his own turmoil and yearning to change as it was a real question from the former student to a teacher. Hank said, "I've got to play one good hand. I'm going to stick with this." In Blazek's eyes it meant he would remain true to what he terms "a restricted kind of shrunk nugget."

Blazek accompanied Hank, Joe Wolberg, the organizer of the reading, and Ferlinghetti to the reading. Hank's nervousness and fear showed. In Bukowski's eyes, the audience seemed to be tearing him apart. Wolberg had placed a refrigerator on the stage and stocked it with beer. Hank, already drunk, vomited just minutes before walking onstage. Once up there, he began insulting the crowd, setting the tone for a wild night, one that Blazek feels was more a sports event than a poetry reading—not merely because of the wildness of both poet and audience, but because it was held in a gymnasium. People shouted obscenities at the equally obscene poet who was transformed once onstage. From a wobbly drunk he turned into a dynamo, perfectly willing to entertain his band of fans. "I felt the need to be more a part of this," Blazek says. He yelled out to Bukowski to read particular poems and instructed a young poet friend to go up to the stage and ask Bukowski for two beers from the refrigerator. His friend obliged. Hank responded by opening the fridge and handing two beers down as the sea of people stomped their feet and howled. During the reading, and after it, booze and dope passed from hand to hand. In the bathrooms people urinated in the sinks, vomited into toilet bowls.

Hank took the rock star status heaped upon him in stride. Drunk as he was, however, a part of him desired a quieter, more settled evening. But if the crowd wanted a show, he was more than happy to respond. As Hackford panned the camera from the stage to the audience and back to the stage again, he was somewhat pained by the crowd's demand that Hank play the wild man. But every time Hank read, it was obvious that he was master of the situation. "I think when he saw the people packed into this huge gym, he really understood how big an impact he was making on his readers," Wolberg said. "He had never really been lionized like this before, and I think it really unnerved him, although he would never admit to it."

When the reading ended, Wolberg cleared a path for Hank and Linda through the crowded gymnasium. A small group went up to Ferlinghetti's apartment. Hank smoked marijuana and drank beer as the film crew recorded his every movement. According to Linda, a friend of Hank's got into a fight and threw a chair through a closed window, only a hint of the madness going on there that night. At one point, a drunken Hank accused Linda of coming on to other men. She ran from the apartment down to the street below and stayed there for several hours. When things quieted down upstairs and the people had gone home, she returned to the apartment through the broken glass that lay below the shattered window. Ignoring Hank, she called a yellow cab, packed her bag and went outside to wait.

When Hackford returned to L.A., he realized that he had gone through his entire budget for his proposed Bukowski film, but this didn't deter him. Convinced that he had fantastic footage, he decided to increase the running time of the film from twenty minutes, his original plan, to one hour. "So what I did was I went back and I eventually wrote backwards from that poetry reading, so that when you see the film . . . you meet Bukowski in Los Angeles and then we go up to Ned's liquor store and then we go back to Bukowski's place and we talk. He talks about his life and philosophy, and then he talks about going to the poetry reading, but this other stuff was done months later." The "other stuff" included interviews with Liza and Linda, and commentary on the two women by Bukowski.

Around the time of the City Lights reading, German translator Hans Hermann went to work on translating *Post Office*. He thought that the novel would surely make the difference in building up a German audience. A major publisher in Cologne brought it out in a first printing of four thousand copies. Unfortunately, the edition sold very slowly, although the reviews were positive. Meanwhile, a pocket-book publisher in Frankfurt published a paperback edition of *Notes of a Dirty*

Old Man in a printing of fifteen thousand copies. Again, sales were disappointing. Ferlinghetti sent Hank's loyal friend and promoter in Germany, Carl Weissner, a copy of *Erections, Ejaculations, Exhibitions and General Tales of Ordinary Madness*. He showed it around to all the publishers. "It was too big for the small presses," he said. Many of the editors he sent the book to wrote back nasty comments, such as "Spare us the unsavory ramblings of this low-life drunk" and "Do you think young people want to read this?" Weissner sent back insulting replies. "It was terrible," Weissner recalled. "Especially this uptight feeling that the publishers had about Hank's work." Things didn't seem to be going well at all in terms of really advancing Bukowski in a big way in Germany.

Weissner felt at a loss until he decided to try the poetry: he set himself to translating a substantial selection of Bukowski's poetry, choosing the strongest and most biting poems. He shaped the collection to reflect the varied tonalities of the poet. Weissner took the title from a chapbook, *Poems Written Before Jumping out of an 8 Story Window*. He offered them to a young editor named Benno Käsmayr who lived in Augsburg, a small town outside of Munich, who had just started a press called Maro Verlag, a one-man operation. Already a Bukowski fan, the editor went crazy over the translations and got the book out in four weeks' time.

Weissner's earlier efforts to publish the poems had met only with tiresome caution and insulting rejections posed as the common wisdom about publishing. As a result, he was determined to fly in the face of normal book marketing. The title, for instance, should be "short and punchy," something that appeals spontaneously to the eye; but it wasn't. He wrote an introduction that included photographs of the poet and letters from Bukowski to Weissner. (In one of them the poet tells the translator of his excitement over the upcoming edition of *Notes*.) He also included a poem in English about visiting Jon and Lou Webb when they were in New Mexico. And German book covers are normally very austere, but his shows nine photos of Bukowski at forty-two years old, which originally appeared in *The Outsider*; they show him in varying poses—cigarette in mouth as he bangs away on the typewriter, leaning back, cigarette in hand, looking satisfied with his work.

Weissner's vision about the poetry translations proved to be correct. The first printing, consisting of eighteen hundred copies, at first sold slowly; but soon the publisher managed to distribute the book through a chain bookstore, Montanus (Maro knew the buyer). Maro produced an expensive silk-screen poster for promotion. The book was not just unusual-looking, but quite handsome. Sales picked up suddenly, and the second printing was five thousand copies. In the end, the book sold fifty thousand copies and is correctly considered to be the book that sold Bukowski to the German public.

Käsmayr, like Carl Weissner, maintained a strong interest in American literature. Aside from publishing individual volumes of work by avant-garde American writers, he published *Terpentin on the Rocks*, a collection of poems by various poets selected by Weissner and Bukowski. The project gave Bukowski an opportunity to interest the German audience in some of the poets he had admired over the years, including Wanda Coleman, Gerald Lockin, Steve Richmond, and William Wantling. The first printing was in March 1978. A few years later the anthology was sold to Fischer Verlag, a major German publisher.

Once again, after the San Francisco reading, Hank and Linda reconciled. Linda moved from the house she rented and found a larger one on Edgewater Terrace at the north end of Silverlake. Rather than renting, she bought property. Hank agreed to move in with her in order to help meet the monthly payments. He gave up the place on De Longpre, a somewhat traumatic move for him, but he wanted to be with Linda. While living together, they maintained what Linda refers to as a liberated household. Everyone there—her two children, her, Hank—had to take their turn at various chores. (For instance, though, the person who did the dishes didn't have to do them on the night that they were used, so often dishes would stack up in enormous piles for a week or more!) The relationship went smoothly for a while. Hank had his desk in the bedroom, and spent a few hours each day writing. Linda recalls that everything he wrote then was sent off to John Martin on a frequent basis. Hank also did a lot of painting, often joining in with Linda's daughter Carissa. Hank went to the track as much as ever, and Linda often joined him. As Linda puts it, once they got to the track, they didn't bother one another. Hank always had a system going, which he used until he began losing, and then he would work out a new one. "I lost a lot more than Hank did," Linda recalls.

Tempers boiled over whenever Hank drank heavily, often leaving the house for long periods of time. Linda discovered that he was having an affair with a woman living in Hollywood. Hank told Linda about the woman, saying that she had a luxury car, plenty of money, and was a very cultured woman, not a ranch-hand type like Linda. Linda drove by her house one day and saw Hank on the sidewalk and almost ran over him. "I had a Volkswagen 'Thing,' a small car I had bought the previous summer in order to drive back to Boulder each year." Linda drove around the block again as Hank carefully gathered the beer that had fallen from his arms when Linda almost ran into him. After circling the block, she stopped her car, jumped out, and picked up a bottle of beer. She threw it through the window of the door that led to her rival's apartment, and ran up the stairs to confront her rival. The woman shouted to Hank, "Get her out of here!" Linda circled the block again. When she returned Hank got in the car with her and they drove home.

Not long afterward, Linda found Hank's car hidden on a side street near to the woman's apartment. Rather than confront them again, Linda returned to Edgewater, packed her bags, and left for Utah. She wrote a note telling him that she had gone away again and left it on the windshield of his car. Linda drove with her children to Boulder, where she worked in her sister Margie's bar. She continued doing her sculpture and writing, and finished several paintings. Hank continued living on at Edgewater Terrace. He finally explained his infidelity to Linda, via correspondence, telling her that he only played around when she deliberately made him jealous.

At the end of July, Linda invited Hank to come to visit her in Boulder. They stayed together in a small trailer parked on Linda's thirty acres perched high on the slopes of Boulder Mountain, a fairly isolated area. Hank didn't like it there. "It was too much country for him," Linda says, "too many trees, too many mountains." One day Hank wandered off on his own and became lost. Linda thought he was doing one of his angry walk-off routines. She didn't begin looking for him until several hours later. When she did, she came across a notebook he had taken with him in which to write—this alarmed her. Until that time, she didn't think anything might go wrong. She began tracking him as she would one of the lost cows from her father's ranch. After an hour or so, she found him in a panicky state. He had obviously been worried. The mountains of Boulder had nearly conquered the city poet. He had climbed over the fence of the pasture which Linda owned; if he had not climbed it, he would easily have been able to find his way back to camp.

Linda put on a party for Hank to introduce him to the local people: lumbermen, ranch hands, and roughnecks who worked in the oil industry. It was wild: the locals all danced insanely, Hank sneered at them. It soon became obvious to Linda that Hank did not enjoy his stay in the wilderness, so she drove him back to the airport, and he flew to Los Angeles.

When Linda came back to L.A., Hank had his bags packed. He wrote to Al Winans on July 16, 1973, confiding:

> been on a week's beerdrunk back from Utah. Linda and I have split. I have to be out of here by the 29th. I've got quite a little book with 3 or 4 numbers but I'll be damned if I quite want to get involved, and this battling with and living with the female has kept me trim in a fashion, but so much of the game is run on trickery, chess moves, false moves, ticklers, blasters, farts and one-tenth feelings . . . I think most of our women have been raised too much upon movie magazines and the screen. they've learned game-playing and dramatics but my head just wants to go where it is.

Before the television premiere of Taylor Hackford's *Bukowski*, a private screening was held on October 19, 1973, at the Barnsdell Park Arts Center. Hank brought a bottle of whiskey along, from which he guzzled until a guard came up and told him it was against the rules to have liquor in the theater—an ironic note considering that the film opened with one of Hank's thousands of beer runs to Ned's liquor store. "Well, I don't know," Hank said just before the film began, "I guess I'm going to Hollywood."

On Sunday, November 15, 1973, the television premier of the documentary took place on KCET. After the showing, several formal complaints were filed with the FCC, largely as a result of Hackford's refusal to censor the film. When Hank is on-stage, he might say "Fuck you" or make some other comment usually not allowed on television. Recognizing that a charge of obscenity could only help his film, Hackford sent it to the FCC for review, per their request: they wanted to judge whether or not it could be considered a "work of art" and therefore suitable for the airwaves.

What really focused attention on the film was the award it won: best cultural program of the year from the Corporation for Public Broadcasting. As a result, the National Endowment for the Arts became interested in the film, and wanted to air it nationally. Even though it had been declared not obscene by the FCC, it could not be shown coast-to-coast with the improper language in it. They granted Hackford ten thousand dollars "to cut the film down" to half an hour, making it mostly poetry and commentary—but it wouldn't be the same, as far as Hackford was concerned, it would be sanitized. However, it brought Hank a lot of attention, establishing him as a minor media star. "Once people saw Bukowski's personality on screen," Hackford says, "they realized this was an important figure."

Bukowski won several other awards, and was showcased at the Museum of Modern Art in New York. Because of the success with the film, Hackford wanted to do a feature film based on Hank's work. He thought particularly of *Post Office*, and at one point tried to interest John Cassavetes in making the film, realizing that he himself didn't have the resources to do so. Playboy Productions saw the documentary film and bought the rights to *Post Office*. Hackford later bought the rights back, hoping that someday he would produce it. His own first feature-length effort was *The Idol Maker*, about a rock and roll manager in the early sixties and his relationship to budding stars.

Less than two weeks after the showing of Hackford's film on television, Hank flew to San Francisco once again, this time to read with poet William Stafford at an event sponsored by the San Francisco State College Poetry Center. He earned a fee of one hundred dollars, plus expenses, less than a tenth of what he would come to receive for readings a few years later, as he became increasingly well-known. He and Stafford made a strange combination, as the latter wrote quiet, meditative poetry, a dramatic contrast to Bukowski's work. Originally, he was asked if he wouldn't mind reading with Robert Bly and he wrote back to tell the organizers that he didn't object to reading with anyone they chose.

The reading was held at the War Memorial Building, an environment as ponderous as the name itself. There was no problem filling up the vast auditorium, but there was some difficulty getting Hank inside. He had ensconced himself in the Jury Room, across the street from the auditorium where he began drinking heavily. A. D. Winans joined him, and they left the bar shortly before the reading, along with two other people, and made their way to Lawrence Ferlinghetti's van parked in a nearby alley—where Hank had stashed away a bottle filled with vodka and orange juice. He refused Winans's request for a drink, saying that he needed all the alcohol he could get before facing the audience. They sat in the back of the van, then got out, whereupon Bukowski leaned over the side of the van and vomited. They walked to the back of the building, went in a side entrance, and found Stafford already reading. Instead of taking his place directly offstage, Bukowski insisted on walking down the center aisle and finding a seat ten rows from the front. This caused a commotion as people began talking, saying things like "There he is! It's Bukowski!" Far from being disturbed by the uproar, he appeared to be enjoying the attention he was getting at the other poet's expense. "To Stafford's credit, he kept on reading," Winans recalls, "never losing his composure, seeming to realize that maybe eighty percent of the crowd had come to hear the 'dirty old man' read, not him."

During the reading itself, when Hank came onstage the crowd went wild. He wore his reading glasses and combed back his long hair. Taking one long look at the audience he said, "Let's get going, let's get it done, and then let's get out and live." A woman heckled him, telling him to calm down. "Remove this lady from the auditorium," he said.

He took a drink from the bottle he had onstage, then began reciting the first poem, "No title." It describes his rent being raised and the L.A. Department of Water and Power calling to say that his water bill was going up. He read slowly, deliberately, almost in a monotone, not glancing at the audience. He had apparently just written it with his trip to San Francisco in mind, since the poem contained mention of the city. He said, "I just don't know a goddamned thing about San Francisco. I just came here tonight." He asked if the lady heckler had been removed yet, and hearing no answer, repeated, "Has that lady been removed as I requested?" Somebody else yelled out to him and he responded, "As long as you have scotch, you stay." He bantered with the audience and then said, "Let me be delicate and holy . . . Let me read my next poem."

Bukowski offered vintage Bukowski. The people had come not only to hear his poetry but also to witness a wildman of literature. He didn't let his followers down that night, giving them lively commentary, getting his digs in now and then. After the third poem, he said, "You didn't think old Bukowski could be subtle now and then, did you?" A few photographers began snapping pictures. "*Bring my scotch!*" he shouted. "*Not flashcubes, brother.*" This came before a bitter poem about quarreling lovers, which he ended by saying, "That poem is dedicated to Liza Williams, and she deserves it."

He took another break, then read a poem about the supermarket, in which he rolls his cart down the aisles and becomes involved with a woman shopper. After the poem he asked, "What is the difference between me and Bob Hope? It worries me a little." He waited a moment and then asked, "Jack Micheline, do you have anything to say?" Micheline rose to the occasion, shouting, "Let me read a poem."

"Jack, I'll tell you what," Bukowski said. "Let me finish my reading and you can have the stage."

Then he read a few more poems, after which he said, "If William Stafford is still in the audience and he hasn't fainted, here's a little serious one . . . Should I do like Mr. Stafford does and say, 'I have two poems left'? I'm just a natural-born nasty drunk. I have two poems left." Before the last one he told the audience that he would be finished unless they voiced a "vociferous demand" for more poems "because I'm good and I know it."

Following the poem, which commented on the death of Ezra Pound, he left the podium momentarily, then came back and addressed Micheline. "I'm gonna say something nasty about you, Jack. You slept on my rug and didn't pay any rent." The crowd began howling. Bukowski yelled into the microphone, "I hate precious poets and I hate precious audiences, too." He read a couple more poems, along with his accompanying commentary. Before the final poem he asked, "Do you ever get the feeling you'll suddenly go mad doing a thing like this?" After finishing the poem he briskly walked from the stage, then out of the building together with Winans and a few young fans and went back to the Jury Room, where they continued drinking.

Hank rushed from city to city giving poetry readings, and spent much of the time between them in L.A., still warring with Linda, even though they no longer lived together. John Martin edited and published a collection of Bukowski's short stories, work that had not gone into the City Lights collection, and some newer stories, under the title *South of No North*. The subtitle, *Stories of the Buried Life*, is a revelatory footnote to how the writer viewed himself during much of his life. There are twenty-seven stories in the collection, including "All the Assholes in the World and Mine" and "Confessions of a Man Insane Enough To Live with Beasts," those two raw works from the *Ole* days. A few of the stories, such as "Politics" and "Bop Bop Against that Curtain," shed light on the writer's earlier life, literally those "buried years" when he developed his persona as the ultimate outsider. The former story—a rare glimpse of his youth—concerns his time at L.A. City College when he pretended sympathy for Nazism purely to stir things up on a campus where most of the other students were espousing a patriotic, anti-Nazi line.

June 1974 saw the publication of *Burning in Water Drowning in Flame*. This collection of poems, covering the years 1955 to 1973, was divided into four sections, including the two Loujon Press books, the first Black Sparrow collection, and a gathering of newer poems from 1972 and 1973. All of these were written during the happiness and madness of his life off-and-on with Liza and Linda.

Burning offers Bukowski fans a rare chance to catch him in a moment of reflection through a preface wherein he touches briefly on how each of the books in the selection came together. He wrote that Jon Webb thought of most writers as "detestable human beings" and wanted to see what Bukowski was like before publishing him. He commented that the bulk of the poems for *Crucifix* "were written during one very hot, lyrical month in New Orleans in the year 1965." And he talked of how he and John Martin met. He mentioned how the first Black Sparrow book, *At Terror Street and Agony Way*, came into being. In summing up his feelings about what amounted to a retrospective of his life as a poet, he wrote:

> Looking at these poems written between 1955 and 1973 I like (for one reason or another) the last poems best. I am pleased with this. I have, of course, no idea what shape my future poems will take, or even if I will write any, because I have no idea how long I will go on living, but since I began writing poetry quite late in life, at the age of 35, I like to think they'll give me a few extra years now, at this end. Meanwhile, the poems that follow will have to do.

The last set of poems he refers to offer a hint of the lean style that Hank's poetry developed later. Several of them shed light on his relationship with Linda. "Letters" begins:

she sits on the floor
going through a cardboard box
reading me love letters I have written her
while her 4 year old daughter lies on the floor
wrapped in a pink blanket and
three-quarters asleep . . .

Of the many times they fought and then broke up, the second and third stanzas go on:

we have gotten together after a split
I sit in her house on a
Sunday night

the cars go up and down the hill outside
when we sleep together tonight
we will hear the crickets . . .

Another poem referring to events current in Hank's life at the time is "On the Circuit," which begins:

It was up in San Francisco
after my poetry reading
it had been a nice crowd
I had gotten my money
I had this place upstairs
there was some drinking
and this guy started beating up on a fag
I tried to stop him
and the guy broke a window
deliberately.

Amid the writing of new poems, a furious schedule of poetry readings, and his continuing drama with Linda, Hank finished the manuscript for his second novel, *Factotum*. He had come up with the title one day while thumbing through the dictionary: he happened across the word and, seeing the definition, decided that it fit him back in the forties, the period discussed: "a jack of all trades . . ." The title came easily, but the writing hadn't: he worked on the book sporadically through late 1973 and into the following year. In the fall of 1974 he put the book on the back burner, but he finished it in time for publication in 1975.

After moving out of Linda's house, Hank rented an apartment in a court with eight bungalows, on Carlton Way off Western Avenue. His neighbors included a stripper, a manager of a massage parlor, and other assorted L.A. low-life types. The surroundings and the people were comforting to him. The place was $105.00 per month, complete with paint flaking off the walls, an ancient kitchen, and torn curtains. A large, noisy fan in the living room provided air conditioning during the summer; naturally, beer bottles stood in every available corner. He saw a lot of Brad and Tina Darby, a young couple he had gotten to know in the mid-seventies. Brad, a photographer, snapped pictures of Hank everywhere he could. Together with this young couple, Hank attended numerous parties and went to flashy clubs. Linda still had her place in Silverlake, and spent a lot of time taking care of her children, seeing Hank now and then as he zoomed in and out of town.

Early in 1975, Linda took a job at Flo's Cocktail Lounge on Sunset Boulevard, working as a hostess. Brad showed Linda photos of Hank with a woman sitting nude on his knee. Brad wanted Linda to comment on the photos; she said they were beautiful before ripping them up. Brad scrambled on the floor to pick up the pieces. "I knew the relationship was on its last legs," Linda says. "Hank had some woman fly in from NYC or some other place, to stay on a weekend . . . I went to Hank's door and looked in the window and I could see Hank walking around nude while this woman lay on the bed." One night Linda was at home feeling isolated, looking out the window at a half-dead pine tree ravaged by smog. "I knew Bukowski was with another woman; I could feel it from across town," Linda recalls. "I knew I had to get out of the city if I was ever going to break up [with him] in some final way. I couldn't be just one of his many women."

Around the time she put the house up for sale, she became pregnant. Linda had been with Hank and two other guys, one from the bar where she worked, and then another man named Frenchy, and didn't know whose baby it was. The house sold quickly, and she had to move her furniture out. As she was packing her possessions and lifting heavy objects, she began to hemorrhage. A friend drove her to Country Hospital, where the fetus was removed.

Linda was recuperating alone in the house, when Hank called to tell her about a new girlfriend. "He wanted to incite my jealousy about a new woman." He told her, "I have a new mattress. We're going to sleep on this mattress." When she told him about her miscarriage, Hank was already on his way to a reading out of town, and figured she would get help elsewhere.

"I was in no mood to hear this," Linda says. "The next day I was still half dead . . . and somebody brought me a bottle of wine to build up my blood . . . I drank the whole bottle . . . and I went to his house, broke in, and took some of his books and paintings and his typewriter. I wanted to hurt him more than anything because he only loved his own self, his typewriter, and radio."

As soon as Linda King gathered back her strength, she decided to take further retribution on Bukowski. Quite by chance, Hank returned and caught Linda in the bushes with his books. He said, "Give me back my things! This isn't right." Linda, who had been drinking for hours before coming over to Hank's, snapped back, "But it is right!" She took his books to the back of the court and threw them through his glass door. Every time she threw one, she said, "And don't tell me about your women anymore . . . and I don't want to hear anymore about what you are doing . . ."

Linda had taken his typewriter from the apartment earlier. She went to where she had left it, picked it up, and ran with it to the street, whereupon she threw it onto the pavement. Not knowing what else to do, Hank called the police, who subsequently filed a report on the incident.

Then Linda and her two children moved to Phoenix. It wasn't long after she had settled there that Hank came to visit. When he got off the plane he took one look at her and saw that she had lost a lot of weight and gotten back into shape.

"It looks like you do better without me," he said. They spent a week together, as lovers, and tried to get along. It seemed clear to both of them, however, that their relationship had finally run its course.

He wrote to her some months later when he got involved with a woman named Cupcakes O'Brien. Hank asked Linda to return to L.A. and rescue him, pleading that they could have more wild crazy fun times together. Linda bowed out; she had had enough, and knew that the same cycle would be repeated again—she didn't want to go through it. And so, the relationship had truly come to an end. Hank set his sights elsewhere.

THIRTEEN

L ITTLE did Hank know that one of the most important persons in his life would come to a reading he gave on September 29, 1976, at the Troubadour, a popular L.A. night spot on Santa Monica Boulevard, a few miles west of his apartment on Carlton Way. This was one of his last public readings, and, typically, had sold out. The Troubadour's main dance floor was crowded to capacity on the night that Linda Lee Beighle, the future Mrs. Bukowski, heard him read. Although she had wanted to meet him for some time, she had waited for more than a year, attending his readings, staying in the background.

Linda, who is about twenty-five years younger than Hank, watched women screaming with passionate intensity at their hero, and closely observed his lively responses. The crowd performed nearly as much as the man whom they had come to hear. Hank's motto was to never let the audience rule. Give them room. Let them bellow and howl, but keep ultimate control in your own hands. After a decade and a half of practice, he knew the game and played it well.

Perceptive fans, though, could sense the poet's vulnerability. Such was the case with Linda. It would not be an exaggeration to say that she saw through the carnival atmosphere surrounding this and many of his other readings and straight to the man himself. She admired him and loved his writing. She sensed that his poems were not mere literary invention but, rather, represented his innermost self. In retrospect, she stresses that her feeling for him was almost mystical, and based in large part on intuition.

After the reading, as Hank was leaving the Troubadour with another woman, she approached him. Just as he walked out of the front door, she handed him a note with her name, address, and telephone number. He responded on the spot by giving her his phone number—and he included a one-line poem, which she can no longer recall, along with a drawing of a little man with outstretched arms.

Perfect! He, the man with that great singular vision, actually responded to her overture. Linda drove home convinced that what had transpired between her and Bukowski was only a prelude to new and profound experiences.

Two days later Hank rang her up at the Dewdrop Inn, a health-food restaurant she owned in Redondo Beach, a seaside suburb of Los Angeles—close enough to the madness of the city to receive its smog, but also blessed with sea breezes and cool Pacific air. He suggested that they get together. "Listen, why don't I drive down to your place?" he said. She told him her place was a restaurant and gave him directions. He went back to work, ecstatic at having called; she went about her business, making sandwiches, conversing with her customers, and thinking of him.

On his way there, Hank pictured Linda Beighle in command of a formidable enterprise, directing waitresses and cooks, busily going over the accounts. Thinking of this, and feeling nervous, he became confused and ended up in Lakewood, a community of tract homes—definitely not Bukowski territory. He went to a pay phone at a gas station, called Linda, and said that her directions were wrong. "I need a drink." he confessed. "I'm going back." She asked him to go and check the street signs, so she would be able to direct him from where he had phoned. He let the phone hang and went to find the name of the street. When he returned she gave new instructions, making him promise that he was really on his way.

"You're coming, right?"

"Sure, baby. I'll be right there."

"Okay, now—I'm waiting."

"Yeah. Just let me get in the car. You'll have Bukowski in no time."

He drove to the Pacific Coast Highway and came to the indicated turnoff. Soon he saw a hand-painted sign over a small building: Dewdrop Inn. Before his eyes lay a whimsical and lyrical storefront, anything but the powerhouse restaurant he had constructed in his mind. *What had he gotten himself into?* And that *rainbow* over the entranceway? *Good God!*

Linda saw him pass with a look of panic on his face. A few minutes later he called from a redneck bar up the street from the restaurant, the kind of place that is crowded in the middle of the day. With a vodka-7 in one hand, he used the other to dial her number to inform her that he had stopped for a drink. "Okay now. I'm almost there," he said. When he finished he drove back to the Dewdrop Inn. From inside it seemed a little more substantial, and the hippielike atmosphere amused him. The interior was an honest-to-God time-warp. Hank felt as if he had been thrown back into the mid-sixties. Linda stood behind the counter, preparing a salad, while a few young men in shorts stood around gazing off into space and others huddled together on the floor. A few people were gathered together on a couch. Hank now saw Linda in the light of day for the first time: blond hair, striking eyes, lean body, and a warm, whimsical smile.

Feeling awkward and out of place, he walked over to a bookcase and saw a few of his titles, all with tattered covers. "Somebody's been reading these," he thought to himself. Eschewing his own creations for a paperback edition of Federico Garcia Lorca's poetry, he thumbed through it, pretending to read. A few lines caught his attention, but he was really thinking of Linda's clientele. *Jesus, who are these kids?* he asked himself. None were over thirty. They were tan, athletic, and exuded contentment, as if none were touched by the hard realities of the world. Linda Lee wasn't just the owner of a health-food restaurant they frequented—she had more *life* than them. Her spirit served as a focal point. *She has verve,* Hank noted. More than that, she exuded authority. So maybe this trip would lead to something. All he knew for sure was that women had led him through many strange doors before and this one seemed like it might be . . .

[275]

well, *very strange indeed*. Meher Baba stared down upon him, beneficent, garlanded in beaming soulfulness. *Who knows?*

Linda was too busy to talk to Hank for a while, but she brought him a sandwich. He ate it, watched her clean the kitchen, then helped her close down for the night; together, they brought the tables and chairs in from outside and took the garbage out. They drove to a liquor store for wine, and soon they were at her house, a small, comfortable place presided over by a poster of Meher Baba, just like in the Dewdrop. She had made all of the furniture herself, including the bed. They opened a bottle of red wine as they settled back on her couch. Before the bottle was half finished there was a knock on the door. Word had gotten around that Charles Bukowski was over at her apartment. Rather than being left alone, they found themselves entertaining a whole tribe of beach boys and her women friends. Instead of being alone with this new woman, Hank surrendered to the stream of young people who paraded before him, including one who aspired to be a published poet. He told Hank that he planned to publish his own book of poems by himself. "Why not?" Hank said, "Whitman did it"—not bothering to mention that the thought of self-publication had never entered his own mind.

People came in throughout the evening, many bringing six-packs in homage to the poet. Linda knew all of them well and took it in stride. Hank, as usual, seemed unruffled. Finally only she and her roommate remained. "Listen, I better be going," Hank said. Linda insisted that he stay. "I haven't had a chance to talk to you," she said. With that said, her roommate got up and went into his room. They sat and talked. Hank was comfortable with her, realizing that she could hold her own in conversation and that she spoke with intelligence and tenacity. When the wine ran out he said that he had become too drunk to drive home.

"You can sleep in my bed," she said. "But no sex."

"Why?"

"One doesn't have sex without marriage."

"One doesn't?"

"Meher Baba doesn't believe in it."

[276]

"Sometimes God can be mistaken."

Linda insisted.

Over the course of the next few months Hank visited on occasion, sitting in the restaurant while Linda worked. She liked having his forceful presence in the Dewdrop, which was more like a living room than a business. In planning her business, she had deliberately set it up like a house. Art hung on the walls, and books and magazines were scattered haphazardly throughout the dining area.

Meher Baba notwithstanding, their friendship gradually grew serious, and more sensual. In comparing Linda Beighle to the women he had been with in the past years, Hank saw her as a kind of shelter amidst a raging storm, and realized he might be able to free himself from a cycle of womanizing that had worn him out. He wanted to make his way toward what he called "an easy clarity," not having to worry about racing through the ruins of a kaleidoscopic series of relationships with lovers who were hyped up on sex, drugs, and alcohol. Linda's personality was serene in comparison to the lives of the women he had been chasing since he and Linda King had gone their separate ways. The more he came to know her, the more convinced he was that they might settle into a longtime affair. Her business, her small apartment with its shrine to Meher Baba, and the whole environment of Redondo Beach presented a dramatic contrast to the rundown area around Carlton Way. "I liked going down to the inn—because Linda was there—but after a while, I wanted to be back in the anarchy of the city." Hank says. "We'd run back and forth between both of our places. Plus, I was still seeing other women for a while."

Hank and Linda discovered that they had gone beyond thinking of sex as the only way to sustain a relationship. She listened to Hank talk about the period of his life from 1970 to 1977, learning of all the people involved and the parts they had played in the unfolding drama of Bukowski as sex genius. Hank made it clear to her that this phenomenon had begun for him after the age of fifty, a fact that Linda found amusing. The stories were amusing. Much of Hank's poetry from the period went into the making of *Love Is a Dog from Hell*.

While Hank enjoyed his revelry, there was an equal amount of pain. In fact, he bore deep scars from his search for love and sexual fulfillment. Naturally he didn't want to rush into anything serious. Even so, he soon realized that he liked being with Linda Lee on more than just a part-time basis. Also, what she refers to as his "research" for a new novel about his affairs with numerous women had just been completed.

Gradually, she and Hank settled into a routine that found them spending long weekends together at Carlton Way. Linda Lee remembers his apartment as a foul environment in dire need of a clean-up job—especially the kitchen, which had a stove that was caked with grease about half an inch thick.

Linda Beighle grew up in Penn Valley, near Bryn Mawr, and on the Main Line, an exclusive corridor of well-to-do communities next to the trains heading into downtown Philadelphia. Her grandfather, O. Snyder, founded the Philadelphia Hospital and College of Osteopathy, and was a prominent figure in the city. Her mother, Honora Snyder, was raised in what Linda describes as "an extremely aristocratic family." Her father, James L. Beighle, of German and Welsh descent, provided well for his wife, who spent her time keeping house and raising Linda, her sisters Jhara and Gwendolyn, and her brother, Peter.

Linda was a rebellious child, suspicious of the tight-laced confining world she lived in, and of the propriety of so many of her friends. She ran away from home at age eleven, and more successfully at fifteen, when she moved to a nearby neighborhood, found a job as a waitress (having lied about her age), and found a place to stay in a rooming house. She managed to live on her own for nearly four months, until her family finally located her.

In 1971, Linda moved to California, a veteran of the sixties hippie movement and a veteran flower child. She had just returned from a trip to India, and was eager to begin a new life on the West Coast. Her devotion to Meher Baba had been spurred on by a picture she saw of the spiritual master while working in a nightclub during her first stay in

California in the sixties. She asked the owner of the club who that man was as his face fascinated her. She became involved with an artist who followed the master's teachings—when she asked him why he so effortlessly maintained a "high" all the time, he attributed it to Meher Baba. The artist gave Linda one of the master's books, *The Everything and the Nothing*. In 1971, having become a follower, Linda took the money she had saved from numerous jobs, and opened the Dewdrop Inn.

Hank continued seeing a few other women during those first few months of dating Linda Beighle, including one whom he had nick-named "Scarlet" and written about in his poetry quite extensively. None of this bothered Linda, who watched the competition drop away one by one. She retained her apartment in Redondo and kept the restaurant running, liking the idea of having her own circle of friends and a world she alone had defined, separate from Hank. Her commitment to her business gave her an understanding of his need for time at the track and time to write. The drives between the apartment on Carlton Way and Redondo Beach became more frequent in the winter of 1976. Once Hank was picked up by the police for drunk driving on his way back from Linda's. Taylor Hackford bailed him out from the drunk tank, and Linda later came over to Carlton Way, only to find Hank lying in his shorts, surrounded by a pile of whiskey bottles and ashtrays. Two lesbians who lived in the court were there celebrating his release. She ran the two women off, but later, she and the lesbians became friends. They dubbed Hank the "porno king" and Linda Beighle the "health food queen."

Linda watched Hank undergo a transformation whenever they drank for a long period of time. "He would have to become real drunk," she says, "and he would go into this other dimension, from the ranting, raving drunkard to the deeply philosophical Bukowski, and he would talk about the inner world, spiritual things, sometimes for hours." What she found attractive in Hank's extended monologues was his combination of openness and wisdom. She saw so much of the child coming out of this self-described "madman-recluse," and so much pain stemming from his earlier years—especially regarding his parents, and his former lovers. Yet, it was all balanced by an ability to move beyond self-pity and to transform the tragedies of his life into building blocks for the continued development of his own character and his art. Linda recalls the time that Hank met her mother, Honora, during their first Christmas together in December 1977. Honora traveled from her home in the East, anxious to meet her daughter's new boyfriend. Hank still drank very heavily at this time. He told her mother, "You know, Honora, I love your little girl. I keep her heart in my back pocket and sometimes I sit on it." The comment was a one-line poem, easy to comprehend, completely honest, just like the words Hank put down on paper.

"A lot of wine drinking going on then," Linda recalls. "I got Hank to switch from beer to wine. We drank in excess. I always enjoyed drinking. This was something else, but I did it, and still managed to get to the café and open on schedule." Every so often the poet Ben Pleasants, who had known Hank for a number of years and published often in *The Wormwood Review*, came by to drink. Linda had been shocked by Hank's eating habits. He used to go to a place called Philly's Hoagie Shop at Western and Sunset, where he would eat either a hoagie or a cheese-steak sandwich. To cure this, she took him into a store near Carlton Way, and bought him vitamins and a supply of health food. He took to the new regimen as if he had been on it all of his life, and noticed a difference in his physical well-being almost immediately.

Linda didn't set out to reform Hank, though. Her goal was merely to put him on a healthier diet—she wanted *him* to remain as strong as his writing. Beyond that, she knew that she and he could be of real help to one another: "I believed that I could help him be a better human being," she says. "Having read his books, I felt I knew his heart. I saw a lot of sadness, and I wanted to help allow him to feel free enough to open up parts of himself that had remained closed." She saw much of their interaction as a process of becoming, an opening up into new perceptions, a kind of expansiveness. Her attitude was basically new for Hank, considering that the ladies he had been with in his immediate past were more concerned about sexual in-fighting and complex interpersonal games.

While his relationship with Linda intensified, Hank completed his new novel, *Women*, in October 1977, a 433-page manuscript in ninety-nine episodes. He sent it to John Martin, who decided to hold off issuing it because of the release of the poetry collection, *Love Is a Dog from Hell*. Somehow, the new novel had put more fire into Hank's system: he wrote twenty to thirty poems a week, pumping them out as he had in the *Crucifix* period. He had begun in 1955 with the idea of the clear, focused poem, devoid of pretense, and had pursued it, becoming ever more sparse in his imagery Linda had a lot to do with a new sense of rejuvenation in his creative work. In a letter to A. D. Winans on October 27, 1977, Hank wrote:

> Yes, Linda Lee is a good woman. I was due for some luck. She is a sayer with a gentle courage and doesn't play man against man as if she were some golden cow. I've had some bad ones, many bad ones. the percentages have come around and I am able to accept them.

Love Is a Dog from Hell, a poetic record of his numerous love affairs that came before his involvement with Linda Beighle, was published in 1977. Reading the book from beginning to end, one easily gets the feeling of walking through a gallery of portraits of women. The first poem, "Sandra," describes a slim and tall woman with earrings wearing a long gown. "the six foot goddess" is the title for a poem beginning:

> *I'm big*
> *I suppose that's why my women always seem*
> *small*
> *but this 6 foot goddess*
> *who deals in real estate*
> *and art*
> *and flies from Texas*
> *to see me . . .*

The collection follows the theme of the title. There are specific poems from this collection that stand out for their humorous dialogue. One of them, "I have shit stains in my underwear too" is a snapshot of life in the "whorehouse district," as the poet called the area around Carlton Way:

> I hear them outside;
> "does he always type this
> late?"
> "no, it's very unusual."
> "he shouldn't type this
> late."
> "he hardly ever does."
> "does he drink?"
> "I think he does. "
> "he went to the mailbox in
> his underwear yesterday."
> "I saw him too."
> "he doesn't have any friends."
> "he's old."
> "he shouldn't type this late."
>
> they go inside and it begins
> to rain as 3 gun shots sound half a block
> away and
> one of the skyscrapers in
> downtown L.A. begins
> burning
> 25 foot flames licking toward
> doom.

Bukowski loved this kind of poem, an affirmation that he hadn't gone soft, that he had, indeed, quit striving for what he looked upon as an easy technical proficiency.

Another of the shorter poems in *Love Is a Dog from Hell*, "the place didn't look bad," has the same hard edge to it:

> she had huge thighs
> and a very good laugh
> she laughed at everything
> and the curtains were yellow
> and I finished
> rolled off
> and before she went to the bathroom
> she reached under the bed and
> threw me a rag.
> it was hard
> it was stiff with other men's
> sperm.
> I wiped off on the sheet.
>
> when she came out
> she bent over
> and I saw all that behind
> as she put Mozart
> on.

In "madness," he dives into the misery of the squalid life at Carlton Way and its surroundings:

> the woman in the court behind me howls,
> weeps every night.
> sometimes the county comes
> and takes her away for a day or two.
>
> I believed she was suffering the loss
> of a great love
> until one day she came over and told me about
> it . . .

[283]

From the center of the low-life in L.A. to the arms of Linda Lee Beighle—a wide chasm, and Hank crossed over gladly. He no longer needed to prove himself. The macho Bukowski, so often thought of as having a Hemingway complex, especially in his relations with the opposite sex, could finally settle down with one woman. The anarchic, helter-skelter style of his love relationships had ended.

Linda was not a writer. She dreamed of becoming an actress, and in their first few years together she attended drama classes. Her devotion to the philosophy of Meher Baba continued unabated. The cynical Bukowski, far from disapproving, was amused by her interest in the "avatar of the age." People who visited the home they later bought together were often astounded to find Baba's face looking down on them with his effervescent smile.

That home was bought because Hank's book sales were bringing in so much money by the late seventies that he was advised to buy a house for tax purposes. The only one he had owned was his father's place, which he inherited, and he had quickly sold it. He and Linda ranged far from Carlton Way, looking for a suitable property, even going as far north as Bakersfield in the San Joaquin Valley. One of the areas they were interested in was Topanga Canyon, just to the north of L.A. But on one venture there, they stopped in a bar and all the people recognized Bukowski. They began calling his name, and suddenly free drinks began to show up. Far from feeling cheered by all of this, he wanted out. Half of the guys in the bar had that Charles Manson look, a general sense of physical and spiritual dissipation. Hank had had enough of that.

They explored San Pedro. The general atmosphere seemed more easygoing than other parts of L.A., and the summers weren't sweltering because it was so close to the ocean. They liked the old downtown area—there was a seediness that was neither oppressive nor depressive. Unlike some of the other beach towns, the spirit of the sixties hadn't settled on it. Perhaps the biggest factor was how close the freeways were; they could bring Bukowski to Santa Anita or Hollywood Park racetracks quickly—a major consideration. He didn't want to sacrifice the racetrack, even if it meant compromising in other ways.

The house they found lay securely in an unpretentious middle-class neighborhood. The lots were spacious enough to allow for privacy, and the house sat far back from the street. Hank wanted to wait a while before committing himself financially, but Linda insisted, fearing that someone else might buy it before they did. And when they bought the property in October 1978, Hank realized he could now barricade himself even more from the demand of the literary public. He had done enough readings and began turning down almost all of them. The same held true for interviews and requests for personal meetings.

Hank took to the house as if he had always lived there, installing himself in a small, second-floor room that contained a large oak desk left by the previous occupants. He set his typewriter on it, filled the drawers with paper, and went to work. They brought a bed Linda had built for Hank's place on Carlton Way late in 1976 and put it in the bedroom. His first poem at the new house was "Fear and Madness":

> barricaded here on the 2nd floor
> chair against the door
> butcher knife on table
> I type my first poem here
> I type this
> for my tax accountant
> for the girls in Omaha
> for my tax accountant
> I am broke again
> I own 1/4 of this house
> I have a pear tree
> I have a lemon tree
> I have a fig tree
> everybody is worried about my soul now
>
> . . .

I can fail in many ways now
I was always good at that.

the plumbing is of copper
and the typer is of me
and there's enough ground out front to live off of
that is, if I can get my ass out of this chair.

barricaded here on the 2nd floor
I am in a small room again.

Linda Beighle cultivated a garden, as well as keeping the Dewdrop Inn running for several more years. She and Hank settled into a routine that led him to the racetrack during the day, home to shower, out for dinner, and then home to sit in the living room surrounded by cats and wine bottles—only occasionally to hold court with visitors. Late in the evening Hank would see Linda Lee off to bed and then sit down in his workroom to write, his wine bottle near at hand. She understood his rhythms and didn't try to change him. "She hooked me on the wine, and that was good," says Hank, "and the vitamins. When it came time to write Linda left me alone."

Her acceptance of Hank's lifestyle had a great deal to do with the success of their relationship. Her belief that his writing reflected his inner being helped her to accept his mood swings and his need for privacy—which she came to guard, especially as his fame continued to grow through the mid-eighties. Having her own friends and interests, entirely separate from Hank's, was also a boon. Linda came to know the threshold that no one could cross with Hank—even her. She saw it as a secretive part of him, which served as the Wellspring for his talent.

Hank described *Women* to A.D. Winans as "some type of high-low comedy" and excused his treatment of some of his friends and acquaintances by saying that he looks worse than all the others. "It's a jolly roaring blast," he wrote, "and when I reread it I realize that I must have been crazy from 1970 to 1977."

John Martin read the manuscript immediately after it arrived in the mail and he knew that Bukowski had written his most ambitious novel to date. He saw it as the great black humor book of the women's movement, and was entranced by how Bukowski humorously captured experiences that must have been very painful at the time.

The growing debate over whether or not Bukowski's books could be called "novels" in the traditional sense continued. There were critics who wrote that *Women* lacked structure. When he told Bukowski of the suggestion he didn't write novels, the writer answered, "Hell, my work is just words on paper, man." Martin himself answers that structure would ruin the book.

In editing *Women*, Martin changed a few words and altered some of the punctuation. True to form, Bukowski caught the changes, and wanted his words restored. The book went through the first printing, and then a second printing, revised, was issued. "If you read both editions," Martin says, "I don't think you'd catch anything, but remember, he is very particular. He wants you to say exactly what it is, and if you can do something that makes the writing clearer and better, he will leave it, but usually, the way he does it is the best way."

Within a year of its publication in 1978, more than twelve thousand paperbound copies of *Women* were in print. An edition of the book was also published in Australia at the same time as the first Black Sparrow Press edition—a testament to his growing success. Written in an episodic manner reminiscent of *Post Office* and *Factotum*, the book begins with a typically Bukowskian complaint: "I was 50 years old and hadn't been to bed with a woman for four years." It was the kind of honesty that people had come to expect from Henry Chinaski/Charles Bukowski. He followed that with the statement that "I had no women friends. I looked at them as they passed . . ." This is quickly followed by the appearance of Lydia Vance, the fictional name for Linda King, who comes leaping onto the pages of the novel with as much flair as she did in real life.

Linda King's appraisal of her characterization by Hank in *Women* is that he wrote it when he was angry with her. "I didn't read the book for five years after it appeared because I knew that it would be too painful."

She feels that much of Hank's criticism of her was accurate; she just wishes that he had expressed more of the passion of the relationship. She says, "I feel that he diminished my role in his life out of anger."

Events recorded in *Women* are accurate, though it is difficult to find the intensity of Hank's feelings for Linda King: for example, "she projected vitality—you knew that she was there." He describes her outfit the night that they first met at the Bridge reading: "a suede cowgirl jacket with fringe," and goes on to dwell in detail on various parts of her anatomy—typical of him.

Linda King, Hank, and all the characters in the novel might just as well have found a back entrance into Boccaccio's *Decameron*, which was a major influence on *Women*. As Hank told an interviewer from the *Los Angeles Times* on January 4, 1981, "It was not so much love with Boccaccio. It was sex. Love is funnier, more ridiculous. That guy! He could really laugh at it." Hank went on to say that Boccaccio must have been messed up in his relationship with the opposite sex thousands of times. "Love is ridiculous because it can't last," he said, "and sex is ridiculous because it doesn't last long enough."

In particular, Hank found the satirical tone of Boccaccio's stories appealing, as in the tale of Rustico, a man so taken by the beauty of a young woman that he gets an erection while standing before her. She asks him what that thing is sticking out in front of him. He explains that it is the devil that he had been telling her about, and that he wants to send this devil back to hell—and "You have hell," he tells her, going on to say that he believed God sent her to help him get rid of the devil. With this said, he is able to lure her into bed and plunge his devil into her "hell." Once done, she says it was a very painful thing. He assures her that it won't always be so. In fact, after a few days of sending the devil to hell, the young woman began to like it so much that she encouraged it again and again.

In an *Open City* column from February 1968, Bukowski praised Boccaccio and urged his readers to buy *The Decameron*.

In describing his personal life in *Women*, Hank explains his fear of having left the security of the post office and beginning to make his way as a writer. Bukowski pulls no punches: he gets right to it in the second paragraph and gives a lucid, concise description of the makings of the professional writer, literally of turning the "machine gun" into a money-making machine. The paragraph ends, "It took me twenty-one nights to write my first novel."

Women doesn't end with the hero Chinaski going off with the woman of his dreams. To the contrary, he is alone in his apartment, having just turned down a nineteen-year-old woman who had called him on the telephone. After they've bantered back and forth a while, she says, "My name's Rochelle," to which he responds, "Goodbye, Rochelle," and hangs up. He walks into the kitchen and opens a bottle of vitamin E, which he downs with half a glass of Perrier.

"It was going to be a good night for Chinaski," he proclaims. "The sun was slanting down through the venetian blinds, making a familiar pattern on the carpet . . ." He enjoyed confronting himself and his small apartment after night upon night of being crowded in with women. There is no hint of misogyny, just a portrait of a man trying to save himself, for himself. Bukowksi/Chinaski walks onto the porch and finds a strange tomcat sitting there, "a huge creature . . .with a shining black coat and luminous yellow eyes." Rather than running from Chinaski, the cat walks up to him and begins to rub against one of his legs. "I was a good guy and he knew it," Chinaski affirms. The two of them walk into the house together. "I opened him up a can of Star-Kist solid white tuna. Packed in spring water. Nt. wt. 7 oz.," and that is how the book ends.

Over the years John Martin's respect for Bukowski's abilities had grown, and it continued to grow, even as Black Sparrow moved north to Santa Barbara in 1975, and even as their lives continued to be lived out in such different ways: Martin, the self-possessed puritan and Bukowski, the rough-edged libertine. Each, nonetheless, learned from the other. Martin has never forgotten something Bukowski said to him once, that "possible is better than perfect." In terms of the criticism leveled at *Women*, Martin believed that Bukowski had more than justified himself by writing books that were totally honest, completely devoid of pretense, books that were very much in the tradition of other writers of the heart, such as D. H. Lawrence and Henry Miller. "You can't hold Bukowski's work up to a literary mindset and ask if he satisfies certain requirements," Martin emphasizes. "From Homer forward, the great heart pieces are still with us, just as Bukowski's will be." Martin has a bottom-line appreciation of the writer's wide appeal, saying that his work attracts people who are looking for emotional and spiritual uplift. Martin goes on to say, "As far as I'm concerned, the emotions are much more important than the brain. D. H. Lawrence used to preach against mind-centered culture. Now everything has to be computerized. The computer does all of our work for us, and it has no feeling and never will, and art that is programmed and has no feeling in my opinion is just not the highest form of art."

Soon after *Women*, Martin issued a new collection of poems with yet another of Bukowski's distinctive and amusing titles—*Play the Piano Drunk Like a Percussion Instrument until the Fingers Begin to Bleed a Bit*—a book he put together from Bukowski's earlier work that had not yet been collected. A reader familiar with the poet's output will encounter poems that are typical of his earlier poems. "Fire Station," about him and Jane, describes a series of funny incidents that take place at a fire station in Los Angeles; "Interviews" concerns the army of eager young men, armed with their tape recorders, who come to see the poet, hoping for a special interview. One of his more popular poems, "a little atomic bomb," written in the sixties, is also included. Like Gregory Corso's poem, "Bomb," written more than a decade earlier, it mocks a subject usually written about in the gravest manner. Bukowski begins:

> o, just give me a little atomic bomb
> not too much
> just a little
> enough to kill a horse in the street
> but there aren't any horses in the street
> well, enough to knock the flowers from a bowl
> but I don't see any

flowers in a
bowl

He brings the bomb down to eye level, as it were, making of it something no bigger than ourselves, no less controllable than our own urges. There is a touch of the lyrical Bukowski of the later fifties in the poem, and his bittersweet humor. We are even treated to a personal note as the poem continues,

enough then
to frighten my love
but I don't have any
love

The next stanza is the most striking. Here Bukowski makes a unique juxtaposition of images, bringing the atomic bomb, a fearful, awful invention of modern science, literally right into the bathtub:

well
give me an atomic bomb then
to scrub in my bathtub
like a dirty and lovable child

(i've got a bathtub) . . .

With *Women* completed, and life with Linda Beighle going well, Hank began to think of making a trip to Germany to see his uncle, Heinrich Fett, and Carl Weissner. As far back as 1965 I remember Hank talking about his Uncle Heinrich. Hank would say, "Well, I have this uncle in Germany named Heinrich Fett and we've begun writing to one another." I never saw any of the letters from Hank's uncle, but he told me that the old man wished he could come to visit his nephew in L.A. Because of Hank's growing reputation in Europe, especially in Germany, a trip there was inevitable.

Together with L.A. photographer Michael Montfort, a German by birth, who would document Hank's wanderings through Germany, Hank and Linda Beighle flew into Frankfurt on May 8, 1978, and were met by Carl Weissner. The reception at the customs stop in Frankfurt was not a smooth one, since Hank had several huge parcels: among them, a skateboard for Carl's son, Mike, and a reel of the film based on one of his stories, "The Mermaid Blues." The film aroused the suspicion of the German customs officials who asked what was in it. "None of your fucking business," Hank told them. Because the guards didn't understand this brand of English, Carl translated it literally. Linda stood by, wide-eyed, and commented soon after they left, "Now I know we're really in Germany." Weissner then drove them all to Mannheim, installing them in a hotel on the main thoroughfare. They stayed for a week, visiting Heidelberg, drinking, and talking.

According to Weissner, Hank remained uneasy during the trip. "Probably being in a strange country," Weissner says, "with the reading coming up. And he realized that Germany had been bombed flat during the war." Weissner remembers how impressed Hank was with how orderly and clean everything was as they drove into the city from the airport. Montfort and Linda also sensed Hank's uneasiness. He told Linda often enough that he had no desire to visit ruins or the famous tourist sights. Outside of seeing his uncle, visiting Carl Weissner, and giving his reading in Hamburg, he could have done without the trip. From the moment he set foot on German soil he kept particularly close to Linda. It was obvious to anyone who was with them for any length of time that they were very much in love. She had become an anchor for Hank in a strange, unknown land. Because of this, their bond grew ever stronger.

On the second night there, Linda called Montfort to tell him that Hank had become sick, a result of a marathon bout of carousing on the night before. Montfort and Weissner quickly responded to her call. They went in search of soup, reasoning that Hank needed something to eat. They found a gay bar around the corner from the hotel where a pot of hot soup sat on a stove. After convincing the proprietor that they would bring the pot back they took it to Hank.

Hank and Linda stayed in Mannheim for a few days before heading north for the reading in Hamburg, which had actually been arranged in L.A. during a visit there by the young German poet Christoph Derschau. Hank had not wanted to do a reading, but Derschau convinced him to do at least one. The Weissners and Michael Montfort came along on the train to Hamburg, a journey of a few hours. When they arrived, Hank was recognized everywhere. The group went into a large department store where they bought several bottles of wine. As they walked out of it with their purchases, people ran out of cafés and pubs with napkins and slips of paper for Hank to autograph. Even back in Mannheim at the train station Hank's presence created a stir. He and Linda had gone into a bookstore where they saw his books on the shelves. As they walked out, the woman behind the counter came running up to Hank with a handful of his books and asked him to sign them, which he did.

The reading took place on May 18 in an old hall that had once been a food market. In fact, part of it was still used as a marketplace. Upstairs, a large space had been turned into a punk rock club run by a former Lutheran priest who had been defrocked for obscure reasons. A few months before the Bukowski reading, Günter Grass had read there. Several hundred people had come to the reading. Weissner had known that Hank would attract a huge audience, and, as it turned out, he was correct—more than four hundred people crowded into the hall, eagerly awaiting Bukowski's first and last public appearance in Europe.

When Bukowski came onstage, the mass of people standing before him began to applaud, stomp their feet, and shout both greetings and obscenities. He looked out on the audience and said, "It's good to be back home again," and then, "I'm sorry, the reading must begin, and for better or for worse this reading is dedicated to my translator and my friend, Carl Weissner."

He started with one of his newer poems and then lit a cigarette, telling the audience, "This is not a joint." After lighting it he wailed into the microphone, causing a stir throughout the auditorium, then read a poem called "Hot Dog," a humorous piece about a long-gone love affair. He paused for a moment and asked, "How are you people doing? Do you got anything to drink out there?" There was silence. "No?" he asked. After the third poem he glanced around and asked, "Isn't an hour up yet?" which caused a lot of laughter, in the midst of which he leafed through his poems and suddenly said, in a loud, forceful voice, "All of these poems are not about sex . . . I don't fuck all the time . . . I don't think about sex all the time . . . and I don't hate women . . .And I don't hate men . . . and I don't hate children . . . And I don't hate dogs." The audience clapped and he said, "Well, there are certain dogs I might dislike. When I step in their shit, you know . . ."

Hank read on, mostly humorous pieces. He told a heckler, "When the wine is gone, the reading is over with . . ." People began shouting out that they would go and get more wine. Hank then read a poem called "Some People." This was followed by "The White Poets" and "The Black Poets," two poems from the late sixties, offering the youthful German audience an inside look at Bukowski's disdain for most contemporary poetry, especially poems involving sociopolitical positions. After these two poems a heckler yelled out to him, and Hank shot back, "Haven't you gone home to your mother yet? She's got a little bottle of milk for you, warmed up." He read some of his favorite earlier poems such as "Another Academy" and "The Genius."

He stopped to talk for a moment about his wine drinking habits, saying that he consumed two or three bottles of expensive red wine a night, and that he had two local liquor stores stocking his wine back home. "If one doesn't have it, I go to the other, and they always like to see me because I usually order by the case, so I'm a very popular boy around my neighborhood. The liquor men love me. Which reminds me, I'm making those bastards rich and I'm killing myself." After a round of applause at this, he said, "You don't have to applaud because I'm killing myself." "The Bones of My Uncle," another of his favorite poems, followed. Toward the end of the reading, he brought out one of his earliest poems, "love & fame & death." It was obvious that he had given a mini retrospective of his work, ranging from the fifties to only days before the reading itself. Carl Weissner recalled that a young man at the far end of the hall tried to ask Hank a question, but it was difficult to hear from that far away. "Write me a letter," Hank shouted to him. This caused a stir in the hall, and Hank went on to say, "You Germans are too tough for me. Hell, you're talking more than I do."

Once he had returned home, Hank wrote "There are hecklers in Germany too":

I see you hanging from the girders
in the blue smoke of
Hamburg
hissing and hating
you writers who didn't make it
you writers who think you are great writers
you cheap shots of piss
you can't write
and everybody knows it but you
you hate and scream
why did you come
if you don't believe in
me?
to holler at what you hate.
all right,
maybe it's worth it,
maybe you don't understand
but it's worth it,
you'd like to be up here
with the mike
in front of the cameras . . .

The long-awaited visit to Heinrich Fett's home in Andernach-am-Rhine finally happened a few days later. Hank arrived there with Linda Beighle and Montfort. They crossed over to Andernach on the ferryboat, an approach to the medieval town so dramatic that Hank—despite his disdain for tourism—stared in wonder.

[295]

The three of them stayed at one of the cheaper tourist hotels facing the Rhine. Montfort recalls that Hank was very respectful of his uncle, making sure to call ahead before coming over for a visit. They arranged to meet the next morning; when they did, they were greeted by Heinrich's woman friend of nearly fifty years, Louisa, a heavyset, pleasant woman over eighty years of age. When Hank identified himself and Linda, she told them to come inside and wait until Heinrich finished his nap. Hank said that they would come back later, but Louisa insisted they wait. Once they came inside and were seated, she went upstairs to rouse Hank's uncle from his sleep. As he and Linda sat there, they could hear footsteps coming rapidly down the stairs. There before them stood a short, solid-looking man of ninety wearing thick glasses and grinning expansively. Before Hank could say anything, Heinrich began shouting in perfect English, "Henry! Henry! My God! I can't believe it! Henry, after all these years!"

"Good to see you, Uncle Heinrich," Hank said as they embraced. Linda could see tears in Hank's eyes. Montfort recalls that Hank's uncle scurried around the house for wine and things to eat. He was genuinely overcome by the return of his nephew to Andernach.

Heinrich told his nephew to sit down, and Hank introduced him to Linda. "Hello," he said. "Louisa will bring something soon."

He asked Hank what had brought him to Germany, and Hank explained that it was sort of a business trip, to sell his books, but added that the visit to Andernach was high on his list.

They talked on a while longer. Heinrich spoke of Hank as a child of two and three, and of how he used to cross over from his parents' house to his place shouting, "Uncle Heinie! Uncle Heinie!" The next afternoon, Heinrich came to the hotel to take Hank, Linda Beighle, and Michael for lunch at a restaurant perched on a hillside outside of town.

With the visit to Andernach completed, they returned to Mannheim before leaving for L.A. "Seeing my uncle was the real point of the whole trip," Hank says. "All the rest was okay, like meeting Carl there and staying at the hotel in Mannheim. You know, all the drinking. But the tourist sights didn't affect me. I could have done without them."

Once back home, Hank had no desire to return to Europe. Pressured by his French publishers, however, he consented to go to Paris in October 1978. It had been arranged for him to appear on "Apostrophes," a ninety-minute-long television talk show that featured major literary figures and intellectuals. The show was widely watched throughout the country and had served as a launching ground for many careers. Bernard Pivot, the opinionated host, served as an arbiter of taste, and he did not like to be upstaged on his own program. In order to prepare himself for Pivot and his show, Hank became quite drunk, beginning early in the afternoon of his scheduled appearance. He requested that two bottles of wine be waiting for him. "When we got there," he recalls, "they took me into this room and began applying powder to my face, which was futile to do because of the sweat, grease and scars on my face. Then Linda and I sat down waiting for the show to start. I began on one of the bottles that they had waiting for me."

The other guests and Pivot arrived. Hank noticed that the moderator was tapping his foot on the floor. "What's the matter," Hank asked him, "are you nervous?" Pivot said nothing. Hank poured another glass of wine and offered it to Pivot, who made no move to drink it. Hank used an earphone on which the French was translated into English. Pivot began with him first. Hank's opening statement was that many American writers would like to be on the show, but that it didn't mean much to him. Pivot immediately switched from Hank to another guest. And then another. Hank became increasingly uncomfortable. He began to mumble loudly, interrupting the inane, self-serving conversations. Then, not being able to take any more, he rose up from his chair, ripped the translation device from his ear, and walked off the set—something none of Pivot's guests had ever done before. As he passed by the security guards he grabbed one of them by his shirt collar, pulled a knife he carried with him from his pocket, and threatened the entire group. Not sure whether he was kidding or not, they managed to take the knife from him and escort him from the studio.

The talk show host, meanwhile, seemed both pleased and irritated as he remained on the set with his other guests. He said, "Ladies and gentlemen, America sure is in bad shape, isn't it?" Hank had walked away because he felt trapped in a god-awful sea of mediocrity: no other alternative presented itself, other than paying enough attention to the hocus in translation to become even more abusive.

From a public-relations standpoint, the televised theatrics worked in his favor. He successfully caused a stir throughout France. A literary critic from *Le Monde* called him the following morning, praising him for his actions on Pivot's show. "You were great, bastard," he said, also telling Hank that not one newspaper wrote negatively about his appearance. Readership of Bukowski's books soared after the incident. At that time *Post Office*, *Notes of a Dirty Old Man*, *Erections*, and *Love Is a Dog from Hell* were the only titles available in French.

While in France, Hank found himself besieged by people who tried to associate him with what he calls "the beatnik thing." He told the editor of the *Paris Metro* that he was drunk throughout the whole beatnik era, and that he didn't pal around with Kerouac or Ginsberg. "I'm supposed to be the last surviving specimen of an extinct species." He said that he felt closer to the punks than to the beatniks, and went on to say that "I am not interested in this bohemian, Greenwich Village, Parisian bullshit. Algiers, Tangiers . . . that's all romantic claptrap."

FOURTEEN

H ANK began writing *Ham on Rye* in 1980. The book is a song for
L.A., crowded with images of the city in the twenties and of
life among lower-middle-class Angelinos during the Great Depression. When the echoes of Andernach, which begin the book, turn into
graphic descriptions of beatings by an angry father, the mythic Bu-
kowski/Chinaski emerges. Once again, Hank didn't plan or prepare
for the novel, rather it crept up on his psyche, surprising him one day
when he sat down at the typewriter. Having completed *Women* he
wanted new subject matter—and there it lay waiting, a colorful pan-
orama of emotions and memories.

John Martin, sensitive to Bukowski's reluctance (at least back in
the early seventies) to write a long work about his youth, once pointed out to Hank that *South of No North* had several stories based
on the early years of his life. "Bop Bop Against that Curtain" has as
much oldtime L.A. color as does *Ham on Rye*. It deals with Hank's
escapades with Baldy and Jimmy Haddox in the downtown burlesque houses, and it's filled with a richly woven texture of humor,
pathos, and hard-nosed realism.

One of the things that separated Bukowski from William Saroyan
and Henry Miller was that both of these writers wrote voluminously
on their childhood. Saroyan had done so in *The Human Comedy* and
My Name Is Aram and Miller in *Black Spring* and many of his essays.

The most notable stories of Miller's youth are in the first section of *Black Spring*, where he talks about his life on the streets. In both Saroyan and Miller are lyrical retellings of their early years, and the reader gets the idea that they had "golden" childhoods. By taking on the largely untapped well of material from his "ungolden" childhood, Hank reopened memories that were often difficult to face. Yet he had done so in short doses through poetry and short fiction, and once he got going, the writing came easily. "It was like being in the old neighborhood again," Hank recalls, "but a lot easier to take than before."

Readers who followed the exploits of Hank's longtime alter-ego Henry Chinaski through the grime of East Hollywood and the dungeons of the Terminal Annex Post Office could now witness his coming of age as he journeyed through childhood, amused and disappointed at the shortcomings of the adult world. That grim yet accepting attitude of Chinaski rules from early childhood right through junior college.

Hank's contemporaries are not spared in *Ham on Rye*. One of the more revealing moments of the book is when Chinaski describes his friends in high school:

> It was like grammar school all over again. Gathered around me were the weak instead of the strong, the ugly instead of the beautiful, the losers instead of the winners. It looked like it was my destiny to travel in their company through life. That didn't bother me so much as the fact that I seemed irresistible to these dull idiot fellows.

Even as Hank worked on *Ham on Rye* the poems kept pouring out, as did many of the pieces that would go into *Hot Water Music*, a collection of short stories published in 1983. Just as *Ham on Rye* is the first extended work about subjects Hank had for the most part avoided, *Hot Water Music* is important, according to Hank, because it represents a newer, freer style of writing.

A young film director named Barbet Schroeder had picked up a copy of *South of No North* in 1975 while working on a film called *Koko the Talking Gorilla* in San Francisco. Schroeder is a tall, good-looking man, the son of a German mother and a Swiss-born father. He was born in Teheran and grew up in South America, mostly in Colombia. He spoke Spanish as a child, and, at age fourteen, after going to the movies almost every night, as well as to matinees, he made up his mind that he wanted to make movies. He went to Paris for his studies, attending the Sorbonne as a philosophy student. He became involved in the New Wave movement, which led him to begin his own production company, *Les Films du Losange*. He produced Eric Rohmer's *Moral Tales*, a work of Marguerite Duras, and other films. He was also a film critic for the French magazine *Cahiers du Cinema*. In 1969, he directed *More*. Then came *The Valley Obscured by Clouds*, with music by Pink Floyd. In 1976, he directed a highly acclaimed movie on Idi Amin Dada, the former dictator of Uganda, entitled *Dada: A Documentary*, followed by a fictional film on sadomasochism.

He had never read prose like this before, nor such hard-hitting, honest dialogue. Schroeder found something unique in Bukowski, especially in the poetry, when he saw that it had little to do with the Beat aesthetic, Henry Miller, or other "outsider" movements in literature. The combination of pessimism and humor attracted him, as well as the stolid anticonformism. He felt that the writing showed a side of life that had not been exposed before, and became convinced that Bukowski could write a good film script. Schroeder realized that none of the stories he had read could be worked into a feature-length movie. He felt intuitively that something fundamental in the writer's meanings might be lost if he were to transfer them onto the screen. Bukowski knew his medium—his writings were *written*. The only solution would be to seek out Bukowski and get him to write a screenplay from scratch. He didn't want to tangle with a story, translate it into a screenplay, and then miss something essential. And besides—he liked the idea of working with a writer who had so profoundly affected him.

In 1977, Schroeder came to L.A. and began stalking Hank. Playing the part of a detective, he obtained Hank's unlisted phone number and dialed excitedly. After a hasty introduction, he said, "I want to meet you for a movie project." Hank's initial reaction was negative. He told Schroeder to forget it, adding, "Fuck off, you French frog." Undeterred, Schroeder blurted, *"This isn't a Hollywood thing! It will be yours as much as it is mine!"* Hank still hesitated.

Schroeder was not deterred. "I'm serious," he said. "This will be a work of respect." Hank answered, "What?" Whereupon the filmmaker replied that he planned on leaving the script in Hank's hand. "I won't change anything without your agreement." Schroeder mentioned *Hiroshima, Mon Amour*, written by Marguerite Duras for Alain Resnais. No one else touched it. The script bore her imprint from beginning to end. That is the way Schroeder wished to proceed with Bukowski, whose reluctance to get involved had much to do with his lack of regard for the medium of film. Hank told Schroeder to come over, warning him that he didn't think the idea would go anywhere.

Much of the negativity Hank felt in relationship to filmmaking stemmed from an earlier film project, *Tales of Ordinary Madness* (1983), directed by Marco Ferreri, which was based on some of Hank's fiction. This work made Hank especially cautious about the film industry. He had not had anything to do with Ferreri's film, and felt it was a corruption of his writing. Ferreri, who had previously directed *La Grand Bouffe*, the story of gluttonous people who devour anything edible until they drop dead, wrote the script for *Tales of Ordinary Madness* with fellow Italian Sergio Amidei.

Hank still lived on Carlton Way when he first met Schroeder, and he hosted the filmmaker not long before the trip to Germany. When they stood face to face, Hank's preconceptions dropped away. Instead of a slick, smooth-talking Hollywood type, he found himself face-to-face with an exuberant personality. As the evening went on, until 5 A.M., Hank realized that writing a screenplay would be a real challenge. Toward the end of the evening, after consuming several bottles of wine, Hank half stood up from the couch, swung his arms out in a threatening manner, and said, "Okay, Barbet. You think you're tough, so come over here and let's fight." Schroeder rose to his full height and moved toward Hank.

"No. Wait," Hank said. "That'll be it. Let's just forget the fight."

After their first encounter, Hank saw Schroeder's documentary on Idi Amin Dada. That film, more than anything else, convinced him of the director's abilities. Hank liked the honest way in which Amin was portrayed, and felt that the real man came through—not some sanitized Hollywood version. He knew that Barbet was okay—he could do the job.

Bukowski admired *All Quiet on the Western Front*, an Academy Award-winning movie adapted by Maxwell Anderson from Erich Maria Remarque's novel. Produced by Carl Laemmle, and directed by George Abbott, it shows the destructive powers of armed conflict as it eats away, both spiritually and physically, at the young soldiers on the front lines. The film begins with a professor lecturing his students on the glories of war and the honor of serving the great Fatherland. The boys are swept away by the patriotic rhetoric and quickly volunteer for service. With only the barest training, they are soon thrown into the battle, where they see the grim reality of war.

One scene really struck Hank. Early in the film Paul, played by Lewis Ayres, had been struck by the glories of defending Germany and had insisted to his fellow students, "We must defend the Fatherland!" When the young hero has gone back to the trenches after a disillusioning leave home, he is cowering behind a protective cover of sandbags; a butterfly suddenly appears on the ground before him. He reaches his arm out to it, exposing himself to an enemy sniper who kills him as his hand nearly touches the butterfly.

In 1979 Hank signed a contract with Schroeder to write the screenplay. He knew instinctively how to proceed, focusing on two particular periods of his life, and melding them into a coherent whole: his years in Philadelphia in the early forties and his first few years haunting the dives on Alvarado Street in Los Angeles, where he and Jane met just after World War II. Just as he did in his books, he stuck close to the basic facts of his life, but felt free to play around with time and to spice things up when needed.

All the people he knew from those periods of his life were either dead or long gone from his world, so nothing prevented him from relating the story out as he chose. While Hank worked on the script, Schroeder wrapped up his business back in France, returned to L.A., and began living in Linda Beighle's house in Redondo Beach. He would be awakened by the women who lived in the house next door reciting chants for Meher Baba. A steady stream of beach boys passed by, most of them with flowing blond hair. Later Schroeder found lodgings in the Marina Del Rey and Venice Beach areas of L.A.

Hank knew very well how Hollywood glamorized even seedy characters. He kept this in mind as he wrote, not wanting to lose the desperation he and Jane had shared. As in his books, he avoided romantic flourishes, preferring a slice of life to that grandiose linearity of most American films, a story with a definitive beginning, middle, and end.

Thinking back on the people he had known, those other barflies, they didn't seem so bad. The character of Eddie the bartender, his nemesis in *Barfly*, was based on one whom he actually had known in Philadelphia back in the mid-forties, a man who worked hard at being macho. Hank thinks of himself back then as being macho without even trying. He explains the difference between the two quite succinctly: "The bartender had muscles and anxiety. I was just a death symbol." Eddie represented a type Hank despised—the kind who made a good first impression, talked glibly, gave off an aura of manliness, but after a time, it proved to be nothing but show. In writing *Barfly*, Hank enjoyed contrasting himself, a true prepunk, feisty young man with this quintessential blow-hard. "Yet, as I got into it," he said, "the guy didn't seem so bad. He was just searching in his own way, like I was."

Hank had no intention of sparing himself. He had been a clown of sorts in his drinking days, and he didn't hide it while writing the screenplay. The master of self-deprecation as an art form did what comes naturally. He made a universal statement about his own foibles, one that others could laugh at and garner truth from. He wrote about the errands he would run for both bar patrons and bartenders. Antihero Henry Chinaski was no larger than life in film than he had been in the stories and novels.

"Already life-worn" is how Hank describes himself-as-character in the screenplay for *Barfly*. "Rather than enter the treadmill of society he had chosen the bottle and the bars." The bars, the drinking, the low life was like one sustained telegram of rage for his parents and their precious values. While writing *Barfly* he began to think visually, to see himself and his long-gone companions as if they were standing before him. "I was writing a movie, after all, and people would be looking at these scenes, so I started seeing it all like some mad theater."

Wanda Wilcox, Chinaski's girlfriend in the screenplay, is modeled on Jane Cooney. He describes her as having "an intelligence born of disillusion" and as being "sexy in a quiet way. She is not, basically, after men or after sex, she is chasing drink and catching it and consuming it. She still wears old clothes from the past, some years out of fashion."

As if he were auditioning for a role in his own movie, Hank unwittingly treated Schroeder to a taste of the legend of the wild, drunken, blindly jealous Bukowski. After long drinking sessions with the director, Hank might go to bed feeling strange, so strange, in fact, that he would dial Schroeder's number. "You put LSD in my wine glass," he once accused, adding, "You're trying to fuck Linda, I know, and I don't like that. Watch your screen door. I'm gonna come over with a knife, motherfucker. I'm serious. You know me. I'm Bukowski. The tough guy and I don't kid around."

Schroeder answered, "Listen, Hank. Can't I give you my word of honor?"

Hank said, "No."

"I'll make a deal with you," Schroeder said. "If what you are saying is true, I'll sign a suicide note and you can come and kill me and then you won't have to go to jail. I'll give you permission to kill me."

"Yeah, that sounds pretty good," Hank said, and he calmed down.

On another evening, after he and Linda had consumed a considerable amount of expensive red wine, he dialed Schroeder's number and again accused him of lusting after Linda; again he threatened to kill him.

"You know what I'm going to do?" Schroeder replied. "I'll burn your house down."

"Hey, Barbet, we're friends. Let's just forget that there was any problem." Hank answered. "Now, I am going to hang up the telephone and go to sleep. I want you to do the same thing. Okay? Remember. We are friends. I'll write the fucking screenplay."

Schroeder matched Bukowski *mano a mano* when it came to unorthodox behavior—which truly endeared him to Bukowski. "I could see that Barbet was trustworthy. Plus, I had this feeling he would see a project through to its end and I wouldn't just be wasting my time." They became friends rather than mere business associates, and this almost certainly helped Bukowski endure the years it would take to make the project a reality. Barbet had warned him that films are not always born overnight, that one sometimes had to give several years to a project. Because of Barbet, Hank's natural suspicion of Hollywood melted away.

When Schroeder read the first few pages of what Hank had written, he commented that some of the dialogue was too literary. "Listen, this is already fifteen minutes of film" he said of a relatively short piece of the manuscript. Hank understood and astounded Schroeder at how fast he was able to rewrite the script into a more practical form.

Barbet soon began to show the manuscript around. True to his word, he didn't listen to those who told him that they had someone in mind to change this or that aspect of the script to improve it. There were those who liked it and others who didn't relate to it at all—but *every* person he approached said there was no chance that *Barfly* would succeed. Undaunted, Schroeder kept hard at work on this "author's movie." He knew that Bukowski could trim the rough edges and make a leaner, even more brilliant script.

Dennis Hopper found the script interesting and showed it to Sean Penn. The young actor offered to play the role of the drunker Bukowski for the symbolic fee of $1.00, his one stipulation being that Hopper direct the film. Because Barbet had put so much into the screenplay over a long period of time, Hank stuck by him. Penn, though, had no intention of leaving Barbet out in the cold. He and Hopper offered the director a good salary to be the producer. Barbet had invested so much into the idea of he and Hank truly collaborating as writer and director that he had to decline the offer. Hank finally called a meeting at his house.

In the spring of 1986, Penn, Hopper, and Schroeder gathered in Hank's living room, and they all tried to come to some agreement. Hank remembers not liking what Hopper wore, including a pair of gold chains around his neck. "As Hopper talked, his chains kept bouncing up and down. It was ridiculous," Hank recalls. "Barbet kept looking at me." Hank let it be known that he wanted Barbet to do the job, as originally planned.

During the long, painful birth of the *Barfly* project, Hank and Linda Beighle were married. For several months beforehand, Hank had considered the possibility of marriage, thinking that she had to be a very courageous woman to stick around with him through his drunkenness, his obsession with the racetrack, and his preoccupation with writing. He popped the question in the late spring of 1985, while they were sitting on the porch overlooking their garden. Out of nowhere Hank said, "Let's get married."

"What?" Linda exclaimed, leaping from her chair.

"Yeah, let's do it."

"When? When?" she asked.

"Let's make it the first Sunday after my birthday," Hank answered. The ceremony took place on August 18, 1985, at the Philosophical Society Library in Los Angeles, presided over by Manly Palmer Hall. There were about a dozen people attending, including John Martin, who served as best man; Marina Bukowski and her boyfriend Jeff Stone; Linda's mother; and her sister Jhara. After the marriage a reception was held at Siam West. Linda had arranged for a reggae band to play and they invited around eighty people, including poets John Thomas, Steve Richmond, and Gerald Locklin. At one point during the party Hank grabbed a wide-brimmed hat covered with gardenias off Linda's head and began dancing as he threw the hat aside. When it came time for Hank to toast his bride he raised his glass and said, "To my wife, who is searching for something she will never find, the truth."

The morning afterward, Hank woke up and laughingly said, "Good morning, Mrs. Bukowski."

"Good morning, dear husband," she replied.

Barfly continued to progress with Barbet searching for locations along with Hank and Linda. They still only had a first draft and no financial backers. While they roamed around Los Angeles, Hank relived the old days, visiting streets, neighborhoods, and haunts he hadn't seen in years. Schroeder wanted a bar that had more than just a corridor. He needed space to move the camera and crew around without cramping the flow of action in the bar. The only way to find such a place would be to search one out on his own. He began to frequent bars, listening to the habitués and drinking. Schroeder came upon a bar in Culver City that had been used in several movies, and he knew he had found what he was looking for. It had a kind of timeless quality that allowed him to avoid a period film—which, past or the future, he hated. Early on, he decided not to build Barfly around the forties or early fifties, but rather in a timeless present. And this was the place.

Barbet gave the script to Mickey Rourke to read and the actor liked it. Barbet tried to bring the actor over to Hank's house, but Rourke wanted it the other way around, claiming that otherwise he might be overwhelmed by Bukowski. Unlike Penn, he was not an avid reader of Bukowski's work, nor a poet himself. Barbet assured Hank that the actor was perfect for the role and they soon drove over to Rourke's apartment in North Hollywood. Hank's impression of Rourke was positive, despite rumors about his hypersensitivity. In *Film Comment* (August 1987), Bukowski said that throughout the filming Rourke made it clear he never forgot who had written the screenplay. Hank came on the set one day and found Rourke in the midst of an interview. He had the cameras on him, but he called out, "Hey, Hank, c'mere! Help me!" Hank joined him for the interview.

Schroeder managed to find backing from the Cannon Group. When the company had second thoughts due to financial considerations, the director made his way into their offices carrying an electric chain saw, which he plugged into an outlet. He said he was prepared to cut off his fingers one at a time unless he had immediate assurances that Barfly would not be canceled. Needless to say, this set off shock waves that reached deep into the hearts of the most hardened decision makers at Cannon, and Schroeder was given the green light.

Filming began in February 1987. Hank continued going to the racetrack. Often, when he arrived home, messages from the set asking particular questions awaited him. Most centered around the script itself and were easily remedied. He knew that some of the dialogue he had written on paper just didn't go that well when spoken out, and so he remained flexible on changes, just as long as they were approved by him.

The shooting outside of the bar took place in vintage Bukowski territory, ten blocks centered around MacArthur Park. Here one found the L.A. blend of palm trees and sunlight, aging apartment buildings and nondescript clutter, or as he put it, "a mixture of palm trees and misery." Much of it evoked the old days, but keeping in line with the feeling he wanted to evoke, Schroeder made use of modern-day cars and street scenes. If Schroeder had been asked to write a profile of Bukowski's life during this early period, he would have been able to do a good job, fresh from his forays into the old neighborhoods. Bukowski/Chinaski came alive for him, and he really felt he knew his subject inside-out by the time shooting began. But once it began, he tried to get all of those things out of his mind, to let the moment rule.

Hank initially believed that Rourke overacted the role, putting too much into it. He changed his mind when he saw how professionally Rourke created a very strange, fantastic, lovable character. Hank envisioned kids on the streets going around with Rourke's Chinaski voice and mannerisms. Vincent Canby, the *New York Times* critic, later compared Rourke's performance with that of Dustin Hoffman in the role of the down-and-out Ratso Rizzo in *Midnight Cowboy*.

When Hank saw the first cut he felt that the film opened too slowly. He felt that the pace needed stepping up. One of the things he learned in working with Barbet was how an edit can alter, and improve, a movie. He learned quickly how to gauge a film and manipulate rhythm and transitions. Because of budget considerations, which were horrendous, Barbet shot the film in less than thirty-four days. He had gone through so many difficulties getting backers, and then keeping them in line once they were in place, that he must have outdone himself to reach the goal of having a final, well-edited film in hand. Not only that, he wanted to have it ready for the Cannes Film Festival. He sent them a rough cut, and soon heard that they liked it.

Barfly opens slowly, building up a sense of suspense before any sort of interpersonal action begins. As the credits pass by, the eye is treated to red, green, blue, and purple neon light chronicling the names of the bars of L.A., the kind of names familiar to Bukowski in his wild youth. The first of them is "The Sunset," starkly red neon against the night, followed by "Hollyway," "Kenmore," "Crabby Joe's," "The Golden Horn," and focuses on a smaller neon sign that simply proclaims the place a "Bar." The camera rests there a few moments before moving past another neon sign proclaiming "Cocktails," then moves briefly into darkness, after which the camera pans across a colorful barroom, empty except for the bartender, who sits on a chair behind the counter nonchalantly reading the newspaper. The sense of emptiness and calm in the bar is broken by the emerging sound of voices in a fevered state of excitement—coming from outside of the bar, but not too far away. Already, before anything has happened, Schroeder has captured the ominous, gritty, and yet strangely matter-of-fact sensibility of the entire film.

Hank began a novel based on his experiences with Barbet Schroeder, called *Hollywood*. Like so many writers before him, he did not find Hollywood to be a rewarding place. He might make a considerable amount of money writing another screenplay, which Barbet suggested, yet he would never again have total control of his own work, mastery over every line.

In the fall of 1987 the premiere of *Barfly* was held. A white stretch limousine pulled up in Hank's long, narrow driveway to take him and Linda Bukowski to a theater next to a shopping mall. One of the neighborhood kids asked, "Hank, are you famous?" "Oh, yeah, sure, kid. I'm famous," he answered. At the theater, Hank found himself surrounded by interviewers and cameramen. One reporter asked, "Is this the story of your life?" "A few days out of a ten-year period," he replied. While he answered more questions he caught sight of Barbet Schroeder. They greeted one another as Hank was barraged by a group of reporters with cameras and video recorders. He was asked about drinking and about why he wrote the movie. As to the latter question he said, "When I write I never think about it." As they entered the theater a man appeared with the wine that Hank had left in the limo. "You are one of the world's greatest men," Hank told him.

At the postpremiere party held at Catherine, "a champagne bistro" on La Brea, Hank arrived carrying an open bottle of Mumm's champagne in one hand and holding onto Linda with the other. They walked inside, found a large, noisy throng and were quickly escorted upstairs, to where the "in-crowd" had gathered, including Faye Dunaway, who had portrayed Wanda, and Mickey Rourke. Hank was cornered by a reporter from the now-defunct *Herald-Examiner*. He told the reporter that *Barfly* would be remembered long after the Academy Award movies were forgotten, and that viewers were sure to find new meaning in it each time they watched it.

Hank felt much the same way about the work of another European director, Dominique Deruddere from Belgium, who, like Schroeder, had come to Bukowski through his writings. Deruddere directed *Love Is a Dog from Hell*, based on several Bukowski stories that the director tied together along with his screenplay collaborator Marc Detain. Hank appreciated the film, feeling that it accurately captured the spirit of his writing. "Not only did I like *Love Is a Dog from Hell*, but Deruddere is an honest guy," Bukowski says, "and is as unaffected by Hollywood as Barbet."

Unlike *Barfly*, this film begins with a childhood scene, the sexual awakening of a young, handsome, naive scamp, played by young Belgian actor Geert Hunserts. He goes to a movie, and from this develops a highly romantic vision of womanhood. In true life, however, the boy, called Harry Voss, quickly finds out that the reality is quite different. His desires lead him into the bed of an older woman while she is sleeping. When she wakes up, she begins screaming and lashing out at him. Young Harry runs away, a sadder, wiser child.

In the second segment Harry Voss is now a post-adolescent, whose face is marred by scars from a horrendous case of acne. Lonely and confused, he yearns for a woman but is afraid to seek one out. A friend tries to arrange a date for him, but it doesn't work. Having swathed his head in toilet paper, he asks the girl of his dreams to the school prom, and she accepts. The third and final segment shows Harry as an adult. He and a friend come across the corpse of a dead woman who had obviously been very glamorous while alive. With extraordinary delicacy, the film implies that Harry makes love to the corpse, thereby solving his need for love.

Hank remained prolific as poet and short-story writer. He surrendered none of his independence during his work with Schroeder. Time for the racetrack and time for writing remained sacred. Poems poured out of the great myth-maker, whose work mainly served as commentary on what it is like being a famous underground writer—just as he had long before written about being a well-known little-magazine poet.

Two collections of poetry, all of it written after the publication of *Ham on Rye*, were released by Black Sparrow. *War All the Time: Poems, 1981–1984* and *You Get So Alone at Times That It Just Makes Sense*, published in 1986, testified that Bukowski had not gone soft or lazy from his newfound celebrity status. In "Dear Pa and Ma," he wrote:

> *my father never liked*
> *what I wrote: "people*
> *don't want to read this*
> *sort of thing."*
>
> *"yes, Henry," said my*
> *mother, "people like to*
> *read things that make*
> *them happy."*
>
> *they were my earliest*
> *literary critics*
> *and*
> *they both were*
> *right.*

Amidst all this flurry of activity, Hank came down with flulike symptoms in December 1988 and lost weight rapidly. Eventually, he began to cough uncontrollably. Finally, he sought medical help: he went from physician to physician, hoping to find out what was wrong. Every specialist had his own idea of what the problem was. Every once in a while his health rebounded, only to leave him feeling weaker, more drained. He and Linda were extremely worried. Several tests were administered, but nothing specific could be found. By the spring his health hadn't improved. Increasingly exasperated with the process, Hank called his regular doctor and spoke to the nurse. "Listen," he said. "I think I need a chest X-ray." After having been probed in every part of his body except for the chest he had figured that the problem might be there, especially since the coughing kept worsening. The X-ray was ordered, and when an internist examined the results he told Hank that he had TB. On May 13 he began a regimen of antibiotics, which he took for six months, until November 13. During this time he stopped drinking—with surprising ease—and, for the first few months, didn't even go to the racetrack or write much poetry. Hank needed beer or wine to fuel his

[313]

source of inspiration. In place of wine, he began drinking fruit juice.

His trips to the hospital for tests reminded him of the many journeys he had taken to the L.A. County Hospital when he was an adolescent. In "The Orderly," written during his recovery period, Hank writes:

> I am sitting on a tin chair outside the x-ray lab as
> death, on stinking wings, wafts through the
> halls forevermore.
> I remember the hospital stenches from when
> I was a boy and when I was a man and now
> as an old man
> I sit in my tin chair waiting . . .

Linda, who faithfully guarded Hank's privacy and had long known the importance of his daily ritual, watched him grow increasingly nervous about his illness. Although sixty-eight years old, he was as determined as ever to maintain his old routine. Long before the treatments came to an end, Hank returned to the track. Whether at Santa Anita or Hollywood Park, the lure of the tote board, first post, even the crowd, renewed him. The horses had remained a constant source of pleasure for Hank since the mid-fifties and he wasn't about to stop going. "Maybe it's just an addiction to gambling," he has said, "but whatever it is, the track has helped keep me sane."

His daughter Marina married Jeffrey Stone on October 7, 1989, in an outdoor ceremony held at a park overlooking San Pedro and the Port of Los Angeles. Hank and Linda arrived shortly before the wedding began, greeted the guests, of which there were about fifty, and took their seats in front of a gazebo surrounded by tall trees. Later, at the reception, Hank held his own with the other drinkers. "Hell, how often does your daughter get married?" he said. "I've got a month to go on the antibiotics, but a day's drunk won't make a difference."

Hank's poetic output slowed considerably while he convalesced. In the back of his mind he knew that the words were waiting, like so many freight cars in a railroad yard, for the time he would be able to throw himself back into his work. Once he was given health clearance and felt physically renewed, his slender hands were able to type away as proficiently as ever. Poems and short stories danced off his fingertips and onto the typewriter keys. The fire remained. Sitting in his compact study late at night, he felt it glowing from within. And once again he went through the ritual of mailing poems to *The Wormwood Review* and *New York Quarterly*, as well as to newer journals such as *The Moment* and *Long Shot*, edited by young poets. Black Sparrow Press soon had the beginnings of a new collection of poems and stories, *Septuagenarian Stew*, four hundred pages of Bukowski unchained. The novel *Hollywood* became a selection of the Quality Paperback Book Club, and in Germany his books continued to sell briskly as they did in Italy, France, Great Britain, and elsewhere. A reader could go into a bookstore there and pick up the German edition of *Notes of a Dirty Old Man*, a collection of stories titled *Fuck Machine*, and a number of other books as well. Carl Weissner's dream of seeing Bukowski imprinted on the German consciousness had come true.

Hank felt better. The writing was back on track. The horses were running to form, and he spent more time relaxing at home with Linda. One evening, drunk, he raised his glass and said, "Thank you father for my poetry and stories, for my house, for my car, for my bank account. Thank you for those beatings that taught me how to endure." He grinned, winked at his guests, and drank more wine.

EPILOGUE

L ATE in 1983 I walked into a small bookstore on Las Palmas Avenue off Hollywood Boulevard. A friend had sent me there, having told me that the proprietor had an available copy of Bukowski's *Ham On Rye*, which I had been looking for. The man behind the front desk turned out to be a crusty, red-headed former New Yorker, Sholom Stodolsky, known as "Red." Sure enough, he had a stack of them. I picked one up and immediately recognized Hank's high school graduation picture on the cover, having seen it back in the 60s. I proceeded to introduce myself.

"I've heard about you," Stodolsky said. "I've got copies of the magazine you and Hank used to edit." He brought out *Laugh Literary and Man the Humping Guns*, the third issue, with a cover of Hank and me together with an eighty-five-year-old window washer who happened to be walking by when the photograph was taken.

"Sure would be good to see Hank again."

"Give him a call, I'm sure he'd like to hear from you."

"No. Things went bad between us. You can't get too close to Hank. He and I had strong words back in the early 70s and then he published an article in *The Los Angeles Free Press* saying there are three famous women poets in the world. I was the third. He claimed I talked about him behind his back. I got so mad that I wrote a diatribe against him for *Invisible City*." Red laughed, saying that none of that made any difference.

I liked the way this wily older guy talked. "Hank's living a good life with Linda Beighle. They fight, but usually over small things. I think Linda has brought stability into his life. For Chris-sake, call him."

"He won't want to hear from me," I protested. "It's been too many years. He's famous now. And he's working on a movie. I heard all about it."

Red wouldn't take no for an answer. He wrote out Hank's telephone number. I accepted it, bought *Ham on Rye* and then drove over to Cantor's Delicatessen where I settled down to read the opening chapters. It was the story of Hank's childhood, told at last.

"You want a glass of water?" my waitress asked.

"Sure."

"Didn't you work at the bookstore that used to be across the street? You knew the writer, that dirty old man, Bukowski, right?"

"Yeah. We were friends. We edited a magazine together."

"Tell me . . . is he on the level?"

"I guess I'm going to find out. I've got his phone number and I'm gonna call after I finish eating."

I ate and read bits of the book, oblivious to time. Five cups of coffee later I told myself that *Ham on Rye* was as close to a ham sandwich as one could get at Cantor's. I continued to skim the book, unearthing pain, humor, and bittersweet dreams. After journeying through Hank's childhood and young adult years, I found his unconventional wisdom undiminished. The book dealt honestly and clearly with the concerns of youth, concerns that still preoccupied the adult Bukowski. Here they were revealed at a boy's eye level.

I finished my sandwich and the two pickles that came with it. Then I walked outside to a telephone booth and dialed Hank's number.

"Jesus, kid, is that you? What's going on?"

He was surprised that I was back in Los Angeles, and poked fun at San Francisco poets sitting in coffeehouses from morning until midnight, complaining about lack of fame and praising one another's work. "It must be good to get away from that," he jabbed playfully. He invited me to his home. "If you've heard it's a mansion, you'll be disappointed. But I do drive a powerful piece of machinery I guess some people would call it a luxury car. I've got to be able to get to the track and back and when it's Santa Anita it's about a ninety mile round trip."

At home, I sat down to complete my reading of *Ham on Rye*. I studied it as a topographical map, not just of Hank's mind, but of Los Angeles itself, and of life during the depression. True to form, Hank kept the humor going.

A week later I arrived at his two story, white stucco house set back from the street on the side of a steep hill. I negotiated my way into the driveway, wracking my brains over what I might say, laughing at myself because this was Hank, not some stranger. I realized how much I had missed him. Back in the 60s he provided a sure-fire refuge from madness. His voice rang with self-assurance. True, he was often drunk and said cruel things, but I accepted that as part of the territory.

I parked my car and walked up to the door with its little peephole smack in the center. "I can't stop now," I told myself. I thought over what he said about our first encounter: "When I first met Neeli, he was sixteen and I was Bukowski." Then I remembered him visiting my parents' house, walking into my bedroom. His voice filled the room as he rumbled, "All right Little Rimbaud. Get the fuck out of bed. Bukowski's here." I knocked, then heard footsteps and that familiar tone, "Hey, baby. Come inside. It's been a long time." There he stood, my old pal, a bit heavier, but with the flush of health on his face.

I entered a spacious, dark room divided by a sagging bookshelf. Hank motioned me over to the couch and a long, low coffee table on which sat a few bottles of wine. As I hastened to take my place, a large cat darted past.

"That's a tough cat," Hank said. "He's a fighter. A real scraper. Don't mess with him."

I sat down on a chair off to one side of the couch where Hank stationed himself. There were a few moments of silence. Finally, Hank said, "You look the same. You haven't changed a bit. It's a miracle."

"You look the same, too."

"Sure, kid. . . sure I do."

[319]

I took a sip of the wine Hank had poured and watched as the cat scurried upstairs. I suddenly felt awkward. I began to study his face. It dawned on me that Hank looked a bit drawn. His hair had turned white. A pang of regret struck me that so many years had gone by since we had seen one another. The one or two visits in the 70s were too short. Then I caught my own face in the sliding glass door. I had also aged, despite Hank's appraisal. Also, I mulled over the fact that much of what we had experienced together, one on one, had been repetitive. We had certain mind games we played over and over again, like a bad tape.

As the wine reached my head I relaxed, feeling less uptight. Hank told me about his new short story collection. "These are different from earlier ones. They're cleaner, closer to the vest. I'm trying for clarity. I think I've really done it this time."

"I just finished reading *Ham on Rye*. You've put in all those tales you used to tell and re-tell on De Longpre."

"It took me a long time to get around to that. But it's all in there. The old neighborhoods. L.A. County Hospital. Sometimes you need distance before you can write on a subject."

We drank the bottle of Sangre de Toro table wine I had brought. Hank complimented me on my choice, faking a connoisseur's voice. After sniffing his glass of wine, he said that Linda would be home soon.

"Be nice to her. She's a good lady. She's wanted to meet you."

"I'm glad you've settled down," I said. "You're so well-mannered. So sedate."

"Listen. Give me an hour and we can get back to old times again. I'm just warming up."

I scanned the bookshelves, all of them filled with Bukowski titles in foreign languages: German, Italian, French, Dutch, Norwegian and others. There were also copies of *Laugh Literary* and some of the mimeographed journals from the early 60s.

"The gods have been good to me," Hank offered. "I don't know how long it will keep up."

As I returned to the couch Linda came in the front door, a petite woman with a wide smile and flowing golden hair.

"Linda, this is Neeli."

She came over to me and shook my hand. She had warm eyes that radiated gentleness.

"I've heard you and Hank on tape," she said. "You are one of the few people who could keep pace with him. You guys were insane on those recordings."

We sat around for a while, until Hank suggested we go out for dinner.

We left the house and drove through the December night to the downtown San Pedro restaurant. Hank and Linda were well-known by the restaurant's staff. They bantered with the waiter and then Hank turned his sights on a group of well-dressed college students who had commandeered a large table at the center of the room. "I've earned my right to be here," Hank proclaimed. "Those college kids still have powder on their asses. Their faces are like dough." Luckily, the kids didn't appear to have heard him. We were quickly distracted by the steaming plates set before us, loaded with food. I had a lot of questions I wanted to ask concerning *Ham on Rye*, but decided to save them for later. Instead, we joked about some of the people we had known. Our laughter swung from fondness to stinging criticism.

Linda described Hank's evolving movie project, *Barfly*. He himself wondered if it would really come together. "We've run into a lot of trouble," he said. "Getting the money for this kind of thing isn't easy."

Toward the end of our meal, Hank directed a few more barbs at the college students. Then, in the parking lot, he shouted a string of obscenities at a heavyset man in a BMW, just like his own. "You don't deserve one of those. Only I do . . ." Linda managed to coax him into the car and we drove back to their place.

I used to think I had some grasp of this man, but as we sat in his living room I realized there was an enigmatic side to Hank's personality. He made life appear simple in both poetry and prose, yet that very directness hinted at an ultimate complexity. I speculated that the key to that other Hank lay in a gentleness he masked behind the rough-hewn exterior. I used to watch him with his daughter Marina when she was still a child. His patience toward her was remarkable, a fatherly care, in distinct contrast to his self-made reputation as a gruff, self-centered writer. He would sit with his daughter on his lap reading from a storybook hour after hour, adding his own commentary. One time, as they were going through a book on city life, Hank paused before a picture of a bright-faced, blond haired policeman and said to Marina, "Oh the policeman is very nice . . .but not all the time. There are also bad policemen, just like there are good criminals."

There were sides to him that might never come to light. I understood that now, as I sat in his living room talking. But I wanted to find out more about his relationship with Jane, the woman whom he had lived with so long, and about those early years of travel. Things didn't add up. This man who used to move around so much was the same man who used to brow-beat me about how foolish I was to travel. Back in 1970, as I was leaving for my first trip to Europe, he kept telling me that he himself had no desire to go there. "Only a damn fool travels." I answered that there must be a lot of damn fools in the world. "You've got that right," he retorted.

As the night came to a close I didn't want to leave, but eventually I found myself on the Harbor Freeway heading to West Covina where I was living on a quiet street three blocks from a shopping center, two blocks from a landfill site. Overwhelmed by the visit, I recited some of Hank's poems, the handful I had memorized, in an effort to prolong the encounter.

When I crawled into bed, I knew that I might as well forget sleep. I had seen the old man again. His boundless energy had infected me. I leafed through his latest book of poems, *Dangling in the Tournefortia*. There I discovered that Hank had made a significant transformation in his poetic style. These new poems lacked the lyrical power that had made his earlier poems so engaging. Hank was not making an attempt at writing that one perfect poem. He had opted for a massive outpouring of emotions, caring little for shape or craft. I could imagine him telling me, "Forget the lyrical poem. To hell with proficiency. Get to what you want to say," and he'd be right. Years ago he had railed against the idea that each poem had to be a perfect little diamond of aesthetic delight. Now there were humorous poems about Hank at the track, Hank in and out of love, Hank now living in semi-domestic bliss.

The night I was to visit Hank again turned into a catastrophe. Somehow I confused the date and had already decided to call and check when the phone rang. It was Hank, angry as hell, informing me that he had waited for over an hour.

"Listen," he said. "You're Jewish, right? We Christians have a lot of shopping and tree buying and tree decorating and gift wrapping to do. So let's just forget the whole thing."

"Hank, I'm sorry."

He had already hung up the phone.

"Well, there goes the rebirth of our friendship," I said to my friend, Jesse Cabrera. "Hank is so damned touchy. He was always that way. He can dish it out, but do one thing out of kilter regarding him and oh boy!"

In 1986, I was living in San Francisco again when another collection of Hank's poems appeared, *You Get So Alone At Times That It Just Makes Sense*. The title intrigued me as did the cut-up photograph of Hank on the cover, designed by Barbara Martin, the wife of Hank's publisher. I began to think that, beginning with *Love Is a Dog From Hell* (1977) and going on right down to this new collection, Hank had truly surrendered himself to an inner voice that dictated in a rugged, conversational manner.

About that time I was contacted by Paul Ciotti, a writer for the *Los Angeles Times* Magazine, who asked if I'd be willing to do an interview for an article he was writing on Bukowski.

"Sure," I said. "But we've been out of touch since 1983."

"I'll be coming up there. Where would you like to meet?"

"You can come by my place," I answered. "Among other things, you'll find a stack of Bukowski books in my workroom."

A week later Ciotti arrived. I liked the idea of talking to someone else about my friend. Perhaps Ciotti could help me edge back toward Hank. I thought of his novels and my favorite poems such as

"Another Academy" and "Old Man, Dead in a Room," and I knew that Hank deserved to be at the top of anyone's reading list of contemporary writers. But Ciotti wanted stories, so I talked into his tape recorder—gave him a whole trainload of Bukowski tales from the 60s and early 70s. After several pots of coffee, he was on his way back home to Los Angeles.

On March 22, 1987, "Bukowski" by Paul Ciotti came out in the *Los Angeles Times*. Accompanying it were several photographs, the best being of Hank and Linda Lee standing arm in arm in the driveway of their home, flanked by the BMW and Linda's sports car. Linda wore a blue dress with a white floral pattern, and Hank was in slacks, a sports coat, a white shirt and loose red tie. His left hand rested on the roof of the BMW. I could imagine people seeing that picture and asking themselves, "Is this the dirty old man I used to hear about?" Or even the old cornball question, "Has success spoiled Charles Bukowski?"

Because I had wrangled Hank's phone number from Ciotti, I called to congratulate him. He seemed genuinely touched that I had bothered and asked what I was working on. "Not much," I said. "I've been wrestling with a novel."

"Well, *Barfly* will be out soon," he said. "I hope you like it."

Hank's last novel, *Pulp*, published in 1994, the year of his death, is dedicated to bad writing, a jab at the carefully constructed American novels that he used to read and find abhorrent. "The clean fingernail boys" is what he called the writers of formula fiction. Even though Hank's health was failing the story came easily. He had fun writing it. "If you have to fight with your words, something's wrong," he used to say. "Trust your instinct. Don't pull back. Even if you fail, you can get up and try again." Against death, he added a character named Lady Death and sparred with her throughout the novel.

As he grew older, Hank's prose and poetry became leaner, as if he didn't want to waste any time. He threw off what he saw as dead weight, excess description and repetition. More and more he wrote of failing health and told me over the telephone on several occasions that he had no real fear of death. He did confess, however, that he wanted more time. "I want to enjoy all this royalty money and I'd like to write a last novel, maybe the one I'd call 'Poet.' "

After *Pulp*, Black Sparrow Press brought out two collections of Hank's letters. Legendary for his prolific correspondence, this collection of person-to-person writing is a novel in itself. The reader is able to trace Hank's long push toward the writer's life, unattached to a job, or boss, making it on his own. They are humorous, poignant, sometimes angry, often filled with complaint. In Bukowski's correspondence one finds the ambition and aspiration for literary success that is masked in his other writing. Even amid rage, Hank gave off a sense of acceptance of the human condition with its triumphs and failures, high points and pitfalls. Taken in their totality, they are like *The Education of Henry Adams*, a guidebook to the development of a human soul.

Hank died on Wednesday, March 9, 1994, at San Pedro Peninsula Hospital from leukemia, Linda and Marina at his bedside. *The Los Angeles Times* ran a front page story on the city's most celebrated writer, dubbing him "Poet of L.A.'s low-life," a predictable touch of journalese. The obituary in *The New York Times* described him as ". . . a descendant of the Romantic visionaries who worshipped at the altar of personal excess." But the most fully rounded picture of Bukowski came from the poet and teacher Gerald Locklin who wrote a piece for the *Los Angeles Reader*, "Charles Bukowski: A Remembrance." Locklin tells of Hank's beginnings as a little magazine figure and his importance as a spokesperson for those on the bottom.

During his illness, Hank continued writing prolifically. People who talked to him at home or while he was in the hospital sensed a new vulnerability, yet a stoical acceptance of his condition. At the end of a conversation with Sam Cherry, who had known him since the early 60s, he said, "The time is coming when I'll have to put the gloves down. I can feel Papa Death. He's standing on the next corner." On March 14 Hank's funeral was held at Green Hills Memorial Park in Palos Verdes, not far from his home. Among the friends in attendance were John Martin, Sean Penn, Carl Weissner, Steve Richmond, John Thomas, and Red Stoldosky. Linda Bukowski chose the words "Don't Try" to place on his headstone with an etching in the stone of a pair of boxing gloves.

Hank's later poems are filled with death imagery. When my mother died back in 1990, I asked Hank if he knew why I wasn't mourning. It was the day of her funeral; he and his wife Linda stood by my side. "Hell, man . . .You're a poet. What do you think is back of all this? We search through ourselves to find immortality. In the end, we know a lot about death and dying."

The young remain faithful to his work. There are editors of small poetry journals who have poems and stories yet to be published. He had become even more prolific in his last years, possibly hoping to forestall the inevitable, and, as always, he remained generous with the little magazines. One might search for a Rilkean meditation on finality, an exalted requiem like the German poet wrote in his last years. It's not there. The common touch remains.

What's the future for Bukowski? He's found in some of the standard anthologies now, and there are a handful of teachers and professors in the academic world who teach his work, treating him as a serious writer. Still, there's a reluctance in the English departments to rank him with important figures. While the Beat poets are gaining more acceptance in the academy, Hank remains what he always called himself, *the* Outsider. Much like Henry Miller, whose writings continue to be an antipode to the "canon," Hank might well keep up his outsider status, providing a counterweight to a safer, more stabilizing literature. As with Miller, he never won a literary prize in his own country. If he had, it is very possible that he would have rejected it. Two years before his death, Hank confessed that he had a certain nostalgia for the days of obscurity. "I think about it a lot. Maybe it was the luck of the gods or just the fact that I kept working. I never pretended to be more than I was, a guy doing a job . . . end of statement."

Books by CHARLES BUKOWSKI

Flower, Fist and Bestial Wail, Eureka, Hearse Press, 1960

Longshot Pomes for Broke Players, New York, 7 Poets Press, 1962

Run with the Hunted, Chicago, Midwest Press, 1962

It Catches My Heart in Its Hands, New Orleans, Loujon Press, 1963

Crucifix in a Deathhand, New Orleans, Loujon Press, 1965

Cold Dogs in the Courtyard, Chicago, Literary Times-Cyfoeth, 1965

Confessions of a Man Insane Enough To Live with Beasts,
    Bensenville, Ole Press, 1965

The Genius of the Crowd, Cleveland, 7 Flowers Press, 1966

All the Assholes in the World and Mine, Bensenville, Ole Press, 1966

At Terror Street and Agony Way, Los Angeles, Black Sparrow Press, 1968

Poems Written Before Jumping out of an 8 Story Window,
    Glendale, Poetry X/Change/Litmus, 1968

Notes of a Dirty Old Man, North Hollywood, Essex House, 1969;
    reissue, San Francisco, City Lights Books, 1973

A Bukowski Sampler, Madison, Quixote Press, 1969

The Days Run Away Like Wild Horses Over the Hills,
    Los Angeles, Black Sparrow Press, 1969

Post Office, Los Angeles, Black Sparrow Press, 1970

Mockingbird Wish Me Luck, Los Angeles, Black Sparrow Press, 1972

Erections, Ejaculations, Exhibitions and General Titles of Ordinary Madness,
    San Francisco, City Lights Books, 1972; reissue, City Lights Books, 1983 as two
    books: *The Most Beautiful Woman in the World* and *Tales of Ordinary Madness*

South of No North, Los Angeles, Black Sparrow Press, 1973

Burning in Water Drowning in Flame: Selected Poems 1955–1973,
    Santa Barbara, Black Sparrow Press, 1974

Factotum, Santa Barbara, Black Sparrow Press, 1975

Love Is a Dog from Hell: Poems 1974–77, Santa Barbara, Black Sparrow Press, 1977

Women, Santa Barbara, Black Sparrow Press, 1978

*Play the Piano Drunk Like a Percussion Instrument Until the Fingers Begin
    to Bleed a Bit*, Santa Barbara, Black Sparrow Press, 1979

Shakespeare Never Did This, San Francisco, City Lights Books, 1979

Dangling in the Tournefortia, Santa Barbara, Black Sparrow Press, 1981

Ham on Rye, Santa Barbara, Black Sparrow Press, 1982

Hot Water Music, Santa Barbara, Black Sparrow Press, 1983

War All the Time: Poems 1981–84, Santa Barbara, Black Sparrow Press, 1984

You Get So Alone at Times That It Just Makes Sense,
    Santa Rosa, Black Sparrow Press, 1986

The Movie: "Barfly", Santa Rosa, Black Sparrow Press, 1987

The Roominghouse Madrigals: Early Selected Poems 1946–1966,
    Santa Rosa, Black Sparrow Press, 1988

Hollywood, Santa Rosa, Black Sparrow Press, 1989

Septuagenarian Stew, Santa Rosa, Black Sparrow Press, 1990

The Last Night of the Earth Poems, Santa Rosa, Black Sparrow Press, 1992

Run With the Hunted: A Charles Bukowski Reader, New York, Harper & Row, 1993

Screams From the Balcony: Selected Letters, 1960–1970,
    Santa Rosa, Black Sparrow Press, 1993

Pulp, Santa Rosa, Black Sparrow Press, 1994

Shakespeare Never Did This (augmented Edition),
    Santa Rosa, Black Sparrow Press, 1995

Living on Luck: Selected Letters, 1960s–1970s, Volume Two,
    Santa Rosa, Black Sparrow Press, 1995

Betting on the Muse: Poems and Stories, Santa Rosa, Black Sparrow Press, 1996

Bone Palace Ballet: New Poems, Santa Rosa, Black Sparrow Press, 1997

The Captain Is Out To Lunch And The Sailors Have Taken Over The Ship,
    Santa Rosa, Black Sparrow Press, 1998

Reach for the Sun: Selected Letters, 1978–1994, Volume Three,
    Santa Rosa, Black Sparrow Press, 1999

What Matters Most Is How Well You Walk Through the Fire,
    Santa Rosa, Black Sparrow Press, 1999

Open All Night, Santa Rosa, Black Sparrow Press, 2000

*Beerspit Night and Cursing: The Correspondence of Charles Bukowski
    and Sheri Martinelli, 1960–1967*, Edited by Steven Moore,
    Santa Rosa, Black Sparrow Press, 2001

The Night Torn Mad with Footsteps, Santa Rosa, Black Sparrow Press, 2001

Sifting Through the Madness for the Word, the Line, the Way,
    New York, Ecco Press, 2003

The Flash of the Lightning Behind the Mountain, New York, Ecco Press, 2004

Slouching Toward Nirvana, New York, Ecco Press, 2005

Come On In!, New York, Ecco Press, 2006

The People Look Like Flowers at Last, New York, Ecco Press, 2007

The Pleasures of the Damned: Selected Poems 1951–1993,
New York, Ecco Press, 2007

Portions from a Wine-Stained Notebook: Uncollected Stories and Essays, 1944–1990,
Edited by David Stephen Calonne, San Francisco, City Lights Books, 2008

The Continual Condition, New York, Ecco Press, 2009

Absence of the Hero: Uncollected Stories and Essays, Vol. 2: 1946–1992,
Edited by David Stephen Calonne, San Francisco, City Lights Books, 2010

More Notes of a Dirty Old Man: The Uncollected Columns,
Edited by David Stephen Calonne, San Francisco, City Lights Books, 2011

On Writing, New York, Ecco Press, 2015

On Cats, New York, Ecco Press, 2015

The Bell Tolls for No One, Edited by David Stephen Calonne,
San Francisco, City Lights Books, 2015

On Love, New York, Ecco Press, 2016

Storm for the Living and the Dead: Uncollected and Unpublished Poems,
Edited by Abel Debritto, New York, Ecco Press, 2017

The Mathematics of the Breath and the Way: On Writers and Writing,
Edited by David Stephen Calonne, San Francisco, City Lights Books, 2018

On Drinking, New York, Ecco Press, 2019

Bukowski 100: Poems, Edited by Daniel Halpern, New York, Ecco Press, 2020

Books About CHARLES BUKOWSKI

Baughan, Michael Gray, *Charles Bukowski*,
 Philadelphia, Chelsea House Publishers, 2004

Calonne, David, editor, *Charles Bukowski: Sunlight Here I Am: Interviews &
 Encounters 1963–1993*, Okemos, Sun Dog Press, 2003

Cherkovski, Neeli, *Hank: The Life of Charles Bukowski*,
 New York, Random House, 1991

Debritto, Abel, *Charles Bukowski, King of the Underground: From Obscurity to
 Literary Icon*, New York, Palgrave Macmillan, 2013

Duval, Jean-François, *Bukowski and the Beats*, Okemos, Sun Dog Press, 2002

Harrison, Russell, *Against the American Dream: Essays on Charles Bukowski*,
 Santa Rosa, Black Sparrow Press, 1994

King, Linda, *Loving and Hating Charles Bukowski: A Memoir*,
 San Francisco, Wild Ocean Press, 2014

Locklin, Gerald, *Charles Bukowski: A Sure Bet*, Sudbury, Water Row Press, 1996

Malone, Aubrey, *The Hunchback of East Hollywood: A Biography of Charles
 Bukowski*, Manchester, Critical Vision, 2003

Miles, Barry, *Charles Bukowski*, London, Virgin Books, 2005

Pivano, Fernanda, *Charles Bukowski: Laughing with the Gods*,
 Okemos, Sun Dog Press, 2000

Pleasants, Ben, *Visceral Bukowski: Inside the Sniper Landscape of L.A. Writers*,
 Okemos, Sun Dog Press, 2004

Richmond, Steve, *Spinning Off Bukowski*, Northville, Sun Dog Press, 1996

Sherman, Jory, *Bukowski: Friendship, Fame & Bestial Myth*,
 Augusta, Blue Horse Publications, 1981

Sounes, Howard, *Charles Bukowski: Locked in the Arms of a Crazy Life*,
 New York, Grove Press, 1999

Winans, A.D., *The Charles Bukowski/Second Coming Years*,
 Warwickshire, England, Beat Scene Press, 1996

Weizmann, Daniel, editor *Drinking With Bukowski: Recollections of the Poet
 Laureate of Skid Row*, New York, Thunder's Mouth Press, 2001

Wood, Pamela, *Charles Bukowski's Scarlet: A Memoir*,
 Okemos, Sun Dog Press, 2010

EDITOR'S NOTE: *This is by no means an exhaustive list, but merely some of the more
easily accessible books about Bukowski.*

SOURCE NOTES

CHAPTER ONE

Charles Bukowski and I spent many hours recording his early history. There were numerous lengthy telephone conversations as well, and some correspondence.

Interviews were held on 3-29-88, 5-21-88, 5-22-88, 7-15-88, 9-9-88, and 1-28-89 (on several occasions when I spoke with him informally while visiting at his home.)

Katherine Wood, Bukowski's cousin, and her mother, Anna Bukowski, were the only other direct links to his early years. They helped in piecing together information regarding the family.

pages 23–24: "We Ain't Got No Money Honey, but We Got Rain," A New Year's Greeting From Black Sparrow Press, 1990, and *The Last Night of the Earth Poems*, pp.280–288

CHAPTER TWO

I relied on exhaustive interviews with my subject and on his autobiographical novel, *Ham on Rye*.

pages 26–27: *Ham on Rye*, p. 121.

page 45: *Ham on Rye*, pp. 204–205.

CHAPTER THREE

My interviews with Bukowski and the novel *Factotum* were essential in writing this chapter. I made contact with Robert and Beverly Knox, who had attended L.A. City College with Bukowski and had seen him occasionally up until 1943.

pages 72–73: *Notes of a Dirty Old Man*, p. 188.

pages 75–78: "Aftermath of a Lengthy Rejection Slip," *Story* (New York City), March–April 1944.

CHAPTER FOUR

Also based primarily on interviews with Bukowski, these "lost years" were revealed. Interviews with members of the Frye family, both in Wheeler, Texas, and in Los Angeles helped in piecing together some information about Bukowski's first marriage. Bukowski's *Factotum*, *Post Office*, and the final script of *Barfly* (published in book form by Black Sparrow Press) were helpful.

A piece by Bukowski published under the title "Notes of a Dirty Old Man" in *Smoke Signals* (vol. 2, no. 4, 1982) is a memory of Bukowski's life with Jane Cooney and was helpful for finding clues to their relationship and his life in general in this period.

Sanford Dorbin's bibliography (out of print) of Bukowski's work was important for this chapter and all subsequent ones.

page 86: "40 Years Ago in That Hotel Room," *The Wormwood Review*, (vol. 28, nos. 110–111, 1988), pp. 44–46.

page 94: "Layover," *The Roominghouse Madrigals*, p. 51.

page 98: *Post Office*, p. 35.

pages 99–100: "Death Wants More Death," *The Roominghouse Madrigals*, p. 92.

page 101: "The Day I Kicked Away a Bankroll," *The Roominghouse Madrigals*, p. 73.

CHAPTER FIVE

I began utilizing the impressive collection of correspondence on file in the Charles Bukowski collection of the University of California, Santa Barbara's Special Collections Division. This key resource helped me to pinpoint and document many of the events in my subject's life.

Interviews with Bukowski and small-press editor Evelyn Thorne were invaluable. Written exchanges with poet Jory Sherman, who knew Bukowski in the years he was first gaining a reputation as a poet, were also of importance.

pages 108–109: "For Jane: With All the Love I Had, Which Was Not Enough," *The Days Run away Like Wild Horses over the Hills*, p. 32.

pages 109–110: "The Twins," *Burning in Water Drowning in Flame*, p. 23.

CHAPTER SIX

Information was provided by New Orleans-based Edwin Blair, an associate of Bukowski's publisher, Jon Edgar Webb. Frances Smith proved to be an excellent resource, shedding light on the poet's life in the early sixties.

Poets Harold Norse, Jory Sherman, Lee Grue, and Jack Grapes offered invaluable insights and firsthand observations.

Frances Smith interview held 1-28-89.

Marina Bukowski interview held 1-29-89.

The Wormwood Review (vol. 12, no. 1, issue 45, 1972). This is an all-Jon Edgar Webb issue, including a tribute/memoir of the editor by Bukowski and others, and an original short story by Webb. I found important biographical information on Webb here. Bukowski's memoir is good, but contains one piece of misinformation. Bukowski did not meet the Webbs before the publication of *It Catches My Heart In its Hands*. They actually met before *Crucifix in a Deathhand* was published.

The Bukowski/Purdy Letters: 1964–1974 (Sutton West, Ontario, Canada and Santa Barbara, Cal.: Paget Press, 1983), provided me with much information and documentation beginning in this chapter and following on through chapter twelve.

page 125: "the kings are gone," *The Roominghouse Madrigals*, p. 123.

pages 127–28: "Old Man, Dead in a Room," *The Roominghouse Madrigals*, p. 53.

pages 131–32: "the tragedy of the leaves," *Burning in Water Drowning in Flame*, p. 15.

page 133: "sundays kill more men than bombs," *The Roominghouse Madrigals*, p. 41.

CHAPTER SEVEN

Edwin Blair continued to do research on my behalf, searching his extensive collection of correspondence between Webb and Bukowski. A telephone conversation with Louise (Gypsy Lou) Webb helped to corroborate certain vital matters in Bukowski's relationship with his most important early publisher.

pages 150–52: Foreword to "Crucifix in a Deathhand," *Burning in Water Drowning in Flame*, p. 52.

page 152: "Beans with Garlic," *Burning in Water Drawing in Flame*, p. 62.

page 153: "Something for the Touts, the Nuns, the Grocery Clerks and You," *Burning in Water Drowning in Flame*, p. 67.

page 154: Introduction to *Cold Dogs in the Courtyard*, unnumbered.

page 156: "the Outsider," tribute to Jon Edgar Webb in *Wormwood Review* (vol. 12, no. 1, 1972), p. 3.

CHAPTER EIGHT

Interviews with Douglas Blazek, Frances Smith, and Bukowski helped to form this chapter, along with information provided by Jory Sherman, Carl Weissner, and Harold Norse. Harold Norse's own correspondence with Bukowski, which he kindly lent me, proved important from this point into the seventies.

Interview with Carl Weissner in Heidelberg and Mannheim held 9-26-88 and 9-27-88.

Interview with Douglas Blazek held 1-12-89.

page 158: "the new place," *Wormwood Review* (vol. 4, no. 4, 1964).

pages 164–66: "A Rambling Essay on Poetics and the Bleeding Life Written While Drinking a Six-Pack (Tall)," *Ole* (no. 2, March 1965).

page 168: "Confessions of a Man Insane Enough to Live with Beasts," *South of No North*, pp. 168–169.

CHAPTER NINE

Here I relied on my own memory of conversations with Bukowski, and of a particular evening we spent together. John Martin of Black Sparrow Press provided both hard facts and an insightful overview of Bukowski's bourgeoning career for this chapter. I also depended on talks with John Thomas and Frances Smith, as well as interviews with Carl Weissner, Douglas Blazek, and Steve Richmond.

John Martin pointed me to his interview with Robert Dana in *Against the Grain* (Iowa City: University of Iowa Press, 1986) for information about his own formative years and the early years of the Black Sparrow Press.

Carl Weissner sent me a copy of an interview conducted by Jay Dougherty, which later appeared in *Gargoyle*, issue 35 (Bethesda, Maryland), 1988.

An interview in *Southern California Lit Scene* (vol. 1, no. 1, December 1970), "Looking for the Giants, Charles Bukowski," conducted by editor William Robson and Josette Bryson was useful here.

Several telephone talks with Marvin Malone of *The Wormwood Review* were also invaluable.

pages 183–84: "The Genius of the Crowd," *The Roominghouse Madrigals*, p. 31.

page 188: "An Old Drunk Who Ran out of Luck," *Open City* (vol. 2, no. 1, 5–11 May 1967), p. 11.

pages 188–89: *Notes of a Dirty Old Man*, p. 237.

pages 189–90: *Notes of a Dirty Old Man*, p. 84.

page 199: "A Word on the Quick and Modern Poem-Makers," *The Roominghouse Madrigals*, p. 99.

page 202: "Call the Police" in *Laugh Literary and Man The Humping Guns* (vol. 1, no. 2, 1969), unnumbered.

CHAPTER TEN

As a participant in many of the events described, I relied heavily on my own knowledge of events in Bukowski's life and extensive use of the Bukowski correspondence at UCSB. Interviews with Bukowski on this period shed light on many matters. I interviewed Linda King, over a three-day period. The interviews helped to complete this and the following two chapters. Interviews with Paul Vangelisti in Los Angeles were helpful, as were talks with Frances Smith, Marina Bukowski, Carl Weissner, John Martin, and Harold Norse. An interview with Lawrence Ferlinghetti helped on this, and on the following two chapters.

Paul Vangelisti interview held 5-22-88.

John Martin interview held 3-11-89.

page 234: Untitled poem from *Sweet And Dirty*, Redwood City, Cal.: Vagabond Press, unnumbered.

CHAPTER ELEVEN

Linda King's input continued to be important for this chapter, as was that of Paul Vangelisti and Harold Norse. Jack Micheline gave me copies of his correspondence with Bukowski, and I conducted an interview with Taylor Hackford that proved to be invaluable. *Second Coming* (vol. 2, no. 3, 1974) is an all-Bukowski issue of this little magazine edited by A.D. Winans. Linda King's piece, "To Think I Fell in Love with a Male Chauvinist," was of use to me, as were works by Harold Norse, Jack Micheline, and others.

Taylor Hackford interview held 4-18-89.

page 250: "The Mockingbird," *Mockingbird Wish Me Luck*, p. 71.

page 253: "Destroying Beauty," *The Roominghouse Madrigals*, p. 256.

page 254: "Jeffers," *Septuagenarian Stew*, p. 177.

CHAPTER TWELVE

Much-needed information came my way from Lawrence Ferlinghetti, Harold Norse, Douglas Blazek, and poet-editor A. D. Winans. The Hackford interview was also a major resource for this period.

Rolling Stone (no. 215, June 17, 1976) includes an extensive article, by Glenn Esterly, "Bukowski in the Raw," which captures much of the flavor of the poet in the mid–seventies. It aided me in completing this section of the book.

page 267: Introduction to *Burning in Water Drowning in Flame*, p. 177.

page 268: "On the Circuit," *Burning in Water Drowning in Flame*, p. 200.

CHAPTERS THIRTEEN AND FOURTEEN

Interviews and conversations with Bukowski and Linda Lee Bukowski were essential to the writing of these chapters. An interview with Barbet Schroeder, talks with John Martin and Carl Weissner, and Bukowski's novel *Hollywood* (see bibliography), were all helpful.

page 281: "the six foot goddess," *Love Is a Dog from Hell*, p. 18.

page 282: "I have shit stains in my underwear too," *Love Is a Dog from Hell*, p. 209.

page 283: "the place didn't look bad," *Love Is a Dog from Hell*, p. 259.

page 283: "madness," *Love Is a Dog from Hell*, p. 282.

pages 285–86: "Fear and Madness," *Dancing in the Tournefortia*, p. 194.

pages 290–91: "a little atomic bomb," *Play the Piano Drunk like a Percussion Instrument Until the Fingers Begin to Bleed a Bit*, p. 52.

page 295: "There are Hecklers in Germany too," *Dancing in the Tournefortia*, p. 198.

page 300: *Ham on Rye*, p. 155.

pages 312–313: "Dear Pa and Ma," *War All the Time*, p. 205.

INDEX

ACKNOWLEDGMENTS

Thanks to Marina Louise Bukowski, Linda Lee Bukowski,
Katherine Bukowski Wood, Anna K. Bukowski, Frances Smith,
John Martin, Lawrence Ferlinghetti, John Thomas, Steve Richmond,
Linda King, Taylor Hackford, Paul Vangelisti, Jack Micheline,
Jory Sherman, Michael Montfort, Barbet Schroeder,
Douglas Blazek, Marcus Grapes, Louise Webb,
Harold Norse, A. D. Winans, and Joe Wolberg
for giving me their time.

Thanks to Bob Ziembicki, Jack Baran, Herschal Mays, Lee Grue,
Marvin Malone, Evelyn Thorne, Sam Cherry, Clare Cherry,
Stan McNail, Nancy Peters, Jack Hirschman, and John Crowell.

My appreciation to Carl Weissner of Mannheim, Germany,
and to Heinrich Fett of Andernach, Germany.

Thanks to Edwin Blair for his assistance,
Red Stodolsky of Baroque Books
and Jeff Weinberg of Water Row Books.

Thanks to the Special Collections Department Library,
University of California, Santa Barbara
and to the Special Collections Department, Library,
Tulane University, New Orleans.

Thanks to George Scrivani for his editorial assistance,
and to Jesse Cabrera, Raymond Foye, Gerald Nicosia,
and Anthony Duignan-Cabrera for their helpful suggestions.

PERMISSIONS

Printed June 2020 in Quebec, Canada for the Black Sparrow Press by Marquis. Set in New Caledonia with Lydian for titling by MJB. This first edition has been bound in paper-wrappers; 50 copies have been specially bound with cloth spines, and are numbered and signed by the author.

Black Sparrow Press was founded by John and Barbara Martin in 1966, and continued by them until 2002. The iconic sparrow logo was drawn by Barbara Martin.

Photo: Kyle Harvey

Neeli Cherkovski is a poet and editor. He co-edited the *Anthology of L.A. Poets* with Charles Bukowski in 1972, and co-edited *Collected Poems of Bob Kaufman* in 2019. Cherkovski is the subject of the independent documentary feature "It's Nice To Be With You Always." His papers are held at the Bancroft Library, University of California, Berkeley. Cherkovski has lived in San Francisco since 1974.